AF444469

Mastering Distributed Algorithms

Roger Wattenhofer

Contents

Introduction

What are Distributed Algorithms?

In the last few decades, we have experienced an unprecedented growth in the area of distributed systems and networks. Distributed computing now encompasses many of the activities occurring in today's computer and communications world. Indeed, distributed computing appears in quite diverse application areas: The Internet is a distributed system, but so are wireless communication, cloud or parallel computing, multi-core systems, mobile networks. Also an ant colony, a brain, or even the human society can be modeled as distributed systems.

These applications have in common that many processors or entities (often called nodes) are active in the system at any moment. The nodes have certain degrees of freedom: they have their own hard- and software. Nevertheless, the nodes may share common resources and information, and, in order to solve a problem that concerns several—or maybe even all—nodes, coordination is necessary.

Despite these commonalities, a human brain is of course very different from a multi-core processor. Due to such differences, many different models and parameters are studied in the area of distributed computing. In some systems the nodes operate synchronously, in other systems they operate asynchronously. There are simple homogeneous systems, and heterogeneous systems where different types of nodes, potentially with different capabilities, objectives etc., need to interact. There are different communication techniques: nodes may communicate by exchanging messages, or by means of a shared memory. Occasionally the communication infrastructure is tailor-made for an application, sometimes one has to work with any given infrastructure. The nodes in a distributed system often work together to solve a global task, occasionally the nodes are autonomous agents that have their own agenda and compete for common resources. Sometimes the nodes can be assumed to work correctly, at times they may exhibit failures. In contrast to a single-node system, distributed systems may still function correctly despite failures as other nodes can take over the work of the failed nodes. There are different kinds of failures that can be considered: nodes may just crash, or they might exhibit an arbitrary, erroneous behavior, maybe even to a degree where it cannot be distinguished from malicious (also known as Byzantine) behavior. It is also possible that the nodes follow the rules indeed, however they tweak the parameters to get the most out of the system; in other words, the nodes act selfishly.

Apparently, there are many models (and even more combinations of models) that can be studied. We will not discuss them in detail now, but simply define them when we use them. Towards the end of the book, the reader should know the most important concepts, and a general picture should emerge, hopefully!

Book Overview

This book introduces the basic principles of distributed computing, highlighting common themes and techniques. In particular, we study some of the fundamental issues underlying the design of distributed systems:

- Communication: Communication does not come for free; often communication cost dominates the cost of local processing or storage. Sometimes we even assume that everything but communication is free.

- Coordination: How can you coordinate a distributed system so that it performs some task efficiently? How much overhead is inevitable?

- Fault-tolerance: A major advantage of a distributed system is that even in the presence of failures the system as a whole may survive.

- Locality: Networks keep growing. Luckily, global information is not always needed to solve a task, often it is sufficient if nodes talk to their neighbors. Whether a local solution is possible is one of the core topics of this book.

- Parallelism: How fast can you solve a task if you increase your computational power, e.g., by increasing the number of nodes that can share the workload? How much parallelism is possible for a given problem?

- Symmetry breaking: Sometimes some nodes need to be selected to orchestrate computation or communication. This is achieved by a technique called symmetry breaking.

- Synchronization: How can you implement a synchronous algorithm in an asynchronous environment?

- Uncertainty: If we need to agree on a single term that fittingly describes this book, it is probably "uncertainty". As the whole system is distributed, the nodes cannot know what other nodes are doing at this exact moment, and the nodes are required to solve the tasks at hand despite the lack of global knowledge.

Finally, there are also a few areas that we will not cover in this book, mostly because these topics have become so important that they deserve their own books. Examples for such topics are distributed programming or security/cryptography.

In summary, in this book we explore essential algorithmic ideas and lower bound techniques, basically the "pearls" of distributed computing and network algorithms.

Have fun!

Chapter Notes

Many excellent text books have been written on the subject. The most closely related book is by David Peleg [Pel00], as it some of the material. A main focus of Peleg's book are network partitions, covers, decompositions, and spanners – an interesting area that we will only touch in this book. There exist a multitude of other text books that overlap with one or two chapters of this course, e.g., [Lei92, Bar96, Lyn96, Tel01, AW04, HKP$^+$05, CLRS09, Suo12, TR18]. Another related course is by James Aspnes [Asp] and one by Jukka Suomela [Suo14].

Some chapters of this book have been developed in collaboration with (former) Ph.D. students. Many colleagues and students have helped to improve the book. Thanks go to Georg Bachmeier, Philipp Brandes, Raphael Eidenbenz, Roland Flury, Klaus-Tycho Förster, Stephan Holzer, Barbara Keller, Fabian Kuhn, Michael Kuhn, Christoph Lenzen, Darya Melnyk, Thomas Locher, Remo Meier, Thomas Moscibroda, Regina O'Dell, Yvonne-Anne Pignolet, Noy Rotbart, Jochen Seidel, Stefan Schmid, Johannes Schneider, Jara Uitto, Pascal von Rickenbach (in alphabetical order).

Bibliography

[Asp]   James Aspnes. Notes on Theory of Distributed Systems.

[AW04]   Hagit Attiya and Jennifer Welch. *Distributed Computing: Fundamentals, Simulations and Advanced Topics (2nd edition)*. John Wiley Interscience, March 2004.

[Bar96]   Valmir C. Barbosa. *An introduction to distributed algorithms*. MIT Press, Cambridge, MA, USA, 1996.

[CLRS09]   Thomas H. Cormen, Charles E. Leiserson, Ronald L. Rivest, and Clifford Stein. *Introduction to Algorithms (3. ed.)*. MIT Press, 2009.

[HKP+05]   Juraj Hromkovic, Ralf Klasing, Andrzej Pelc, Peter Ruzicka, and Walter Unger. *Dissemination of Information in Communication Networks - Broadcasting, Gossiping, Leader Election, and Fault-Tolerance*. Texts in Theoretical Computer Science. An EATCS Series. Springer, 2005.

[Lei92]   F. Thomson Leighton. *Introduction to parallel algorithms and architectures: array, trees, hypercubes*. Morgan Kaufmann Publishers Inc., San Francisco, CA, USA, 1992.

[Lyn96]   Nancy A. Lynch. *Distributed Algorithms*. Morgan Kaufmann Publishers Inc., San Francisco, CA, USA, 1996.

[Pel00]   David Peleg. *Distributed Computing: a Locality-Sensitive Approach*. Society for Industrial and Applied Mathematics, Philadelphia, PA, USA, 2000.

[Suo12] Jukka Suomela. Deterministic Distributed Algorithms, 2012.

[Suo14] Jukka Suomela. Distributed algorithms. Online textbook, 2014.

[Tel01] Gerard Tel. *Introduction to Distributed Algorithms*. Cambridge University Press, New York, NY, USA, 2nd edition, 2001.

[TR18] Gadi Taubenfeld and Michel Raynal. *Distributed Computing Pearls*. Morgan & Claypool, 2018.

Chapter 1

Vertex Coloring

Vertex coloring is an infamous graph theory problem. It is also a useful toy example to see the style of this course already in the first lecture. Vertex coloring does have quite a few practical applications, for example in the area of wireless networks where coloring is the foundation of so-called TDMA MAC protocols. Generally speaking, vertex coloring is used as a means to break symmetries, one of the main themes in distributed computing. In this chapter we will not really talk about vertex coloring applications, but treat the problem abstractly. At the end of the class you probably learned the fastest algorithm ever! Let us start with some simple definitions and observations.

1.1   Problem & Model

Problem 1.1 (Vertex Coloring)**.** *Given an undirected graph $G = (V, E)$, assign a color c_v to each vertex $v \in V$ such that the following holds: $e = (v, w) \in E \Rightarrow c_v \neq c_w$.*

Remarks:

- Throughout this course, we use the terms *vertex* and *node* interchangeably.

- The application often asks us to use few colors! In a TDMA MAC protocol, for example, less colors immediately imply higher throughput. However, in distributed computing we are often happy with a solution which is suboptimal. There is a tradeoff between the optimality of a solution (efficacy), and the work/time needed to compute the solution (efficiency).

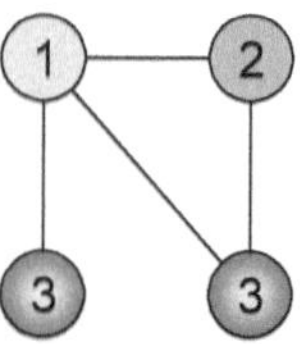

Figure 1.2: 3-colorable graph with a valid coloring.

Assumption 1.3 (Node Identifiers). *Each node has a unique identifier, e.g., its IP address. We usually assume that each identifier consists of only* $\log n$ *bits if the system has* n *nodes.*

Remarks:

- Sometimes we might even assume that the nodes exactly have identifiers $1, \ldots, n$.

- It is easy to see that node identifiers (as defined in Assumption 1.3) solve the coloring problem 1.1, but using n colors is not exciting. How many colors are needed is a well-studied problem:

Definition 1.4 (Chromatic Number). *Given an undirected Graph* $G = (V, E)$, *the **chromatic number** $\chi(G)$ is the minimum number of colors to solve Problem 1.1.*

To get a better understanding of the vertex coloring problem, let us first look at a simple non-distributed ("centralized") vertex coloring algorithm:

Algorithm 1.5 Greedy Sequential

1: **while** there is an uncolored vertex v **do**
2:     color v with the minimal color (number) that does not conflict with the already colored neighbors
3: **end while**

Definition 1.6 (Degree). *The number of neighbors of a vertex v, denoted by $\delta(v)$, is called the **degree** of v. The maximum degree vertex in a graph G defines the graph degree $\Delta(G) = \Delta$.*

Theorem 1.7. *Algorithm 1.5 is correct and terminates in n "steps". The algorithm uses at most $\Delta + 1$ colors.*

Proof: Since each node has at most Δ neighbors, there is always at least one color free in the range $\{1, \ldots, \Delta + 1\}$.

Remarks:

- In Definition 1.11 we will see what is meant by "step".

- Sometimes $\chi(G) \ll \Delta + 1$.

Definition 1.8 (Synchronous Distributed Algorithm). *In a synchronous distributed algorithm, nodes operate in synchronous rounds. In each round, each node executes the following steps:*

1. *Send messages to neighbors in graph (of reasonable size).*

2. *Receive messages (that were sent by neighbors in step 1 of the same round).*

3. *Do some local computation (of reasonable complexity).*

Remarks:

- Any other step ordering is fine.

- What does "reasonable" mean in this context? We are somewhat flexible here, and different model variants exist. Generally, we will deal with algorithms that only do very simple computations (a comparison, an addition, etc.). Exponential-time computation is usually considered cheating in this context. Similarly, sending a message with a node ID, or a value is considered okay, whereas sending really long messages is fishy. We will have more exact definitions later, when we need them.

- We can build a distributed version of Algorithm 1.5:

Algorithm 1.9 Reduce

1: Assume that initially all nodes have IDs
2: **Each node** v executes the following code:
3: node v sends its ID to all neighbors
4: node v receives IDs of neighbors
5: **while** node v has an uncolored neighbor with higher ID **do**
6:     node v sends "undecided" to all neighbors
7:     node v receives new decisions from neighbors
8: **end while**
9: node v chooses the smallest admissible free color
10: node v informs all its neighbors about its choice

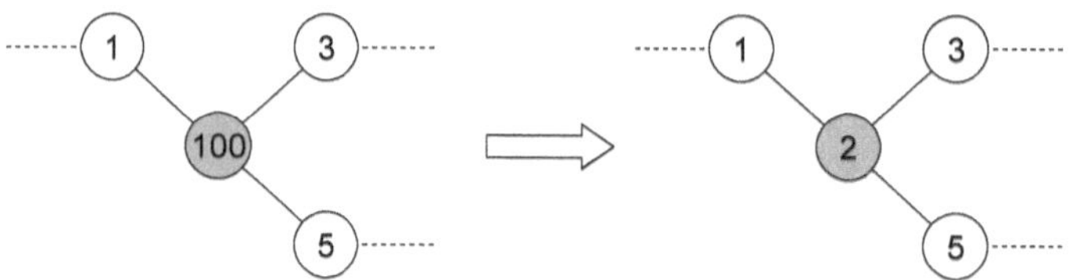

Figure 1.10: Vertex 100 receives the lowest possible color.

Definition 1.11 (Time Complexity). *For synchronous algorithms (as defined in 1.8) the **time complexity** is the number of rounds until the algorithm terminates. The algorithm terminates when the last node terminates.*

Theorem 1.12. *Algorithm 1.9 is correct and has time complexity n. The algorithm uses at most $\Delta + 1$ colors.*

Proof. Nodes choose colors that are different from their neighbors, and no two neighbors choose concurrently. In each round at least one node chooses a color, so we are done after at most n rounds. $\square$

Remarks:

- In the worst case, this algorithm is still not better than sequential.

- Moreover, it seems difficult to come up with a fast algorithm.

- Maybe it's better to first study a simple special case, a tree, and then go from there.

1.2 Coloring Trees

Lemma 1.13. $\chi(Tree) \leq 2$

Proof. Call some node the root of the tree. If the distance of a node to the root is odd (even), color it 1 (0). An odd node has only even neighbors and vice versa. $\qquad\square$

Remarks:

- If we assume that each node knows its parent (root has no parent) and children in a tree, this constructive proof gives a very simple algorithm:

Algorithm 1.14 Slow Tree Coloring

1: Color the root 0, root sends 0 to its children
2: **Each node** v concurrently executes the following code:
3: **if** node v receives a message c_p (from parent) **then**
4:     node v chooses color $c_v = 1 - c_p$
5:     node v sends c_v to its children (all neighbors except parent)
6: **end if**

Theorem 1.15. *Algorithm 1.14 is correct. If each node knows its parent and its children, the time complexity is the tree height which is bounded by the diameter of the tree.*

Remarks:

- How can we determine a root in a tree if it is not already given? We will figure that out later.

- The time complexity of the algorithm is the height of the tree.

- Nice trees, e.g., balanced binary trees, have logarithmic height, that is we have a logarithmic time complexity.

- However, if the tree has a degenerated topology, the time complexity may again be up to n, the number of nodes.

- This algorithm is not very exciting. Can we do better than logarithmic?

Here is the idea of the algorithm: We start with color labels that have $\log n$ bits. In each round we compute a new label with exponentially smaller size than the previous label, still guaranteeing to have a valid vertex coloring! The algorithm terminates in $\log^* n$ time. Log-Star?! That's the number of logarithms (to the base 2) you need to take to get down to 2. Formally:

Definition 1.16 (Log-Star).
$$\forall x \leq 2 : \ \log^* x := 1 \qquad \forall x > 2 : \ \log^* x := 1 + \log^*(\log x)$$

Remarks:

- Log-star is an amazingly slowly growing function. Log-star of all the atoms in the observable universe (estimated to be 10^{80}) is 5. So log-star increases indeed very slowly! There are functions which grow even more slowly, such as the inverse Ackermann function, however, the inverse Ackermann function of all the atoms is already 4.

Algorithm 1.17 6-Color

1: Initially each node v has ID (color) c_v of size $\log n$ bits
2: **Each node** v executes the following code
3: **repeat**
4:     send own color c_v to all children
5:     receive color c_p from parent (for root r set $c_p \in \{0,1\} \neq c_r$)
6:     interpret c_v and c_p as bit-strings
7:     let i be the index of the rightmost bit b where c_v and c_p differ

8:     node v's new color is $c_v = 2i + b$
9: **until** $c_v \in \{0, \dots, 5\}$ for all nodes v

Example:

Algorithm 1.17 executed on the following part of a tree:

Grand-parent	0010110000	$\rightarrow$	10010	$\rightarrow$	...
Parent	1010010000	$\rightarrow$	01010	$\rightarrow$	111
Child	0110010000	$\rightarrow$	10001	$\rightarrow$	001

Theorem 1.18. *Algorithm 1.17 terminates in* $\log^* n + k$ *time, where k is a constant independent of n.*

Proof. We need to show that parent p and child c always have different colors. Initially, this is true, since all nodes start out with their unique ID. In a round, let i be the smallest index where child c has a different bit from parent p. If parent p differs in a different index bit $j \neq i$ from its own parent, parent and child will compute different colors in that round. On the other hand, if $j = i$, the symmetry is broken by p having a different bit at index i.

Regarding runtime, note that the size of the largest color shrinks dramatically in each round, apart from the symmetry-breaking bit, exactly as a logarithmic function. With some (tedious and boring) machinery, one can show that indeed every node will have a color in the range $\{0, \dots, 5\}$ in $\log^* n + k$ rounds. $\qquad\square$

Remarks:

- Let us have a closer look at the end game of the algorithm. Colors 11* (in binary notation, i.e., 6 or 7 in decimal notation) will not be chosen, because the node will then do another round. This gives a total of 6 colors (i.e., colors $0, \dots, 5$).

- What about that last line of the loop? How do the nodes know that all nodes now have a color in the range $\{0, \dots, 5\}$? The answer to this question is surprisingly complex. One may hardwire the number of rounds into the until statement, such that all nodes execute the loop for exactly the same number of rounds. However, in order to do so, all nodes need to know n, the number of nodes, which is ugly. There are (non-trivial) solutions where nodes do not need to know n, see exercises.

- Can one reduce the number of colors? Note that Algorithm 1.9 does not work (since the degree of a node can be much higher than 6)! For fewer colors we need to have siblings monochromatic!

Algorithm 1.19 Shift Down

1: **Each node** v concurrently executes the following code:
2: Recolor v with the color of parent
3: Root chooses a new (different) color from $\{0, 1, 2\}$

Lemma 1.20. *Algorithm 1.19 preserves coloring legality; also siblings are monochromatic.*

Now Algorithm 1.9 can be used to reduce the number of used colors from 6 to 3.

Algorithm 1.21 Six-2-Three

1: **Each node** v concurrently executes the following code:
2: **for** $x = 5, 4, 3$ **do**
3:   Perform subroutine Shift down (Algorithm 1.19)
4:   **if** $c_v = x$ **then**
5:     choose the smallest admissible new color $c_v \in \{0, 1, 2\}$
6:   **end if**
7: **end for**

Theorem 1.23. *Algorithms 1.17 and 1.21 color a tree with three colors in time $O(\log^* n)$.*

Remarks:

- The term $O()$ used in Theorem 1.18 is called "big O" and is often used in distributed computing. Roughly speaking, $O(f)$ means "in the order of f, ignoring constant factors and smaller additive terms." More formally, for two functions f and g, it holds that $f \in O(g)$ if there are constants x_0 and c so that $|f(x)| \leq c|g(x)|$ for all $x \geq x_0$. For an elaborate discussion on the big O notation we refer to other introductory math or computer science classes, or Wikipedia.

- A fast tree-coloring with only 2 colors is more than exponentially more expensive than coloring with 3 colors. In a tree degenerated to a list, nodes far away need to figure out whether they are an even or odd number of hops away from each other in order to get a 2-coloring. To do that one has to send a message to these nodes. This costs time linear in the number of nodes.

- The idea of this algorithm can be generalized, e.g., to a ring topology. Also a general graph with constant degree Δ can be colored with $\Delta + 1$ colors in $O(\log^* n)$ time. The idea is as follows: In each step, a node compares its label to each of its neighbors, constructing a logarithmic

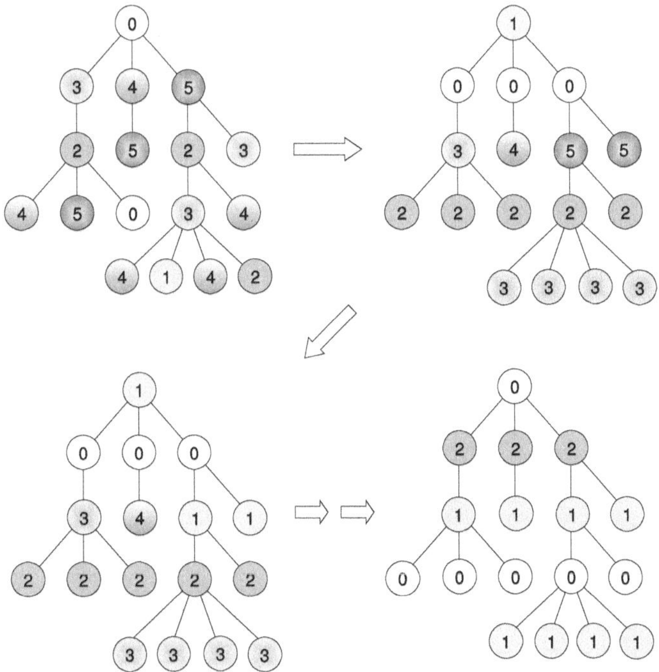

Figure 1.22: Possible execution of Algorithm 1.21.

difference-tag as in Algorithm 1.17. Then the new label is the concatenation of all the difference-tags. For constant degree Δ, this gives a 3Δ-bit label in $O(\log^* n)$ steps. Algorithm 1.9 then reduces the number of colors to $\Delta + 1$ in $2^{3\Delta}$ (this is still a constant for constant Δ!) steps.

- Unfortunately, coloring a general graph is not yet possible with this technique. We will see another technique for that in a later chapter. With this technique it is possible to color a general graph with $\Delta + 1$ colors in $O(\log n)$ time.

- A lower bound shows that many of these log-star algorithms are asymptotically (up to constant factors) optimal. We will see that later.

Chapter Notes

The basic technique of the log-star algorithm is by Cole and Vishkin [CV86]. A tight bound of $\frac{1}{2}\log^* n$ was proven recently [RS15]. The technique can be generalized and extended, e.g., to a ring topology or to graphs with constant degree [GP87, GPS88, KMW05]. Using it as a subroutine, one can solve many problems in log-star time. For instance, one can color so-called growth bounded graphs (a model which includes many natural graph classes, for instance unit disk graphs) asymptotically optimally in $O(\log^* n)$ time [SW08]. Actually, Schneider et al. show that many classic combinatorial problems beyond coloring can be solved in log-star time in growth bounded and other restricted graphs. For the case of toroidal grids of fixed dimension $d > 2$, a generalization of the ring topology to higher dimensions, Brandt et al. recently proved that a coloring with 4 colors can be found in $O(\log^* n)$ time while a 3-coloring requires global time [BHK$^+$17].

In a later chapter we learn a $\Omega(\log^* n)$ lower bound for coloring and related problems [Lin92]. Linial's paper also contains a number of other results on coloring, e.g., that any algorithm for coloring d-regular trees of radius r that run in time at most $2r/3$ require at least $\Omega(\sqrt{d})$ colors.

For general graphs, later we will learn fast coloring algorithms that use a maximal independent set as a base. Since coloring exhibits a trade-off between efficacy and efficiency, many different results for general graphs exist, e.g., [PS96, KSOS06, BE09, Kuh09, SW10, BE11b, KP11, BE11a, BEPS12, PS13, CPS14, BEK14].

Some parts of this chapter are also discussed in Chapter 7 of [Pel00], e.g., the proof of Theorem 1.18.

Bibliography

[BE09] Leonid Barenboim and Michael Elkin. Distributed (delta+1)-coloring in linear (in delta) time. In *41st ACM Symposium On Theory of Computing (STOC)*, 2009.

[BE11a] Leonid Barenboim and Michael Elkin. Combinatorial Algorithms for Distributed Graph Coloring. In *25th International Symposium on DIStributed Computing*, 2011.

[BE11b] Leonid Barenboim and Michael Elkin. Deterministic Distributed Vertex Coloring in Polylogarithmic Time. *J. ACM*, 58(5):23, 2011.

[BEK14] Leonid Barenboim, Michael Elkin, and Fabian Kuhn. Distributed (delta+1)-coloring in linear (in delta) time. *SIAM J. Comput.*, 43(1):72–95, 2014.

[BEPS12] Leonid Barenboim, Michael Elkin, Seth Pettie, and Johannes Schneider. The locality of distributed symmetry breaking. In *Foundations of Computer Science (FOCS), 2012 IEEE 53rd Annual Symposium on*, pages 321–330, 2012.

[BHK$^+$17] S. Brandt, J. Hirvonen, J. H. Korhonen, T. Lempiäinen, P. R. J. Östergård, C. Purcell, J. Rybicki, J. Suomela, and P. Uznański. LCL problems on grids. *ArXiv e-prints*, February 2017.

[CPS14] Kai-Min Chung, Seth Pettie, and Hsin-Hao Su. Distributed algorithms for the lovász local lemma and graph coloring. In *ACM Symposium on Principles of Distributed Computing*, pages 134–143, 2014.

[CV86] R. Cole and U. Vishkin. Deterministic coin tossing and accelerating cascades: micro and macro techniques for designing parallel algorithms. In *18th annual ACM Symposium on Theory of Computing (STOC)*, 1986.

[GP87] Andrew V. Goldberg and Serge A. Plotkin. Parallel $(\Delta+1)$-coloring of constant-degree graphs. *Inf. Process. Lett.*, 25(4):241–245, June 1987.

[GPS88] Andrew V. Goldberg, Serge A. Plotkin, and Gregory E. Shannon. Parallel Symmetry-Breaking in Sparse Graphs. *SIAM J. Discrete Math.*, 1(4):434–446, 1988.

[KMW05] Fabian Kuhn, Thomas Moscibroda, and Roger Wattenhofer. On the Locality of Bounded Growth. In *24th ACM Symposium on the Principles of Distributed Computing (PODC), Las Vegas, Nevada, USA*, July 2005.

[KP11] Kishore Kothapalli and Sriram V. Pemmaraju. Distributed graph coloring in a few rounds. In *30th ACM*

SIGACT-SIGOPS Symposium on Principles of Distributed Computing (PODC), 2011.

[KSOS06] Kishore Kothapalli, Christian Scheideler, Melih Onus, and Christian Schindelhauer. Distributed coloring in $O(\sqrt{\log n})$ Bit Rounds. In *20th international conference on Parallel and Distributed Processing (IPDPS)*, 2006.

[Kuh09] Fabian Kuhn. Weak graph colorings: distributed algorithms and applications. In *21st ACM Symposium on Parallelism in Algorithms and Architectures (SPAA)*, 2009.

[Lin92] N. Linial. Locality in Distributed Graph Algorithms. *SIAM Journal on Computing*, 21(1)(1):193–201, February 1992.

[Pel00] David Peleg. *Distributed Computing: a Locality-Sensitive Approach*. Society for Industrial and Applied Mathematics, Philadelphia, PA, USA, 2000.

[PS96] Alessandro Panconesi and Aravind Srinivasan. On the Complexity of Distributed Network Decomposition. *J. Algorithms*, 20(2):356–374, 1996.

[PS13] Seth Pettie and Hsin-Hao Su. Fast distributed coloring algorithms for triangle-free graphs. In *Automata, Languages, and Programming - 40th International Colloquium, ICALP*, pages 681–693, 2013.

[RS15] Joel Rybicki and Jukka Suomela. Exact bounds for distributed graph colouring. In *Structural Information and Communication Complexity - 22nd International Colloquium, SIROCCO 2015, Montserrat, Spain, July 14-16, 2015, Post-Proceedings*, pages 46–60, 2015.

[SW08] Johannes Schneider and Roger Wattenhofer. A Log-Star Distributed Maximal Independent Set Algorithm for Growth-Bounded Graphs. In *27th ACM Symposium on Principles of Distributed Computing (PODC), Toronto, Canada*, August 2008.

[SW10] Johannes Schneider and Roger Wattenhofer. A New Technique For Distributed Symmetry Breaking. In *29th Symposium on Principles of Distributed Computing (PODC), Zurich, Switzerland*, July 2010.

Chapter 2

Tree Algorithms

In this chapter we learn a few basic algorithms on trees, and how to construct trees in the first place so that we can run these (and other) algorithms. The good news is that these algorithms have many applications, the bad news is that this chapter is a bit on the simple side. But maybe that's not really bad news?!

2.1 Broadcast

Definition 2.1 (Broadcast). *A **broadcast** operation is initiated by a single node, the source. The source wants to send a message to all other nodes in the system.*

Definition 2.2 (Distance, Radius, Diameter). *The **distance** between two nodes u and v in an undirected graph G is the number of hops of a minimum path between u and v. The **radius** of a node u is the maximum distance between u and any other node in the graph. The radius of a graph is the minimum radius of any node in the graph. The **diameter** of a graph is the maximum distance between two arbitrary nodes.*

Remarks:

- Clearly there is a close relation between the radius R and the diameter D of a graph, such as $R \leq D \leq 2R$.

Definition 2.3 (Message Complexity). *The **message complexity** of an algorithm is determined by the total number of messages exchanged.*

Theorem 2.4 (Broadcast Lower Bound). *The message complexity of broadcast is at least $n - 1$. The source's radius is a lower bound for the time complexity.*

Proof: Every node must receive the message.

Remarks:

- You can use a pre-computed spanning tree to do broadcast with tight message complexity. If the spanning tree is a breadth-first search spanning tree (for a given source), then the time complexity is tight as well.

Definition 2.5 (Clean). *A graph (network) is **clean** if the nodes do not know the topology of the graph.*

Theorem 2.6 (Clean Broadcast Lower Bound). *For a clean network, the number of edges m is a lower bound for the broadcast message complexity.*

Proof: If you do not try every edge, you might miss a whole part of the graph behind it.

Definition 2.7 (Asynchronous Distributed Algorithm). *In the asynchronous model, algorithms are event driven ("upon receiving message . . . , do . . . "). Nodes cannot access a global clock. A message sent from one node to another will arrive in finite but unbounded time.*

Remarks:

- The asynchronous model and the synchronous model (Definition 1.8) are the cornerstone models in distributed computing. As they do not necessarily reflect reality there are several models in between synchronous and asynchronous. However, from a theoretical point of view the synchronous and the asynchronous model are the most interesting ones (because every other model is in between these extremes).

- Note that in the asynchronous model, messages that take a longer path may arrive earlier.

Definition 2.8 (Asynchronous Time Complexity). *For asynchronous algorithms (as defined in 2.7) the **time complexity** is the number of time units from the start of the execution to its completion in the worst case (every legal input, every execution scenario), assuming that each message has a delay of at most one time unit.*

Remarks:

- You cannot use the maximum delay in the algorithm design. In other words, the algorithm has to be correct even if there is no such delay upper bound.

- The clean broadcast lower bound (Theorem 2.6) directly brings us to the well known *flooding* algorithm.

Algorithm 2.9 Flooding

1: The source (root) sends the message to all neighbors.
2: **Each other node** v upon receiving the message the first time forwards the message to all (other) neighbors.
3: Upon later receiving the message again (over other edges), a node can discard the message.

Remarks:

- If node v receives the message first from node u, then node v calls node u *parent*. This parent relation defines a spanning tree T. If the flooding algorithm is executed in a synchronous system, then T is a breadth-first search spanning tree (with respect to the root).

- More interestingly, also in asynchronous systems the flooding algorithm terminates after R time units, R being the radius of the source. However, the constructed spanning tree may not be a breadth-first search spanning tree.

2.2 Convergecast

Convergecast is the same as broadcast, just reversed: Instead of a root sending a message to all other nodes, all other nodes send information to a root (starting from the leaves, i.e., the tree T is known). The simplest convergecast algorithm is the echo algorithm:

Algorithm 2.10 Echo

1: A leaf sends a message to its parent.
2: If an inner node has received a message from each child, it sends a message to the parent.

Remarks:

- Usually the echo algorithm is paired with the flooding algorithm, which is used to let the leaves know that they should start the echo process; this is known as flooding/echo.

- One can use convergecast for termination detection, for example. If a root wants to know whether all nodes in the system have finished some task, it initiates a flooding/echo; the message in the echo algorithm then means "This subtree has finished the task."

- Message complexity of the echo algorithm is $n - 1$, but together with flooding it is $O(m)$, where $m = |E|$ is the number of edges in the graph.

- The time complexity of the echo algorithm is determined by the depth of the spanning tree (i.e., the radius of the root within the tree) generated by the flooding algorithm.

- The flooding/echo algorithm can do much more than collecting acknowledgements from subtrees. One can for instance use it to compute the number of nodes in the system, or the maximum ID, or the sum of all values stored in the system, or a route-disjoint matching.

- Moreover, by combining results one can compute even fancier aggregations, e.g., with the number of nodes and the sum one can compute the average. With the average one can compute the standard deviation. And so on ...

2.3 BFS Tree Construction

In synchronous systems the flooding algorithm is a simple yet efficient method to construct a breadth-first search (BFS) spanning tree. However, in asynchronous systems the spanning tree constructed by the flooding algorithm may be far from BFS. In this section, we implement two classic BFS constructions—Dijkstra and Bellman-Ford—as asynchronous algorithms.

We start with the Dijkstra algorithm. The basic idea is to always add the "closest" node to the existing part of the BFS tree. We need to parallelize this idea by developing the BFS tree layer by layer. The algorithm proceeds in phases. In phase p the nodes with distance p to the root (at level p) are detected.

Algorithm 2.11 Dijkstra BFS

1: We start with phase $p = 1$ with a tree T which is the root plus all direct neighbors of the root:
2: **repeat**
3:     The root starts phase p by broadcasting "start p" within T.
4:     When receiving "start p", a leaf node u of T (that is, a node at level p) sends a "join $p+1$" message to all quiet neighbors. (A neighbor v is quiet if u has not yet communicated with v.)
5:     If a node v that is not yet in T receives a "join $p+1$" message, then node v replies with "ACK" and becomes a new leaf of the tree T at level $p + 1$.
6:     If a node v is already in T, the node v replies with "NACK" to all "join" messages.
7:     The leaves of T at level p collect all the answers of their neighbors; then the leaves start an echo algorithm back to the root.
8:     When the echo process terminates at the root, the root increments the phase.
9: **until** there was no new node detected

Theorem 2.12. *The time complexity of Algorithm 2.11 is $O(D^2)$, the message complexity is $O(m + nD)$, where D is the diameter of the graph, n the number of nodes, and m the number of edges.*

Proof: A broadcast/echo algorithm in a BFS tree needs at most time $2D$. Finding new neighbors at the leaves costs 2 time units. Since the BFS tree height is bounded by the diameter, we have D phases, giving a total time complexity of $O(D^2)$. Each node participating in broadcast/echo only receives at most 1 message while broadcasting and sends at most 1 message while echoing. Since there are D phases, the cost is bounded by $O(nD)$. On each edge there are at most 2 "join" messages. Replies to a "join" request are answered by 1 "ACK" or "NACK" , which means that we have at most 4 additional messages per edge. Therefore the message complexity is $O(m + nD)$.

Remarks:

- The time complexity is not very exciting, so let's try Bellman-Ford!

The basic idea of Bellman-Ford is even simpler, and heavily used in the Internet, as it is a basic version of the omnipresent border gateway protocol (BGP). The idea is to simply keep the distance to the root accurate. If a neighbor has found a better route to the root, a node might also need to update its distance.

Algorithm 2.13 Bellman-Ford BFS

1: Each node u stores an integer d_u which corresponds to the distance from u to the root. Initially $d_{\text{root}} = 0$, and $d_u = \infty$ for every other node u.
2: The root starts the algorithm by sending "1" to all neighbors.
3: **if** a node u receives a message "y" with $y < d_u$ from a neighbor v **then**
4:     node u sets $d_u := y$
5:     node u sends "$y + 1$" to all neighbors (except v)
6: **end if**

Theorem 2.14. *The time complexity of Algorithm 2.13 is $O(D)$, the message complexity is $O(nm)$, where D, n, m are defined as in Theorem 2.12.*

Proof: We can prove the time complexity by induction. We claim that a node at distance d from the root has received a message "d" by time d. The root knows by time 0 that it is the root. A node v at distance d has a neighbor u at distance $d - 1$. Node u by induction sends a message "d" to v at time $d - 1$ or before, which is then received by v at time d or before. Message complexity is easier: A node can reduce its distance at most $n - 1$ times; each of these times it sends a message to all its neighbors. If all nodes do this, then we have $O(nm)$ messages.

Remarks:

- Algorithm 2.11 has the better message complexity and Algorithm 2.13 has the better time complexity. The currently best algorithm (optimizing both) needs $O(m + n \log^3 n)$ messages and $O(D \log^3 n)$ time. This "trade-off" algorithm is beyond the scope of this chapter, but we will later learn the general technique.

2.4 MST Construction

There are several types of spanning trees, each serving a different purpose. A particularly interesting spanning tree is the minimum spanning tree (MST). The MST only makes sense on weighted graphs, hence in this section we assume that each edge e is assigned a weight ω_e.

Definition 2.15 (MST). *Given a weighted graph $G = (V, E, \omega)$, the MST of G is a spanning tree T minimizing $\omega(T)$, where $\omega(G') = \sum_{e \in G'} \omega_e$ for any subgraph $G' \subseteq G$.*

Remarks:

- In the following we assume that no two edges of the graph have the same weight. This simplifies the problem as it makes the MST unique; however, this simplification is not essential as one can always break ties by adding the IDs of adjacent vertices to the weight.

- Obviously we are interested in computing the MST in a distributed way. For this we use a well-known lemma:

Definition 2.16 (Blue Edges). *Let T be a spanning tree of the weighted graph G and $T' \subseteq T$ a subgraph of T (also called a **fragment**). Edge $e = (u, v)$ is an **outgoing edge** of T' if $u \in T'$ and $v \notin T'$ (or vice versa). The minimum weight outgoing edge $b(T')$ is the so-called **blue edge** of T'.*

Lemma 2.17. *For a given weighted graph G (such that no two weights are the same), let T denote the MST, and T' be a fragment of T. Then the blue edge of T' is also part of T, i.e., $T' \cup b(T') \subseteq T$.*

Proof: For the sake of contradiction, suppose that in the MST T there is edge $e \neq b(T')$ connecting T' with the remainder of T. Adding the blue edge $b(T')$ to the MST T we get a cycle including both e and $b(T')$. If we remove e from this cycle, then we still have a spanning tree, and since by the definition of the blue edge $\omega_e > \omega_{b(T')}$, the weight of that new spanning tree is less than than the weight of T. We have a contradiction.

Remarks:

- In other words, the blue edges seem to be the key to a distributed algorithm for the MST problem. Since every node itself is a fragment of the MST, every node directly has a blue edge! All we need to do is to grow these fragments! Essentially this is a distributed version of Kruskal's sequential algorithm.

- At any given time the nodes of the graph are partitioned into fragments (rooted subtrees of the MST). Each fragment has a root, the ID of the fragment is the ID of its root. Each node knows its parent and its children in the fragment. The algorithm operates in phases. At the beginning of a phase, nodes know the IDs of the fragments of their neighbor nodes.

Remarks:

- Algorithm 2.18 was stated in pseudo-code, with a few details not really explained. For instance, it may be that some fragments are much larger than others, and because of that some nodes may need to wait for others, e.g., if node u needs to find out whether neighbor v also wants to merge over the blue edge $b = (u, v)$. The good news is that all these details can be solved. We can for instance bound the asynchronicity by guaranteeing that nodes only start the new phase after the last phase is done, similarly to the phase-technique of Algorithm 2.11.

Theorem 2.19. *The time complexity of Algorithm 2.18 is $O(n \log n)$, the message complexity is $O(m \log n)$.*

Proof: Each phase mainly consists of two flooding/echo processes. In general, the cost of flooding/echo on a tree is $O(D)$ time and $O(n)$ messages. However, the diameter D of the fragments may turn out to be not related to the diameter of the graph because the

---

Algorithm 2.18 GHS (Gallager–Humblet–Spira)

1: Initially each node is the root of its own fragment. We proceed in phases:
2: **repeat**
3:     All nodes learn the fragment IDs of their neighbors.
4:     The root of each fragment uses flooding/echo in its fragment to determine the blue edge $b = (u, v)$ of the fragment.
5:     The root sends a message to node u; while forwarding the message on the path from the root to node u all parent-child relations are inverted {such that u is the new temporary root of the fragment}
6:     node u sends a merge request over the blue edge $b = (u, v)$.
7:     **if** node v also sent a merge request over the same blue edge $b = (v, u)$ **then**
8:         either u or v (whichever has the smaller ID) is the new fragment root
9:         the blue edge b is directed accordingly
10:     **else**
11:         node v is the new parent of node u
12:     **end if**
13:     the newly elected root node informs all nodes in its fragment (again using flooding/echo) about its identity
14: **until** all nodes are in the same fragment (i.e., there is no outgoing edge)

MST may meander, hence it really is $O(n)$ time. In addition, in the first step of each phase, nodes need to learn the fragment ID of their neighbors; this can be done in 2 steps but costs $O(m)$ messages. There are a few more steps, but they are cheap. Altogether a phase costs $O(n)$ time and $O(m)$ messages. So we only have to figure out the number of phases: Initially all fragments are single nodes and hence have size 1. In a later phase, each fragment merges with at least one other fragment, that is, the size of the smallest fragment at least doubles. In other words, we have at most $\log n$ phases. The theorem follows directly.

Chapter Notes

Trees are one of the oldest graph structures, already appearing in the first book about graph theory [Koe36]. Broadcasting in distributed computing is younger, but not that much [DM78]. Overviews about broadcasting can be found for example in Chapter 3 of [Pel00] and Chapter 7 of [HKP+05]. For a introduction to centralized tree-construction, see e.g. [Eve79] or [CLRS09]. Overviews for the distributed case can be found in Chapter 5 of [Pel00] or Chapter 4 of [Lyn96]. The classic papers on routing are [For56, Bel58, Dij59]. In a later chapter, we will later learn a general technique to derive algorithms with an almost optimal time and message complexity.

Algorithm 2.18 is called "GHS" after Gallager, Humblet, and Spira, three pioneers in distributed computing [GHS83]. Their algorithm won the prestigious Edsger W. Dijkstra Prize in Distributed Computing in 2004, among other reasons because it was one of the first non-trivial asynchronous distributed algorithms. As such it can be seen as one of the seeds of this research area. We presented a simplified version of GHS. The original paper featured an improved message complexity of $O(m + n \log n)$. Later, Awerbuch managed to further improve the GHS algorithm to get $O(n)$ time and $O(m + n \log n)$ message complexity, both asymptotically optimal [Awe87].

Bibliography

[Awe87] B. Awerbuch. Optimal distributed algorithms for minimum weight spanning tree, counting, leader election, and related problems. In *Proceedings of the nineteenth annual ACM symposium on Theory of computing*, STOC '87, pages 230–240, New York, NY, USA, 1987. ACM.

[Bel58] Richard Bellman. On a Routing Problem. *Quarterly of Applied Mathematics*, 16:87–90, 1958.

[CLRS09] Thomas H. Cormen, Charles E. Leiserson, Ronald L. Rivest, and Clifford Stein. *Introduction to Algorithms (3. ed.)*. MIT Press, 2009.

[Dij59] E. W. Dijkstra. A Note on Two Problems in Connexion
         with Graphs. *Numerische Mathematik*, 1(1):269–271,
         1959.

[DM78]   Y.K. Dalal and R.M. Metcalfe. Reverse path forwarding
         of broadcast packets. *Communications of the ACM*,
         12:1040–148, 1978.

[Eve79] S. Even. *Graph Algorithms*. Computer Science Press,
         Rockville, MD, 1979.

[For56] Lester R. Ford. Network Flow Theory. *The RAND
         Corporation Paper P-923*, 1956.

[GHS83] R. G. Gallager, P. A. Humblet, and P. M. Spira. Distrib-
         uted Algorithm for Minimum-Weight Spanning Trees.
         *ACM Transactions on Programming Languages and
         Systems*, 5(1):66–77, January 1983.

[HKP+05] Juraj Hromkovic, Ralf Klasing, Andrzej Pelc, Peter
         Ruzicka, and Walter Unger. *Dissemination of Informa-
         tion in Communication Networks - Broadcasting, Gos-
         siping, Leader Election, and Fault-Tolerance*. Texts
         in Theoretical Computer Science. An EATCS Series.
         Springer, 2005.

[Koe36] Denes Koenig. *Theorie der endlichen und unendlichen
         Graphen*. Teubner, Leipzig, 1936.

[Lyn96] Nancy A. Lynch. *Distributed Algorithms*. Morgan Kauf-
         mann Publishers Inc., San Francisco, CA, USA, 1996.

[Pel00] David Peleg. *Distributed Computing: a Locality-
         Sensitive Approach*. Society for Industrial and Applied
         Mathematics, Philadelphia, PA, USA, 2000.

Chapter 3

Leader Election

Some algorithms (e.g. the slow tree coloring Algorithm 1.14) ask for a special node, a so-called "leader". Computing a leader is a very simple form of symmetry breaking. Algorithms based on leaders do generally not exhibit a high degree of parallelism, and therefore often suffer from poor time complexity. However, sometimes it is still useful to have a leader to make critical decisions in an easy (though non-distributed!) way.

3.1 Anonymous Leader Election

The process of choosing a leader is known as *leader election*. Although leader election is a simple form of symmetry breaking, there are some remarkable issues that allow us to introduce notable computational models.

In this chapter we concentrate on the ring topology. Many interesting challenges in distributed computing already reveal the root of the problem in the special case of the ring. Paying attention to the ring also makes sense from a practical point of view as some real world systems are based on a ring topology, e.g., the antiquated token ring standard.

Problem 3.1 (Leader Election). *Each node eventually decides whether it is a leader or not, subject to the constraint that there is exactly one leader.*

Remarks:

- More formally, nodes are in one of three states: undecided, leader, not leader. Initially every node is in the undecided state. When leaving the undecided state, a node goes into a final state (leader or not leader).

Definition 3.2 (Anonymous). *indexanonymous A system is anonymous if nodes do not have unique identifiers.*

Definition 3.3 (Uniform). *An algorithm is called uniform if the number of nodes n is not known to the algorithm (to the nodes, if you wish). If n is known, the algorithm is called non-uniform.*

Whether a leader can be elected in an anonymous system depends on whether the network is symmetric (ring, complete graph, complete bipartite graph, etc.) or asymmetric (star, single node with highest degree, etc.). We will now show that non-uniform anonymous leader election for synchronous rings is impossible. The idea is that in a ring, symmetry can always be maintained.

Lemma 3.4. *After round k of any deterministic algorithm on an anonymous ring, each node is in the same state s_k.*

Proof by induction: All nodes start in the same state. A round in a synchronous algorithm consists of the three steps sending, receiving, local computation (see Definition 1.8). All nodes send the same message(s), receive the same message(s), do the same local computation, and therefore end up in the same state.

Theorem 3.5 (Anonymous Leader Election). *Deterministic leader election in an anonymous ring is impossible.*

Proof (with Lemma 3.4): If one node ever decides to become a leader (or a non-leader), then every other node does so as well, contradicting the problem specification 3.1 for $n > 1$. This holds for non-uniform algorithms, and therefore also for uniform algorithms. Furthermore, it holds for synchronous algorithms, and therefore also for asynchronous algorithms.

Remarks:

- Sense of direction is the ability of nodes to distinguish neighbor nodes in an anonymous setting. In a ring, for example, a node can distinguish the clockwise and the counterclockwise neighbor. Sense of direction does not help in anonymous leader election.

- Theorem 3.5 also holds for other symmetric network topologies (e.g., complete graphs, complete bipartite graphs, ...).

- Note that Theorem 3.5 does generally not hold for randomized algorithms; if nodes are allowed to toss a coin, some symmetries can be broken.

- However, more surprisingly, randomization does not always help. A randomized uniform anonymous algorithm can for instance not elect a leader in a ring. Randomization does not help to decide whether the ring has $n = 3$ or $n = 6$ nodes: Every third node may generate the same random bits, and as a result the nodes cannot distinguish the two cases. However, an approximation of n which is strictly better than a factor 2 will help.

3.2   Asynchronous Ring

We first concentrate on the asynchronous model from Definition 2.7. Throughout this section we assume non-anonymity; each node has a unique identifier. Having IDs seems to lead to a trivial leader election algorithm, as we can simply elect the node with, e.g., the highest ID.

Algorithm 3.6 Clockwise Leader Election

1: **Each node** v executes the following code:
2: v sends a message with its identifier (for simplicity also v) to its clockwise neighbor.
3: v sets $m := v$ {the largest identifier seen so far}
4: **if** v receives a message w with $w > m$ **then**
5:    v forwards message w to its clockwise neighbor and sets $m := w$
6:    v decides not to be the leader, if it has not done so already.
7: **else if** v receives its own identifier v **then**
8:    v decides to be the leader
9: **end if**

Theorem 3.7. *Algorithm 3.6 is correct. The time complexity is $O(n)$. The message complexity is $O(n^2)$.*

Proof: Let node z be the node with the maximum identifier. Node z sends its identifier in clockwise direction, and since no other node can swallow it, eventually a message will arrive at z containing it. Then z declares itself to be the leader. Every other node will declare non-leader at the latest when forwarding message z. Since there are n identifiers in the system, each node will at most forward n messages, giving a message complexity of at most n^2. We start measuring the time when the first node that "wakes up" sends its identifier. For asynchronous time complexity (Definition 2.8) we assume that each message takes at most one time unit to arrive at its destination. After at most $n-1$ time units the message therefore arrives at node z, waking z up. Routing the message z around the ring takes at most n time units. Therefore node z decides no later than at time $2n - 1$. Every other node decides before node z.

Remarks:

- Note that in Algorithm 3.6 nodes distinguish between clockwise and counterclockwise neighbors. This is not necessary: It is okay to simply send your own identifier to any neighbor, and forward a message to the neighbor you did not receive the message from. So nodes only need to be able to distinguish their two neighbors.

- Careful analysis shows, that while having worst-case message complexity of $O(n^2)$, Algorithm 3.6 has an *average* message complexity of $O(n \log n)$. Can we improve this algorithm?

Theorem 3.9. *Algorithm 3.8 is correct. The time complexity is* $O(n)$. *The message complexity is* $O(n \log n)$.

Proof: Correctness is as in Theorem 3.7. The time complexity is $O(n)$ since the node with maximum identifier z sends messages with round-trip times $2, 4, 8, 16, \ldots, 2 \cdot 2^k$ with $k \leq \log(n + 1)$. (Even if we include the additional wake-up overhead, the time complexity stays linear.) Proving the message complexity is slightly harder: if a node v manages to survive round r, no other node in distance 2^r (or less) survives round r. That is, node v is the only node in its 2^r-neighborhood that remains active in round $r + 1$. Since this is the same for every node, less than $n/2^r$ nodes are active in round $r + 1$. Being active in round r costs $2 \cdot 2 \cdot 2^r$ messages. Therefore,

---

Algorithm 3.8 Radius Growth

1: **Each node** v does the following:
2: Initially all nodes are *active*. {all nodes may still become leaders}
3: Whenever a node v sees a message w with $w > v$, then v decides to not be a leader and becomes *passive*.
4: Active nodes search in an exponentially growing neighborhood (clockwise and counterclockwise) for nodes with higher identifiers, by sending out *probe* messages. A probe message includes the ID of the original sender, a bit whether the sender can still become a leader, and a time-to-live number (*TTL*). The first probe message sent by node v includes a TTL of 1.
5: Nodes (active or passive) receiving a probe message decrement the TTL and forward the message to the next neighbor; if their ID is larger than the one in the message, they set the leader bit to zero, as the probing node does not have the maximum ID. If the TTL is zero, probe messages are returned to the sender using a *reply* message. The reply message contains the ID of the receiver (the original sender of the probe message) and the leader-bit. Reply messages are forwarded by all nodes until they reach the receiver.
6: Upon receiving the reply message: If there was no node with higher ID in the search area (indicated by the bit in the reply message), the TTL is doubled and two new probe messages are sent (again to the two neighbors). If there was a better candidate in the search area, then the node becomes passive.
7: If a node v receives its own probe message (not a reply) v decides to be the leader.

---

round r costs at most $2 \cdot 2 \cdot 2^r \cdot \frac{n}{2^{r-1}} = 8n$ messages. Since there are only logarithmic many possible rounds, the message complexity follows immediately.

Remarks:

- This algorithm is asynchronous and uniform as well.

- The question may arise whether one can design an algorithm with an even lower message complexity. We answer this question in the next section.

3.3   Lower Bounds

Lower bounds in distributed computing are often easier than in the standard centralized (random access machine, RAM) model because one can argue about messages that need to be exchanged. In this section we present a first difficult lower bound. We show that Algorithm 3.8 is asymptotically optimal.

Definition 3.10 (Execution). *An execution of a distributed algorithm is a list of events, sorted by time. An event is a record (time, node, type, message), where type is "send" or "receive".*

Remarks:

- We assume throughout this course that no two events happen at exactly the same time (or one can break ties arbitrarily).

- An execution of an asynchronous algorithm is generally not only determined by the algorithm but also by a "god-like" scheduler. If more than one message is in transit, the scheduler can choose which one arrives first.

- If two messages are transmitted over the same directed edge, then it is sometimes required that the message first transmitted will also be received first ("FIFO").

For our lower bound, we assume the following model:

- We are given an asynchronous ring, where nodes may wake up at arbitrary times (but at the latest when receiving the first message).

- We only accept uniform algorithms where the node with the maximum identifier can be the leader. Additionally, every node that is not the leader must know the identity of the leader. These two requirements can be dropped when using a more complicated proof; however, this is beyond the scope of this course.

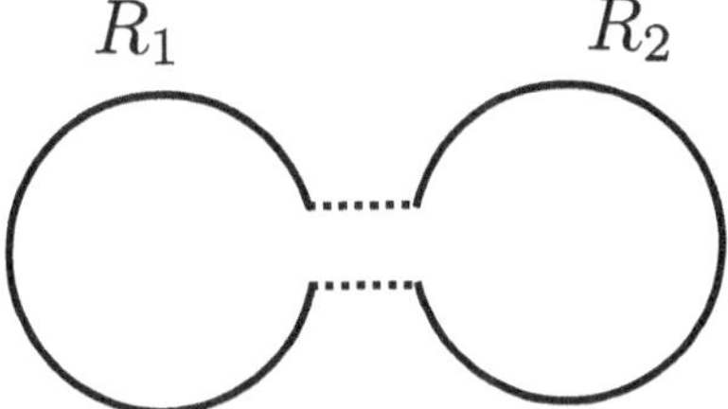

Figure 3.13: The rings R_1, R_2 are glued together at their open edge.

- During the proof we will "play god" and specify which message in transmission arrives next in the execution. We respect the FIFO conditions for links.

Definition 3.11 (Open Schedule). *A schedule is an execution chosen by the scheduler. An open (undirected) edge is an edge where no message traversing the edge has been received so far. A schedule for a ring is open if there is an open edge in the ring.*

The proof of the lower bound is by induction. First we show the base case:

Lemma 3.12. *Given a ring R with two nodes, we can construct an open schedule in which at least one message is received. The nodes cannot distinguish this schedule from one on a larger ring with all other nodes being where the open edge is.*

Proof: Let the two nodes be u and v with $u < v$. Node u must learn the identity of node v, thus receive at least one message. We stop the execution of the algorithm as soon as the first message is received. (If the first message is received by v, bad luck for the algorithm!) Then the other edge in the ring (on which the received message was not transmitted) is open. Since the algorithm needs to be uniform, maybe the open edge is not really an edge at all, nobody can tell. We could use this to glue two rings together, by breaking up this imaginary open edge and connect two rings by two edges. An example can be seen in Figure 3.13.

Lemma 3.14. *By gluing together two rings of size $n/2$ for which we have open schedules, we can construct an open schedule on a ring of size n. If $M(n/2)$ denotes the number of messages already received in each of these schedules, at least $2M(n/2)+n/4$ messages have to be exchanged in order to solve leader election.*

We divide the ring into two sub-rings R_1 and R_2 of size $n/2$. These subrings cannot be distinguished from rings with $n/2$ nodes if no messages are received from "outsiders". We can ensure this by not scheduling such messages until we want to. Note that executing both given open schedules on R_1 and R_2 "in parallel" is possible because we control not only the scheduling of the messages, but also when nodes wake up. By doing so, we make sure that $2M(n/2)$ messages are sent before the nodes in R_1 and R_2 learn anything of each other!

Without loss of generality, R_1 contains the maximum identifier. Hence, each node in R_2 must learn the identity of the maximum identifier, thus at least $n/2$ additional messages must be received. The only problem is that we cannot connect the two sub-rings with both edges since the new ring needs to remain open. Thus, only messages over one of the edges can be received. We look into the future: we check what happens when we close only one of these connecting edges.

Since we know that $n/2$ nodes have to be informed in R_2, there must be at least $n/2$ messages that must be received. Closing both edges must inform $n/2$ nodes, thus for one of the two edges there must be a node in distance $n/4$ which will be informed upon creating that edge. This results in $n/4$ additional messages. Thus, we pick this edge and leave the other one open which yields the claim.

Lemma 3.15. *Any uniform leader election algorithm for asynchronous rings has at least message complexity $M(n) \geq \frac{n}{4}(\log n + 1)$.*

Proof by induction: For the sake of simplicity we assume n being a power of 2. The base case $n = 2$ works because of Lemma 3.12 which implies that $M(2) \geq 1 = \frac{2}{4}(\log 2 + 1)$. For the induction step, using Lemma 3.14 and the induction hypothesis we have

$$
\begin{aligned}
M(n) &= 2 \cdot M\left(\frac{n}{2}\right) + \frac{n}{4} \\
&\geq 2 \cdot \left(\frac{n}{8}\left(\log\frac{n}{2} + 1\right)\right) + \frac{n}{4} \\
&= \frac{n}{4}\log n + \frac{n}{4} = \frac{n}{4}(\log n + 1).
\end{aligned}
$$

$\square$

Remarks:

- To hide the ugly constants we use the "big Omega" notation, the lower bound equivalent of $O()$. A function f is in $\Omega(g)$ if there are constants x_0 and $c > 0$ such that $|f(x)| \geq c|g(x)|$ for all $x \geq x_0$.

- In addition to the already presented parts of the "big O" notation, there are 3 additional ones. Remember that a function f is in $O(g)$ if f grows at most as fast as g. A function f is in $o(g)$ if f grows slower than g.

- An analogous small letter notation exists for Ω. A function f is in $\omega(g)$ if f grows faster than g.

- Last but not least, we say that a function f is in $\Theta(g)$ if f grows as fast as g, i.e., $f \in O(g)$ and $f \in \Omega(g)$.

- Again, we refer to standard text books for formal definitions.

Theorem 3.16 (Asynchronous Leader Election Lower Bound). *Any uniform leader election algorithm for asynchronous rings has $\Omega(n \log n)$ message complexity.*

3.4 Synchronous Ring

The lower bound relied on delaying messages for a very long time. Since this is impossible in the synchronous model, we might get a better message complexity in this case. The basic idea is very simple: In the synchronous model, *not* receiving a message is information as well! First we make some additional assumptions:

- We assume that the algorithm is non-uniform (i.e., the ring size n is known).

- We assume that every node starts at the same time.

- The node with the minimum identifier becomes the leader; identifiers are integers.

Algorithm 3.17 Synchronous Leader Election

1: **Each node** v concurrently executes the following code:
2: The algorithm operates in synchronous phases. Each phase consists of n time steps. Node v counts phases, starting with 0.
3: **if** phase $= v$ **and** v did not yet receive a message **then**
4:     v decides to be the leader
5:     v sends the message "v is leader" around the ring
6: **end if**

Remarks:

- Message complexity is indeed n.

- But the time complexity is huge! If m is the minimum identifier it is $m \cdot n$.

- The synchronous start and the non-uniformity assumptions can be dropped by using a wake-up technique (upon receiving a wake-up message, wake up your clockwise neighbors) and by letting messages travel slowly.

- There are several lower bounds for the synchronous model: comparison-based algorithms or algorithms where the time complexity cannot be a function of the identifiers have message complexity $\Omega(n \log n)$ as well.

- In general graphs, efficient leader election may be tricky. While time-optimal leader election can be done by parallel flooding-echo (see Chapter 2), bounding the message complexity is more difficult.

Chapter Notes

[Ang80] was the first to mention the now well-known impossibility result for anonymous rings and other networks, even when using randomization. The first algorithm for asynchronous rings was presented in [Lan77], which was improved to the presented clockwise algorithm in [CR79]. Later, [HS80] found the radius growth algorithm, which decreased the worst case message complexity. Algorithms for the unidirectional case with runtime $O(n \log n)$ can be found in [DKR82, Pet82]. The $\Omega(n \log n)$ message complexity lower bound for comparison based algorithms was first published in [FL87]. In [Sch89] an algorithm with constant error probability for anonymous networks is presented. General results about limitations of computer power in synchronous rings are in [ASW88, AS88].

Bibliography

[Ang80] Dana Angluin. Local and global properties in networks of processors (Extended Abstract). In *12th ACM Symposium on Theory of Computing (STOC)*, 1980.

[AS88] Hagit Attiya and Marc Snir. Better Computing on the Anonymous Ring. In *Aegean Workshop on Computing (AWOC)*, 1988.

[ASW88] Hagit Attiya, Marc Snir, and Manfred K. Warmuth. Computing on an anonymous ring. volume 35, pages 845–875, 1988.

[CR79] Ernest Chang and Rosemary Roberts. An improved algorithm for decentralized extrema-finding in circular configurations of processes. *Commun. ACM*, 22(5):281–283, May 1979.

[DKR82] Danny Dolev, Maria M. Klawe, and Michael Rodeh. An $O(n \log n)$ Unidirectional Distributed Algorithm for Extrema Finding in a Circle. *J. Algorithms*, 3(3):245–260, 1982.

[FL87] Greg N. Frederickson and Nancy A. Lynch. Electing a leader in a synchronous ring. *J. ACM*, 34(1):98–115, 1987.

[HS80] D. S. Hirschberg and J. B. Sinclair. Decentralized extrema-finding in circular configurations of processors. *Commun. ACM*, 23(11):627–628, November 1980.

[Lan77] Gérard Le Lann. Distributed Systems - Towards a Formal Approach. In *International Federation for Information Processing (IFIP) Congress*, 1977.

[Pet82] Gary L. Peterson. An $O(n \log n)$ Unidirectional Algorithm for the Circular Extrema Problem. 4(4):758–762, 1982.

[Sch89] B. Schieber. Calling names on nameless networks. In *Proceedings of the eighth annual ACM Symposium on Principles of distributed computing*, PODC '89, pages 319–328, New York, NY, USA, 1989. ACM.

Chapter 4

Distributed Sorting

> "Indeed, I believe that virtually *every* important aspect of programming arises somewhere in the context of sorting [and searching]!"
>
> – Donald E. Knuth, The Art of Computer Programming

In this chapter we study a classic problem in computer science—sorting—from a distributed computing perspective. In contrast to an orthodox single-processor sorting algorithm, no node has access to all data, instead the to-be-sorted values are *distributed*. Distributed sorting then boils down to:

Definition 4.1 (Sorting). *We choose a graph with n nodes $v_1, \ldots, v_n$. Initially each node stores a value. After applying a sorting algorithm, node v_k stores the kth smallest value.*

Remarks:

- What if we route all values to the same central node v, let v sort the values locally, and then route them to the correct destinations?! According to the message passing model studied in the first few chapters this is perfectly legal. With a star topology sorting finishes in $O(1)$ time!

Definition 4.2 (Node Contention). *In each step of a synchronous algorithm, each node can only send and receive $O(1)$ messages containing $O(1)$ values, no matter how many neighbors the node has.*

Remarks:

- Using Definition 4.2 sorting on a star graph takes linear time.

4.1   Array & Mesh

To get a better intuitive understanding of distributed sorting, we start with two simple topologies, the array and the mesh. Let us begin with the array:

Algorithm 4.3 Odd/Even Sort

1: Given an array of n nodes $(v_1, \ldots, v_n)$, each storing a value (not sorted).
2: **repeat**
3:    Compare and exchange the values at nodes i and $i+1$, i odd

4:    Compare and exchange the values at nodes i and $i+1$, i even
5: **until** done

Remarks:

- The compare and exchange primitive in Algorithm 4.3 is defined as follows: Let the value stored at node i be v_i. After the compare and exchange node i stores value $\min(v_i, v_{i+1})$ and node $i+1$ stores value $\max(v_i, v_{i+1})$.

- How fast is the algorithm, and how can we prove correctness/efficiency?

- The most interesting proof uses the so-called 0-1 Sorting Lemma. It allows us to restrict our attention to an input of 0's and 1's only, and works for any "oblivious comparison-exchange" algorithm. (Oblivious means: Whether you exchange two values must only depend on the relative order of the two values, and not on anything else.)

Lemma 4.4 (0-1 Sorting Lemma). *If an oblivious comparison-exchange algorithm sorts all inputs of 0's and 1's, then it sorts arbitrary inputs.*

Proof. We prove the opposite direction (does not sort arbitrary inputs $\Rightarrow$ does not sort 0's and 1's). Assume that there is an input $x = x_1, \ldots, x_n$ that is not sorted correctly by the sorting algorithm. Then there is a smallest value k such that the value at node v_k after running the algorithm is strictly larger than the kth smallest value $x(k)$. Define an input $x_i^* = 0 \Leftrightarrow x_i \le x(k)$, $x_i^* = 1$ else. Whenever the algorithm compares a pair of 1's or 0's, it is not important whether it exchanges the values or not, so we may simply assume that it does the same as on the input x. On the other hand, whenever the algorithm exchanges some values $x_i^* = 0$ and $x_j^* = 1$, this means that $x_i \le x(k) < x_j$. Therefore, in this case the respective compare-exchange operation will do the same on both inputs. We conclude that the algorithm will order x^* the same way as x, i.e., the output with only 0's and 1's will also not be correct. $\qquad\square$

Theorem 4.5. *Algorithm 4.3 sorts correctly in n steps.*

Proof. Thanks to Lemma 4.4 we only need to consider an array with 0's and 1's. In this array, let j_1 be the node containing the "rightmost" 1, i.e., j_1 is the highest-index node from $\{v_1, \ldots, v_n\}$ with value 1. If the index r of node $v_r = j_1$ is odd (even), the value 1 of this node will "move to the right" in the first (second) step. In any case it will move right in every following step until it reaches the rightmost node v_n. Let j_k be the node with the kth rightmost 1. We show by induction that j_k is not "blocked" anymore (constantly moves until it reaches destination!) after step k. We have already anchored the induction at $k = 1$. Since the 1 at node j_{k-1} moves after step $k - 1$, j_k gets a right 0-neighbor for each step after step k. (For matters of presentation we omitted a couple of simple details.) $\qquad\square$

Remarks:

- Linear time is not very exciting, maybe we can do better by using a different topology? Let's try a mesh (a.k.a. grid) topology first.

Theorem 4.7. *Algorithm 4.6 sorts n values in $\sqrt{n}(\log n + 1)$ time in snake-like order.*

Proof. Since the algorithm is oblivious, we can use Lemma 4.4. We show that after a row and a column phase, half of the previously

---

Algorithm 4.6 Shearsort

1: We are given a mesh with m rows and m columns, m even, $n = m^2$.

2: The sorting algorithm operates in phases, and uses the odd/even sort algorithm on rows or columns.

3: **repeat**

4:      In the odd phases $1, 3, \ldots$ we sort all the rows, in the even phases $2, 4, \ldots$ we sort all the columns, such that:

5:      Columns are sorted such that the small values move up.

6:      Odd rows $(1, 3, \ldots, m-1)$ are sorted such that small values move left.

7:      Even rows $(2, 4, \ldots, m)$ are sorted such that small values move right.

8: **until** done

---

unsorted rows will be sorted. More formally, let us call a row with only 0's (or only 1's) *clean*, a row with 0's *and* 1's is *dirty*. At any stage, the rows of the mesh can be divided into three regions. In the north we have a region of all-0 rows, in the south all-1 rows, in the middle a region of dirty rows (possibly interspersed with clean rows). Initially all rows can be dirty. Since neither row nor column sort will touch the already clean rows in the northern and southern regions, we can concentrate on the middle region containing the dirty rows.

First we run an odd phase. Then, in the even phase, deviating from the algorithm description, let's run a peculiar column sorter: We group two consecutive rows in the middle region into pairs. Since odd and even rows are sorted in opposite directions, two consecutive rows look as follows:

$$00000 \ldots 11111$$

$$11111 \ldots 00000$$

Such a pair can be in one of three states. Either we have more 0's than 1's (in both rows together), or more 1's than 0's, or an equal number of 0's and 1's. Column-sorting each pair will give us at least one clean row (and two clean rows if "$|0| = |1|$"). Then we move the cleaned rows north/south and the middle region containing the dirty rows will be (roughly) halved in size.

What does this peculiar column sorter have to do with our algorithm? Well, a close look reveals that any column sorter sorts the columns in exactly the same way (we are very grateful to have Lemma 4.4!). Hence, we actually described what our algorithm does in the even phase.

All in all we need $2 \log m = \log n$ phases to remain with (at most) 1 dirty row in the middle which will be sorted (not cleaned) with the last row-sort. $\qquad\square$

Remarks:

- There are algorithms that sort in $3m + o(m)$ time on an m by m mesh (by diving the mesh into smaller blocks). This is asymptotically optimal, since a value might need to move $2m$ times.

- Such a $\sqrt{n}$-sorter is cute, but we are more ambitious. There are non-distributed sorting algorithms such as quicksort, heapsort, or mergesort that sort n values in (expected) $O(n \log n)$ time. Using our n-fold parallelism effectively we might therefore hope for a distributed sorting algorithm that sorts in time $O(\log n)$!

4.2 Sorting Networks

In this section we construct a graph topology which is carefully manufactured for sorting. This is a deviation from previous chapters where we always had to work with the topology that was given to us. In many application areas (e.g. peer-to-peer networks, communication switches, systolic hardware) it is indeed possible (in fact, crucial!) that an engineer can build the topology best suited for her application.

Definition 4.8 (Sorting Networks). *A **comparator** is a device with two inputs x, y and two outputs x', y' such that $x' = \min(x, y)$ and $y' = \max(x, y)$. We construct so-called **comparison networks** that consist of wires that connect comparators (the output port of a comparator is sent to an input port of another comparator). Some wires are not connected to comparator outputs (we call them input wires), and some are not connected to comparator inputs (we call them output wires). A **sorting network** with **width** n has n input wires and n output wires. A sorting network routes n values given on the input wires through the wires and comparators of the network such that the values are sorted on the output wires.*

Remarks:

- Often we will draw all the wires on n horizontal lines, where n is the width of the network. Comparators are then vertically connecting two of these lines. An example sorting network is depicted in Figure 4.9.

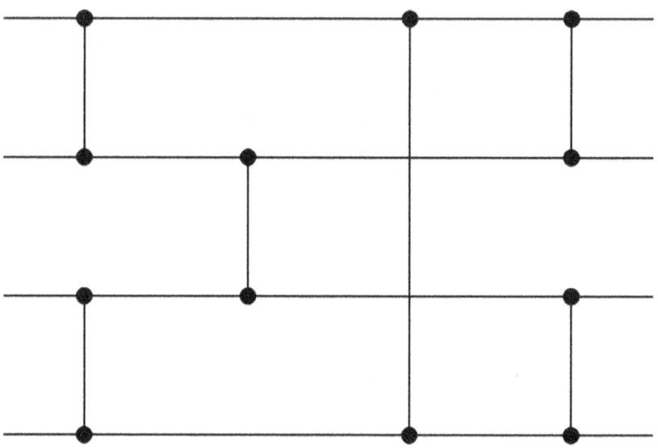

Figure 4.9: A sorting network with width 4, 6 comparators, and 16 wires.

Definition 4.10 (Depth). *The depth of an input wire is 0. The depth of a comparator is the maximum depth of its input wires plus one. The depth of an output wire of a comparator is the depth of the comparator. The depth of a comparison network is the maximum depth (of an output wire).*

Remarks:

- The odd/even sorter explained in Algorithm 4.3 can also be described as a sorting network. An odd/even sorting network with width n has depth n.

- Note that a sorting network is an oblivious comparison-exchange network. Consequently we can apply Lemma 4.4 throughout this section.

Definition 4.11 (Bitonic Sequence). *A **bitonic sequence** is a sequence of numbers that first monotonically increases, and then monotonically decreases, or vice versa.*

Remarks:

- $< 1, 4, 6, 8, 3, 2 >$ or $< 5, 3, 2, 1, 4, 8 >$ are bitonic sequences.

- $< 9, 6, 2, 3, 5, 4 >$ or $< 7, 4, 2, 5, 9, 8 >$ are not bitonic.

- Since we restrict ourselves to 0's and 1's (Lemma 4.4), bitonic sequences have the form $0^i 1^j 0^k$ or $1^i 0^j 1^k$ for $i, j, k \geq 0$.

Algorithm 4.12 Half Cleaner

1: A half cleaner is a comparison network of depth 1, where we compare wire i with wire $i + n/2$ for $i = 1, \ldots, n/2$ (we assume n to be even).

Lemma 4.13. *Feeding a bitonic sequence into a half cleaner (Algorithm 4.12), the half cleaner cleans (makes all-0 or all-1) either the upper or the lower half of the n wires. The other half is bitonic.*

Proof. Assume that the input is of the form $0^i 1^j 0^k$ for $i, j, k \geq 0$. If the midpoint falls into the 0's, the input is already clean/bitonic and will stay so. If the midpoint falls into the 1's the half cleaner acts as Shearsort with two adjacent rows, exactly as in the proof of Theorem 4.7. The case $1^i 0^j 1^k$ is symmetric. $\qquad \square$

Algorithm 4.14 Bitonic Sequence Sorter

1: A bitonic sequence sorter of width n (where width is the number of input wires and we assume n to be a power of 2) consists of a half cleaner of width n, and then two bitonic sequence sorters of width $n/2$ each.

2: A bitonic sequence sorter of width 1 is empty.

Lemma 4.15. *A bitonic sequence sorter (Algorithm 4.14) of width n sorts bitonic sequences. It has depth $\log n$.*

Proof. The proof follows directly from Algorithm 4.14 and Lemma 4.13. $\qquad \square$

Remarks:

- Clearly we want to sort arbitrary and not only bitonic sequences! To do this we need one more concept, merging networks.

Algorithm 4.16 Merging Network

1: A merging network of width n is a merger of width n followed by two bitonic sequence sorters of width $n/2$. A merger is a depth-one network where we compare wire i with wire $n-i+1$, for $i = 1, \ldots, n/2$.

Remarks:

- Note that a merging network is a bitonic sequence sorter where we replace the (first) half-cleaner by a merger.

Lemma 4.17. *A merging network of width n (Algorithm 4.16) merges two sorted input sequences of length n/2 each into one sorted sequence of length n.*

Proof. We have two sorted input sequences. Essentially, a merger does to two sorted sequences what a half cleaner does to a bitonic sequence, since the lower part of the input is reversed. In other words, we can use the same argument as in Theorem 4.7 and Lemma 4.13: Again, after the merger step either the upper or the lower half is clean, the other is bitonic. The bitonic sequence sorters complete sorting. $\qquad\square$

Remarks:

- How do you sort n values when you are able to merge two sorted sequences of size $n/2$? Piece of cake, just apply the merger recursively.

Algorithm 4.18 Batcher's "Bitonic" Sorting Network

1: A batcher sorting network of width n consists of two batcher sorting networks of width $n/2$ followed by a merging network of width n. (See Figure 4.19.)
2: A batcher sorting network of width 1 is empty.

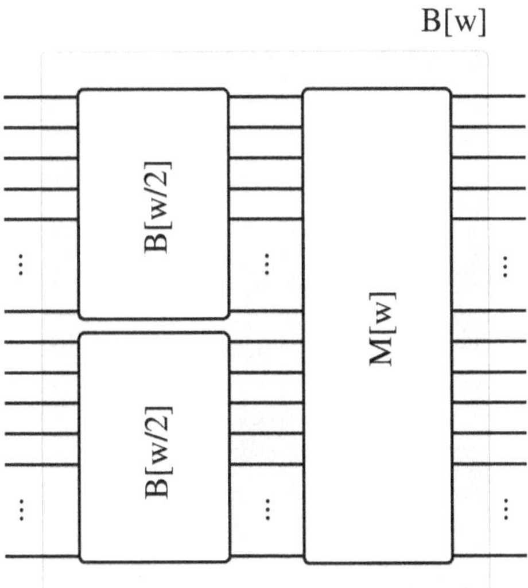

Figure 4.19: A batcher sorting network

Theorem 4.20. *A sorting network (Algorithm 4.18) sorts an arbitrary sequence of n values. It has depth $O(\log^2 n)$.*

Proof. Correctness is immediate: at recursive stage k ($k = 1, 2, 3,$ $\dots, \log n$) we merge 2^k sorted sequences into 2^{k-1} sorted sequences. The depth $d(n)$ of the sorting network of width n is the depth of a sorting network of width $n/2$ plus the depth $m(n)$ of a merging network of width n. The depth of a sorter of level 1 is 0 since the sorter is empty. Since a merging network of width n has the same depth as a bitonic sequence sorter of width n, we know by Lemma 4.15 that $m(n) = \log n$. This gives a recursive formula for $d(n)$ which solves to $d(n) = \frac{1}{2} \log^2 n + \frac{1}{2} \log n$. $\qquad\square$

Remarks:

- Simulating Batcher's sorting network on an ordinary sequential computer takes time $O(n \log^2 n)$. As said, there are sequential sorting algorithms that sort in asymptotically optimal time $O(n \log n)$. So a natural question is whether there is a sorting network with depth $O(\log n)$. Such a network would have some remarkable advantages over sequential asymptotically optimal sorting algorithms such as heapsort. Apart from being highly parallel, it would be completely oblivious, and as such perfectly suited for a fast hardware solution. In 1983, Ajtai, Komlos, and Szemeredi presented a celebrated $O(\log n)$ depth sorting network. (Unlike Batcher's sorting network the constant hidden in the big-O of the "AKS" sorting network is too large to be practical, however.)

- It can be shown that Batcher's sorting network and similarly others can be simulated by a Butterfly network and other hypercubic networks, see next chapter.

- What if a sorting network is asynchronous?!? Clearly, using a synchronizer we can still sort, but it is also possible to use it for something else. Check out the next section!

4.3 Counting Networks

In this section we address distributed counting, a distributed service which can for instance be used for load balancing.

Definition 4.21 (Distributed Counting). *A **distributed counter** is a variable that is common to all processors in a system and that supports an atomic **test-and-increment** operation. The operation delivers the system's counter value to the requesting processor and increments it.*

Remarks:

- A naive distributed counter stores the system's counter value with a distinguished central node. When other nodes initiate the test-and-increment operation, they send a request message to the central node and in turn receive a reply message with the current counter value. However, with a large number of nodes operating on the distributed counter, the central processor will become a bottleneck. There will be a congestion of request messages at the central processor, in other words, the system will not scale.

- Is a scalable implementation (without any kind of bottleneck) of such a distributed counter possible, or is distributed counting a problem which is inherently centralized?!?

- Distributed counting could for instance be used to implement a load balancing infrastructure, i.e., by sending the job with counter value i (modulo n) to server i (out of n possible servers).

Definition 4.22 (Balancer). *A balancer is an asynchronous device which forwards messages that arrive on the left side to the wires on the right, the first to the upper, the second to the lower, the third to the upper, and so on.*

Remarks:

- In electronics, a balancer is called a flip-flop.

Algorithm 4.23 Bitonic Counting Network.

1: Take Batcher's bitonic sorting network of width w and replace all the comparators with balancers.
2: When a node wants to count, it sends a message to an arbitrary input wire.
3: The message is then routed through the network, following the rules of the asynchronous balancers.
4: Each output wire is completed with a "mini-counter."
5: The mini-counter of wire k replies the value "$k + i \cdot w$" to the initiator of the ith message it receives (starting with $i = 0$).

Definition 4.24 (Step Property). *A sequence $y_0, y_1, \ldots, y_{w-1}$ is said to have the **step property**, if $0 \leq y_i - y_j \leq 1$, for any $i < j$.*

Remarks:

- If the output wires have the step property, then with r requests, exactly the values $1, \ldots, r$ will be assigned by the mini-counters. All we need to show is that the counting network has the step property. For that we need some additional facts...

Facts 4.25. *For a balancer, we denote the number of consumed messages on the ith input wire by x_i, $i = 0, 1$. Similarly, we denote the number of sent messages on the ith output wire by y_i, $i = 0, 1$. A balancer has these properties:*

(1) A balancer does not generate output-messages; that is, $x_0 + x_1 \geq y_0 + y_1$ in any state.

(2) Every incoming message is eventually forwarded. In other words, if we are in a quiescent state (no message in transit), then $x_0 + x_1 = y_0 + y_1$.

(3) The number of messages sent to the upper output wire is at most one higher than the number of messages sent to the lower output wire: in any state $y_0 = \lceil (y_0 + y_1)/2 \rceil$ (thus $y_1 = \lfloor (y_0 + y_1)/2 \rfloor$).

Facts 4.26. *If a sequence $y_0, y_1, \ldots, y_{w-1}$ has the step property,*

(1) then all its subsequences have the step property.

(2) then its even and odd subsequences satisfy

$$\sum_{i=0}^{w/2-1} y_{2i} = \left\lceil \frac{1}{2} \sum_{i=0}^{w-1} y_i \right\rceil \quad and \quad \sum_{i=0}^{w/2-1} y_{2i+1} = \left\lfloor \frac{1}{2} \sum_{i=0}^{w-1} y_i \right\rfloor.$$

Facts 4.27. *If two sequences $x_0, x_1, \ldots, x_{w-1}$ and $y_0, y_1, \ldots, y_{w-1}$ have the step property,*

(1) and $\sum_{i=0}^{w-1} x_i = \sum_{i=0}^{w-1} y_i$, then $x_i = y_i$ for $i = 0, \ldots, w - 1$.

(2) and $\sum_{i=0}^{w-1} x_i = \sum_{i=0}^{w-1} y_i + 1$, then there exists a unique j $(j = 0, 1, \ldots, w - 1)$ such that $x_j = y_j + 1$, and $x_i = y_i$ for $i = 0, \ldots, w - 1$, $i \neq j$.

Remarks:

- An alternative representation of Batcher's network has been introduced in [AHS94]. It is isomorphic to Batcher's network, and relies on a Merger Network $M[w]$ which is defined inductively: $M[w]$ consists of two $M[w/2]$ networks (an upper and a lower one) whose output is fed to $w/2$ balancers/comparators. The upper network merges the even subsequence $x_0, x_2, \ldots, x_{w-2}$, while the lower network merges the odd subsequence $x_1, x_3, \ldots, x_{w-1}$. Call the outputs of these two $M[w/2]$, z and z' respectively. The final stage of the network combines z and z' by sending each pair of wires z_i and z_i' into a balancer whose outputs yield y_{2i} and y_{2i+1}.

- It is enough to prove that a merger network $M[w]$ preserves the step property.

Lemma 4.28. *Let $M[w]$ be a merger network of width w. In a quiescent state (i.e., there is no message in transit), if the inputs $x_0, x_1, \ldots, x_{w/2-1}$ resp. $x_{w/2}, x_{w/2+1}, \ldots, x_{w-1}$ have the step property, then the output $y_0, y_1, \ldots, y_{w-1}$ has the step property.*

Proof. By induction on the width w.

For $w = 2$: $M[2]$ is a balancer and a balancer's output has the step property (Fact 4.25.3).

For $w > 2$: Let z resp. z' be the output of the upper respectively lower $M[w/2]$ subnetwork. Since $x_0, x_1, \ldots, x_{w/2-1}$ and $x_{w/2}, x_{w/2+1}, \ldots, x_{w-1}$ both have the step property by assumption, their even and odd subsequences also have the step property (Fact 4.26.1). By induction hypothesis, the outputs of both $M[w/2]$ subnetworks have the step property. Let $Z := \sum_{i=0}^{w/2-1} z_i$ and $Z' := \sum_{i=0}^{w/2-1} z_i'$. From Fact 4.26.2 we conclude that $Z = \lceil \frac{1}{2} \sum_{i=0}^{w/2-1} x_i \rceil + \lfloor \frac{1}{2} \sum_{i=w/2}^{w-1} x_i \rfloor$. Similarly, we know that $Z' = \lfloor \frac{1}{2} \sum_{i=0}^{w/2-1} x_i \rfloor + \lceil \frac{1}{2} \sum_{i=w/2}^{w-1} x_i \rceil$. Since $\lceil a \rceil + \lfloor b \rfloor$ and $\lfloor a \rfloor + \lceil b \rceil$ differ by at most 1 we know that Z and Z' differ by at most 1.

If $Z = Z'$, Fact 4.27.1 implies that $z_i = z_i'$ for $i = 0, \ldots, w/2-1$. Therefore, the output of $M[w]$ is $y_i = z_{\lfloor i/2 \rfloor}$ for $i = 0, \ldots, w - 1$. Since $z_0, \ldots, z_{w/2-1}$ has the step property, so does the output of $M[w]$ and the lemma follows.

If Z and Z' differ by 1, Fact 4.27.2 implies that $z_i = z_i'$ for $i = 0, \ldots, w/2 - 1$, except that there is a unique j such that z_j and z_j' differ by 1. Let $l := \min(z_j, z_j')$. Then, the output y_i (with $i < 2j$) is $l+1$. The output y_i (with $i > 2j+1$) is l. The outputs y_{2j} and y_{2j+1} are balanced by the final balancer resulting in $y_{2j} = l+1$ and $y_{2j+1} = l$. Therefore $M[w]$ preserves the step property. $\square$

A bitonic counting network is constructed to fulfill Lemma 4.28, i.e., the final output comes from a Merger whose upper and lower inputs are recursively merged. Therefore, the following theorem follows immediately.

Theorem 4.29 (Correctness). *In a quiescent state, the w output wires of a bitonic counting network of width w have the step property.*

Remarks:

- Is every sorting network also a counting network? No. But surprisingly, the other direction is true!

Theorem 4.30 (Counting vs. Sorting). *If a network is a counting network then it is also a sorting network, but not vice versa.*

Proof. There are sorting networks that are not counting networks (e.g. odd/even sort, or insertion sort). For the other direction, let C be a counting network and $I(C)$ be the isomorphic network, where every balancer is replaced by a comparator. Let $I(C)$ have an arbitrary input of 0's and 1's; that is, some of the input wires have a 0, all others have a 1. There is a message at C's i^{th} input wire if and only if $I(C)$'s i input wire is 0. Since C is a counting network, all messages are routed to the upper output wires. $I(C)$ is isomorphic to C, therefore a comparator in $I(C)$ will receive a 0 on its upper (lower) wire if and only if the corresponding balancer receives a message on its upper (lower) wire. Using an inductive argument, the 0's and 1's will be routed through $I(C)$ such that all 0's exit the network on the upper wires whereas all 1's exit the network on the lower wires. Applying Lemma 4.4 shows that $I(C)$ is a sorting network. $\qquad\square$

Remarks:

- We claimed that the counting network is correct. However, it is only correct in a quiescent state.

Definition 4.31 (Linearizable). *A system is **linearizable** if the order of the values assigned reflects the real-time order in which they were requested. More formally, if there is a pair of operations o_1, o_2, where operation o_1 terminates before operation o_2 starts, and the logical order is "o_2 before o_1", then a distributed system is not linearizable.*

Lemma 4.32 (Linearizability). *The bitonic counting network is not linearizable.*

Proof. Consider the bitonic counting network with width 4 in Figure 4.33: Assume that two *inc* operations were initiated and the corresponding messages entered the network on wire 0 and 2 (both in light gray color). After having passed the second resp. the first balancer, these traversing messages "fall asleep"; In other words, both messages take unusually long time before they are received

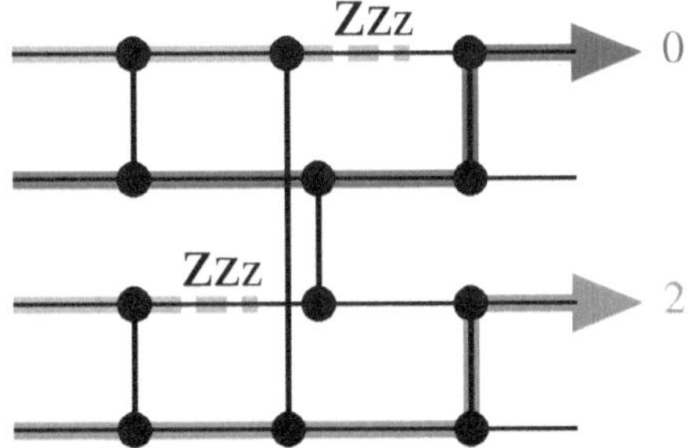

Figure 4.33: Linearizability Counter Example.

by the next balancer. Since we are in an asynchronous setting, this may be the case.

In the meantime, another *inc* operation (medium gray) is initiated and enters the network on the bottom wire. The message leaves the network on wire 2, and the *inc* operation is completed.

Strictly afterwards, another *inc* operation (dark gray) is initiated and enters the network on wire 1. After having passed all balancers, the message will leave the network wire 0. Finally (and not depicted in Figure 4.33), the two light gray messages reach the next balancer and will eventually leave the network on wires 1 resp. 3. Because the dark gray and the medium gray operation do conflict with Definition 4.31, the bitonic counting network is not linearizable. □

Remarks:

- Note that the example in Figure 4.33 behaves correctly in the quiescent state: Finally, exactly the values $0, 1, 2, 3$ are allotted.

- It has been shown that linearizability comes at a high price (the depth grows linearly with the width).

Chapter Notes

The technique used for the famous lower bound of comparison-based sequential sorting first appeared in [FJ59]. Comprehensive introductions to the vast field of sorting can certainly be found in [Knu73]. Knuth also presents the 0/1 principle in the context of sorting networks, supposedly as a special case of a theorem for decision trees of W. G. Bouricius, and includes a historic overview of sorting network research.

Using a rather complicated proof not based on the 0/1 principle, [Hab72] first presented and analyzed Odd/Even sort on arrays. Shearsort for grids first appeared in [SSS86] as a sorting algorithm both easy to implement and to prove correct. Later it was generalized to meshes with higher dimension in [SS89]. A bubble sort based algorithm is presented in [SI86]; it takes time $O(\sqrt{n}\log n)$, but is fast in practice. Nevertheless, already [TK77] presented an asymptotically optimal algorithm for grid network which runs in $3n + O(n^{2/3}\log n)$ rounds for an $n \times n$ grid. A simpler algorithm was later found by [SS86] using $3n + O(n^{3/4})$ rounds.

Batcher presents his famous $O(\log^2 n)$ depth sorting network in [Bat68]. It took until [AKS83] to find a sorting network with asymptotically optimal depth $O(\log n)$. Unfortunately, the constants hidden in the big-O-notation render it rather impractical.

The notion of counting networks was introduced in [AHS91], and shortly afterward the notion of linearizability was studied by [HSW91]. Follow-up work in [AHS94] presents bitonic counting networks and studies contention in the counting network. An overview of research on counting networks can be found in [BH98].

Bibliography

[AHS91]   James Aspnes, Maurice Herlihy, and Nir Shavit. Counting networks and multi-processor coordination. In *Proceedings of the twenty-third annual ACM symposium on Theory of computing*, STOC '91, pages 348–358, New York, NY, USA, 1991. ACM.

[AHS94]   James Aspnes, Maurice Herlihy, and Nir Shavit. Counting networks. *J. ACM*, 41(5):1020–1048, September 1994.

[AKS83]   Miklos Ajtai, Janos Komlós, and Endre Szemerédi. An 0(n log n) sorting network. In *Proceedings of the fifteenth annual ACM symposium on Theory of computing*, STOC '83, pages 1–9, New York, NY, USA, 1983. ACM.

[Bat68]   Kenneth E. Batcher. Sorting networks and their applications. In *Proceedings of the April 30–May 2, 1968, spring joint computer conference*, AFIPS '68 (Spring), pages 307–314, New York, NY, USA, 1968. ACM.

[BH98] Costas Busch and Maurice Herlihy. A Survey on Counting Networks. In *WDAS*, pages 13–20, 1998.

[FJ59] Lester R. Ford and Selmer M. Johnson. A Tournament Problem. *The American Mathematical Monthly*, 66(5):pp. 387–389, 1959.

[Hab72] Nico Habermann. Parallel neighbor-sort (or the glory of the induction principle). Paper 2087, Carnegie Mellon University - Computer Science Departement, 1972.

[HSW91] M. Herlihy, N. Shavit, and O. Waarts. Low contention linearizable counting. In *Foundations of Computer Science, 1991. Proceedings., 32nd Annual Symposium on*, pages 526–535, oct 1991.

[Knu73] Donald E. Knuth. *The Art of Computer Programming, Volume III: Sorting and Searching*. Addison-Wesley, 1973.

[SI86] Kazuhiro Sado and Yoshihide Igarashi. Some parallel sorts on a mesh-connected processor array and their time efficiency. *Journal of Parallel and Distributed Computing*, 3(3):398–410, 1986.

[SS86] Claus Peter Schnorr and Adi Shamir. An optimal sorting algorithm for mesh connected computers. In *Proceedings of the eighteenth annual ACM symposium on Theory of computing*, STOC '86, pages 255–263, New York, NY, USA, 1986. ACM.

[SS89] Isaac D. Scherson and Sandeep Sen. Parallel sorting in two-dimensional VLSI models of computation. *Computers, IEEE Transactions on*, 38(2):238–249, feb 1989.

[SSS86] Isaac Scherson, Sandeep Sen, and Adi Shamir. Shear sort – A true two-dimensional sorting technique for VLSI networks. *1986 International Conference on Parallel Processing*, 1986.

[TK77] Clark David Thompson and Hsiang Tsung Kung. Sorting on a mesh-connected parallel computer. *Commun. ACM*, 20(4):263–271, April 1977.

Chapter 5

Shared Memory

In distributed computing, various different models exist. So far, the focus of the course was on loosely-coupled distributed systems such as the Internet, where nodes asynchronously communicate by exchanging messages. The "opposite" model is a tightly-coupled parallel computer where nodes access a common memory totally synchronously—in distributed computing such a system is called a emphParallel Random Access Machine (PRAM).

5.1 Model

A third major model is somehow between these two extremes, the *shared memory* model. In a shared memory system, asynchronous processes (or processors) communicate via a common memory area of shared variables or registers:

Definition 5.1 (Shared Memory). *A shared memory system is a system that consists of asynchronous processes that access a common (shared) memory. A process can atomically access a register in the shared memory through a set of predefined operations. An atomic modification appears to the rest of the system instantaneously. Apart from this shared memory, processes can also have some local (private) memory.*

Remarks:

- Various shared memory systems exist. A main difference is how they allow processes to access the shared memory. All systems can atomically read or write a shared register R. Most systems do allow for advanced *atomic* read-modify-write (RMW) operations, for example:

  - test-and-set(R): $t := R$; $R := 1$; return t
  - fetch-and-add(R, x): $t := R$; $R := R + x$; return t
  - compare-and-swap(R, x, y): if $R = x$ then $R := y$; return **true**; else return **false**; endif;
  - load-link(R)/store-conditional(R, x): Load-link returns the current value of the specified register R. A subsequent store-conditional to the same register will store a new value x (and return **true**) only if no updates have occurred to that register since the load-link. If any updates have occurred, the store-conditional is guaranteed to fail (and return **false**), even if the value read by the load-link has since been restored.

- The power of RMW operations can be measured with the so-called *consensus-number*: The consensus-number k of a RMW operation defines whether one can solve consensus for k processes. Test-and-set for instance has consensus-number 2 (one can solve consensus with 2 processes, but not 3), whereas the consensus-number of compare-and-swap is infinite. This insight had practical impact, as hardware designers stopped developing shared memory systems supporting weak RMW operations.

- Many of the results derived in the message passing model have an equivalent in the shared memory model. Consensus for instance is traditionally studied in the shared memory model.

- Whereas programming a message passing system is rather tricky (in particular if fault-tolerance has to be integrated), programming a shared memory system is generally considered easier, as programmers are given access to global variables directly and do not need to worry about exchanging messages correctly. Because of this, even distributed systems which physically communicate by exchanging messages can often be programmed through a shared memory middleware, making the programmer's life easier.

- We will most likely find the general spirit of shared memory systems in upcoming multi-core architectures. As for programming style, the multi-core community seems to favor an accelerated version of shared memory, *transactional memory*.

- From a message passing perspective, the shared memory model is like a bipartite graph: On one side you have the processes (the nodes) which pretty much behave like nodes in the message passing model (asynchronous, maybe failures). On the other side you have the shared registers, which just work perfectly (no failures, no delay).

5.2 Mutual Exclusion

A classic problem in shared memory systems is mutual exclusion. We are given a number of processes which occasionally need to access the same resource. The resource may be a shared variable, or a more general object such as a data structure or a shared printer. The catch is that only one process at the time is allowed to access the resource. More formally:

Definition 5.2 (Mutual Exclusion). *We are given a number of processes, each executing the following code sections:*
<Entry> → <Critical Section> → <Exit> → <Remaining Code>
A mutual exclusion algorithm consists of code for entry and exit sections, such that the following holds

- *Mutual Exclusion: At all times **at most one** process is in the critical section.*

- *No deadlock: If some process manages to get to the entry section, later **some** (possibly different) process will get to the critical section.*

Sometimes we in addition ask for

- *No lockout: If some process manages to get to the entry section, later **the same** process will get to the critical section.*

- *Unobstructed exit: No process can get stuck in the exit section.*

Using RMW primitives one can build mutual exclusion algorithms quite easily. Algorithm 5.3 shows an example with the test-and-set primitive.

Algorithm 5.3 Mutual Exclusion: Test-and-Set

Input: Shared register $R := 0$
<**Entry**>
  1: **repeat**
  2:    $r := \text{test-and-set}(R)$
  3: **until** $r = 0$
<**Critical Section**>
  4: ...
<**Exit**>
  5: $R := 0$
<**Remainder Code**>
  6: ...

Theorem 5.4. *Algorithm 5.3 solves the mutual exclusion problem as in Definition 5.2.*

Proof. Mutual exclusion follows directly from the test-and-set definition: Initially R is 0. Let p_i be the ith process to successfully execute the test-and-set, where successfully means that the result of the test-and-set is 0. This happens at time t_i. At time t_i' process p_i resets the shared register R to 0. Between t_i and t_i' no other process can successfully test-and-set, hence no other process can enter the critical section concurrently.

Proving no deadlock works similar: One of the processes loitering in the entry section will successfully test-and-set as soon as the process in the critical section exited.

Since the exit section only consists of a single instruction (no potential infinite loops) we have unobstructed exit. $\qquad\square$

Remarks:

- No lockout, on the other hand, is not given by this algorithm. Even with only two processes there are asynchronous executions where always the same process wins the test-and-set.

- Algorithm 5.3 can be adapted to guarantee fairness (no lockout), essentially by ordering the processes in the entry section in a queue.

- A natural question is whether one can achieve mutual exclusion with only reads and writes, that is without advanced RMW operations. The answer is yes!

Our read/write mutual exclusion algorithm is for two processes p_0 and p_1 only. In the remarks we discuss how it can be extended. The general idea is that process p_i has to mark its desire to enter the critical section in a "want" register W_i by setting $W_i := 1$. Only if the other process is not interested ($W_{1-i} = 0$) access is granted. This however is too simple since we may run into a deadlock. This deadlock (and at the same time also lockout) is resolved by adding a priority variable Π. See Algorithm 5.5.

Algorithm 5.5 Mutual Exclusion: Peterson's Algorithm

Initialization: Shared registers W_0, W_1, Π, all initially 0.
Code for process p_i , $i = \{0, 1\}$
<**Entry**>
  1: $W_i := 1$
  2: $\Pi := 1 - i$
  3: **repeat until** $\Pi = i$ or $W_{1-i} = 0$
<**Critical Section**>
  4: ...
<**Exit**>
  5: $W_i := 0$
<**Remainder Code**>
  6: ...

Remarks:

- Note that Line 3 in Algorithm 5.5 represents a "spinlock" or "busy-wait", similarly to the Lines 1-3 in Algorithm 5.3.

Theorem 5.6. *Algorithm 5.5 solves the mutual exclusion problem as in Definition 5.2.*

Proof. The shared variable Π elegantly grants priority to the process that passes Line 2 first. If both processes are competing, only process p_Π can access the critical section because of Π. The other process $p_{1-\Pi}$ cannot access the critical section because $W_\Pi = 1$ (and $\Pi \neq 1 - \Pi$). The only other reason to access the critical section is because the other process is in the remainder code (that is, not interested). This proves mutual exclusion!

No deadlock comes directly with Π: Process p_Π gets direct access to the critical section, no matter what the other process does.

Since the exit section only consists of a single instruction (no potential infinite loops) we have unobstructed exit.

Thanks to the shared variable Π also no lockout (fairness) is achieved: If a process p_i loses against its competitor p_{1-i} in Line 2, it will have to wait until the competitor resets $W_{1-i} := 0$ in the exit section. If process p_i is unlucky it will not check $W_{1-i} = 0$ early enough before process p_{1-i} sets $W_{1-i} := 1$ again in Line 1. However, as soon as p_{1-i} hits Line 2, process p_i gets the priority due to Π, and can enter the critical section. $\qquad \square$

Remarks:

- Extending Peterson's Algorithm to more than 2 processes can be done by a tournament tree, like in tennis. With n processes every process needs to win $\log n$ matches before it can enter the critical section. More precisely, each process starts at the bottom level of a binary tree, and proceeds to the parent level if winning. Once winning the root of the tree it can enter the critical section. Thanks to the priority variables Π at each node of the binary tree, we inherit all the properties of Definition 5.2.

5.3 Store & Collect

In this section, we will look at a second shared memory problem that has an elegant solution. Informally, the problem can be stated as follows. There are n processes $p_1, \ldots, p_n$. Every process p_i has a read/write register R_i in the shared memory where it can *store* some information that is destined for the other processes. Further, there is an operation by which a process can *collect* (i.e., read) the values of all the processes that stored some value in their register.

We say that an operation *op1* precedes an operation *op2* iff *op1* terminates before *op2* starts. An operation *op2* follows an operation *op1* iff *op1* precedes *op2*.

Definition 5.7 (Collect). *There are two operations: A* STORE(*val*) *by process p_i sets val to be the latest value of its register R_i. A* COLLECT *operation returns a **view**, a partial function V from the set of processes to a set of values, where $V(p_i)$ is the latest value stored by p_i, for each process p_i. For a* COLLECT *operation **cop**, the following validity properties must hold for every process p_i:*

- *If $V(p_i) = \bot$, then no* STORE *operation by p_i precedes **cop**.*

- *If $V(p_i) = v \neq \bot$, then v is the value of a* STORE *operation **sop** of p_i that does not follow **cop**, and there is no* STORE *operation by p_i that follows **sop** and precedes **cop**.*

Hence, a COLLECT operation *cop* should not read from the future or miss a preceding STORE operation *sop*.

We assume that the read/write register R_i of every process p_i is initialized to $\bot$. We define the step complexity of an operation *op* to be the number of accesses to registers in the shared memory. There is a trivial solution to the *collect* problem as shown by Algorithm 5.8.

Algorithm 5.8 Collect: Simple (Non-Adaptive) Solution

Operation STORE(*val*) (by process p_i) :
1: $R_i := val$
Operation COLLECT:
2: **for** $i := 1$ **to** n **do**
3:    $V(p_i) := R_i$ // *read register R_i*
4: **end for**

Remarks:

- Algorithm 5.8 clearly works. The step complexity of every STORE operation is 1, the step complexity of a COLLECT operation is n.

- At first sight, the step complexities of Algorithm 5.8 seem optimal. Because there are n processes, there clearly are cases in which a COLLECT operation needs to read all n registers. However, there are also scenarios in which the step complexity of the COLLECT operation seems very costly. Assume that there are only two processes p_i and p_j that have stored a value in their registers R_i and R_j. In this case, a COLLECT in principle only needs to read the registers R_i and R_j and can ignore all the other registers.

- Assume that up to a certain time t, $k \leq n$ processes have finished or started at least one operation. We call an operation *op* at time t *adaptive* to contention if the step complexity of *op* only depends on k and is independent of n.

- In the following, we will see how to implement adaptive versions of STORE and COLLECT.

5.4 Splitters

Algorithm 5.9 Splitter Code

Shared Registers: $X : \{\bot\} \cup \{1, \ldots, n\}$; Y : **boolean**
Initialization: $X := \bot$; $Y :=$ **false**

Splitter access by process p_i:
 1: $X := i$;
 2: **if** Y **then**
 3:    **return right**
 4: **else**
 5:    $Y :=$ **true**
 6:    **if** $X = i$ **then**
 7:      **return stop**
 8:    **else**
 9:      **return left**
 10:    **end if**
 11: **end if**

To obtain adaptive collect algorithms, we need a synchronization primitive, called a *splitter*.

Definition 5.11 (Splitter). *A splitter is a synchronization primitive with the following characteristic. A process entering a splitter*

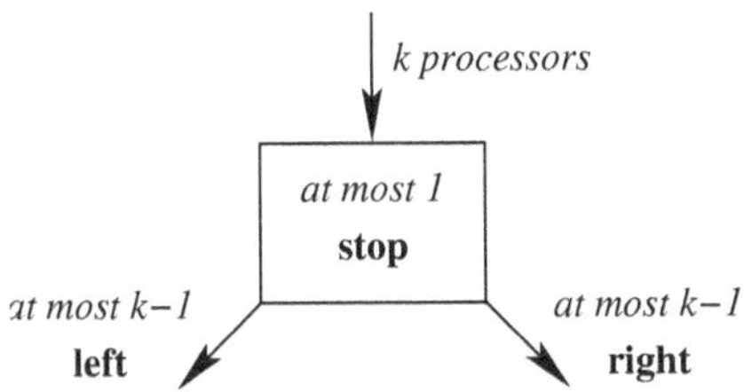

Figure 5.10: A Splitter

exits with either **stop**, **left**, *or* **right**. *If k processes enter a splitter, at most one process exits with* **stop** *and at most $k-1$ processes exit with* **left** *and* **right**, *respectively.*

Hence, it is guaranteed that if a single process enters the splitter, then it obtains **stop**, and if two or more processes enter the splitter, then there is at most one process obtaining **stop** and there are two processes that obtain different values (i.e., either there is exactly one **stop** or there is at least one **left** and at least one **right**). For an illustration, see Figure 5.10. The code implementing a splitter is given by Algorithm 5.9.

Lemma 5.12. *Algorithm 5.9 correctly implements a splitter.*

Proof. Assume that k processes enter the splitter. Because the first process that checks whether $Y = $ **true** in Line 2 will find that $Y = $ **false**, not all processes return **right**. Next, assume that i is the last process that sets $X := i$. If i does not return **right**, it will find $X = i$ in Line 6 and therefore return **stop**. Hence, there is always a process that does not return **left**. It remains to show that at most 1 process returns **stop**. For the sake of contradiction, assume p_i and p_j are two processes that return **stop** and assume that p_i sets $X := i$ before p_j sets $X := j$. Both processes need to check whether Y is **true** before one of them sets $Y := $ **true**. Hence, they both complete the assignment in Line 1 before the first one of them checks the value of X in Line 6. Hence, by the time p_i arrives at Line 6, $X \neq i$ (p_j and maybe some other processes have overwritten X by then). Therefore, p_i does not return **stop** and we get a contradiction to the assumption that both p_i and p_j return **stop**. $\square$

Algorithm 5.13 Adaptive Collect: Binary Tree Algorithm

Operation STORE(val) (by process p_i) :

1:   $R_i := val$
2:   **if** first STORE operation by p_i **then**
3:    $v :=$ root node of binary tree
4:    $\alpha :=$ result of entering splitter $S(v)$;
5:    $M_{S(v)} :=$ **true**
6:    **while** $\alpha \neq$ **stop do**
7:     **if** $\alpha =$ **left then**
8:      $v :=$ left child of v
9:     **else**
10:      $v :=$ right child of v
11:     **end if**
12:     $\alpha :=$ result of entering splitter $S(v)$;
13:     $M_{S(v)} :=$ **true**
14:    **end while**
15:    $Z_{S(v)} := i$
16: **end if**

Operation COLLECT:
Traverse marked part of binary tree:
17: **for all** marked splitters S **do**
18:   **if** $Z_S \neq \bot$ **then**
19:    $i := Z_S;\ V(p_i) := R_i$ *// read value of process p_i*
20:   **end if**
21: **end for**   *// $V(p_i) = \bot$ for all other processes*

5.5   Binary Splitter Tree

Assume that we are given $2^n - 1$ splitters and that for every splitter S, there is an additional shared variable $Z_S : \{\bot\} \cup \{1, \ldots, n\}$ that is initialized to $\bot$ and an additional shared variable $M_S :$ **boolean** that is initialized to **false**. We call a splitter S marked if $M_S =$ **true**. The $2^n - 1$ splitters are arranged in a complete binary tree of height $n - 1$. Let $S(v)$ be the splitter associated with a node v of the binary tree. The STORE and COLLECT operations are given by Algorithm 5.13.

Theorem 5.14. *Algorithm 5.13 correctly implements* STORE *and* COLLECT. *Let k be the number of participating processes. The step complexity of the first* STORE *of a process p_i is $O(k)$, the step* *complexity of every additional* STORE *of p_i is $O(1)$, and the step complexity of* COLLECT *is $O(k)$.*

Proof. Because at most one process can stop at a splitter, it is sufficient to show that every process stops at some splitter at depth at most $k - 1 \le n - 1$ when invoking the first STORE operation to prove correctness. We prove that at most $k - i$ processes enter a subtree at depth i (i.e., a subtree where the root has distance i to the root of the whole tree). By definition of k, the number of processes entering the splitter at depth 0 (i.e., at the root of the binary tree) is k. For $i > 1$, the claim follows by induction because of the at most $k - i$ processes entering the splitter at the root of a depth i subtree, at most $k-i-1$ obtain **left** and **right**, respectively. Hence, at the latest when reaching depth $k - 1$, a process is the only process entering a splitter and thus obtains **stop**. It thus also follows that the step complexity of the first invocation of STORE is $O(k)$.

To show that the step complexity of COLLECT is $O(k)$, we first observe that the marked nodes of the binary tree are connected, and therefore can be traversed by only reading the variables M_S associated to them and their neighbors. Hence, showing that at most $2k - 1$ nodes of the binary tree are marked is sufficient. Let x_k be the maximum number of marked nodes in a tree, where k processes access the root. We claim that $x_k \le 2k - 1$, which is true for $k = 1$ because a single process entering a splitter will always compute **stop**. Now assume the inequality holds for $1, \ldots, k - 1$. Not all k processes may exit the splitter with **left** (or **right**), i.e., $k_l \le k - 1$ processes will turn left and $k_r \le \min\{k - k_l, k - 1\}$ turn right. The left and right children of the root are the roots of their subtrees, hence the induction hypothesis yields

$$x_k = x_{k_l} + x_{k_r} + 1 \le (2k_l - 1) + (2k_r - 1) + 1 \le 2k - 1,$$

concluding induction and proof. $\qquad\square$

Remarks:

- The step complexities of Algorithm 5.13 are very good. Clearly, the step complexity of the COLLECT operation is asymptotically optimal. In order for the algorithm to work, we however need to allocate the memory for the complete binary tree of depth $n-1$. The space complexity of Algorithm 5.13 therefore is exponential in n. We will

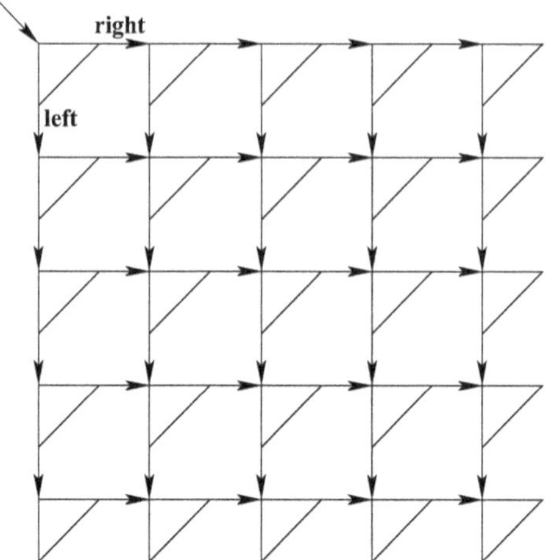

Figure 5.15: 5×5 Splitter Matrix

next see how to obtain a polynomial space complexity at the cost of a worse COLLECT step complexity.

5.6   Splitter Matrix

Instead of arranging splitters in a binary tree, we arrange n^2 splitters in an $n \times n$ matrix as shown in Figure 5.15. The algorithm is analogous to Algorithm 5.13. The matrix is entered at the top left. If a process receives **left**, it next visits the splitter in the next row of the same column. If a process receives **right**, it next visits the splitter in the next column of the same row. Clearly, the space complexity of this algorithm is $O(n^2)$. The following theorem gives bounds on the step complexities of STORE and COLLECT.

Theorem 5.16. *Let k be the number of participating processes. The step complexity of the first STORE of a process p_i is $O(k)$, the step complexity of every additional STORE of p_i is $O(1)$, and the step complexity of COLLECT is $O(k^2)$.*

Proof. Let the top row be row 0 and the left-most column be column 0. Let x_i be the number of processes entering a splitter in row i. By induction on i, we show that $x_i \leq k - i$. Clearly, $x_0 \leq k$. Let us therefore consider the case $i > 0$. Let j be the largest column such that at least one process visits the splitter in row $i - 1$ and column j. By the properties of splitters, not all processes entering the splitter in row $i-1$ and column j obtain **left**. Therefore, not all processes entering a splitter in row $i-1$ move on to row i. Because at least one process stays in every row, we get that $x_i \leq k - i$. Similarly, the number of processes entering column j is at most $k - j$. Hence, every process stops at the latest in row $k - 1$ and column $k - 1$ and the number of marked splitters is at most k^2. Thus, the step complexity of COLLECT is at most $O(k^2)$. Because the longest path in the splitter matrix is $2k$, the step complexity of STORE is $O(k)$. $\qquad\square$

Remarks:

- With a slightly more complicated argument, it is possible to show that the number of processes entering the splitter in row i and column j is at most $k - i - j$. Hence, it suffices to only allocate the upper left half (including the diagonal) of the $n \times n$ matrix of splitters.

- The binary tree algorithm can be made space efficient by using a randomized version of a splitter. Whenever returning left or right, a randomized splitter returns left or right with probability $1/2$. With high probability, it then suffices to allocate a binary tree of depth $O(\log n)$.

- Recently, it has been shown that with a considerably more complicated deterministic algorithm, it is possible to achieve $O(k)$ step complexity and $O(n^2)$ space complexity.

Chapter Notes

Already in 1965 Edsger Dijkstra gave a deadlock-free solution for mutual exclusion [Dij65]. Later, Maurice Herlihy suggested consensus-numbers [Her91], where he proved the "universality of consensus", i.e., the power of a shared memory system is determined by the consensus number. For this work, Maurice Herlihy was awarded the Dijkstra Prize in Distributed Computing in 2003. In 2016, Ellen et al. [EGSZ16] showed that some of the practical intuition about Herlihy's consensus number is misleading, as sets of instructions with a low consensus number can together achieve a high consensus number. In other words, in the world of instructions "the whole is greater than the sum of its parts". Petersons Algorithm is due to [PF77, Pet81], and adaptive collect was studied in the sequence of papers [MA95, AFG02, AL05, AKP+06].

Bibliography

[AFG02] Hagit Attiya, Arie Fouren, and Eli Gafni. An adaptive collect algorithm with applications. *Distributed Computing*, 15(2):87–96, 2002.

[AKP+06] Hagit Attiya, Fabian Kuhn, C. Greg Plaxton, Mirjam Wattenhofer, and Roger Wattenhofer. Efficient adaptive collect using randomization. *Distributed Computing*, 18(3):179–188, 2006.

[AL05] Yehuda Afek and Yaron De Levie. Space and Step Complexity Efficient Adaptive Collect. In *DISC*, pages 384–398, 2005.

[Dij65] Edsger W. Dijkstra. Solution of a problem in concurrent programming control. *Commun. ACM*, 8(9):569, 1965.

[EGSZ16] Faith Ellen, Rati Gelashvili, Nir Shavit, and Leqi Zhu. A complexity-based hierarchy for multiprocessor synchronization:[extended abstract]. In *Proceedings of the 2016 ACM Symposium on Principles of Distributed Computing*, pages 289–298. ACM, 2016.

[Her91] Maurice Herlihy. Wait-Free Synchronization. *ACM Trans. Program. Lang. Syst.*, 13(1):124–149, 1991.

[MA95] Mark Moir and James H. Anderson. Wait-Free Algorithms for Fast, Long-Lived Renaming. *Sci. Comput. Program.*, 25(1):1–39, 1995.

[Pet81] J.L. Peterson. Myths About the Mutual Exclusion Problem. *Information Processing Letters*, 12(3):115–116, 1981.

[PF77] G.L. Peterson and M.J. Fischer. Economical solutions for the critical section problem in a distributed system. In *Proceedings of the ninth annual ACM symposium on Theory of computing*, pages 91–97. ACM, 1977.

Chapter 6

Shared Objects

Assume that there is a common resource (e.g. a common variable or data structure), which different nodes in a network need to access from time to time. If the nodes are allowed to change the common object when accessing it, we need to guarantee that no two nodes have access to the object at the same time. In order to achieve this mutual exclusion, we need protocols that allow the nodes of a network to store and manage access to such a shared object.

6.1 Centralized Solutions

A simple and obvious solution is to store the shared object at a central location (see Algorithm 6.1).

Algorithm 6.1 Shared Object: Centralized Solution

Initialization: Shared object stored at root node r of a spanning tree of the network graph (i.e., each node knows its parent in the spanning tree).

Accessing Object: (by node v)
 1: v sends request up the tree
 2: request processed by root r (atomically)
 3: result sent down the tree to node v

Remarks:

- Instead of a spanning tree, one can use routing.

- Algorithm 6.1 works, but it is not very efficient. Assume that the object is accessed by a single node v repeatedly. Then we get a high message/time complexity. Instead v could store the object, or at least cache it. But then, in case another node w accesses the object, we might run into consistency problems.

- Alternative idea: The accessing node should become the new master of the object. The shared object then becomes mobile. There exist several variants of this idea. The simplest version is a home-based solution like in Mobile IP (see Algorithm 6.2).

Algorithm 6.2 Shared Object: Home-Based Solution

Initialization: An object has a home base (a node) that is known to every node. All requests (accesses to the shared object) are routed through the home base.

Accessing Object: (by node v)

1: v acquires a lock at the home base, receives object.

Remarks:

- Home-based solutions suffer from the triangular routing problem. If two close-by nodes take turns to access the object, all the traffic is routed through the potentially far away home-base.

6.2 Arrow and Friends

We will now look at a protocol (called the Arrow algorithm) that always moves the shared object to the node currently accessing it without creating the triangular routing problem of home-based solutions. The protocol runs on a precomputed spanning tree. Assume that the spanning tree is rooted at the current position of the shared object. When a node u wants to access the shared object, it sends out a *find* request towards the current position of the object. While searching for the object, the edges of the spanning tree are

---

Algorithm 6.3 Shared Object: Arrow Algorithm

Initialization: As for Algorithm 6.1, we are given a rooted spanning tree. Each node has a pointer to its parent, the root r is its own parent. The variable is initially stored at r. For all nodes v, v.successor := **null**, v.wait := **false**.

Start Find Request at Node u:
1: **loop**
2:     u sends "find by u" message to parent node
3:     u.parent := u
4:     u.wait := **true**
5: **end loop**

Upon w Receiving "Find by u" Message from Node v:
6: **loop**
7:     **if** w.parent $\neq w$ **then**
8:         w sends "find by u" message to parent
9:         w.parent := v
10:     **else**
11:         w.parent := v
12:         **if not** w.wait **then**
13:             send variable to u // *w holds var. but does not need it any more*
14:         **else**
15:             w.successor := u // *w will send variable to u a.s.a.p.*
16:         **end if**
17:     **end if**
18: **end loop**

Upon w Receiving Shared Object:
19: perform operation on shared object
20: **loop**
21:     w.wait := **false**
22:     **if** w.successor $\neq$ **null then**
23:         send variable to w.successor
24:         w.successor := **null**
25:     **end if**
26: **end loop**

---

redirected such that in the end, the spanning tree is rooted at u (i.e., the new holder of the object). The details of the algorithm are given by Algorithm 6.3. For simplicity, we assume that a node u only starts a find request if u is not currently the holder of the shared object and if u has finished all previous find requests (i.e., it is not currently waiting to receive the object).

Remarks:

- The parent pointers in Algorithm 6.3 are only needed for the find operation. Sending the variable to u in Line 13 or to w.successor in Line 23 is done using routing (on the spanning tree or on the underlying network).

- When we draw the parent pointers as arrows, in a quiescent moment (where no "find" is in motion), the arrows all point towards the node currently holding the variable (i.e., the tree is rooted at the node holding the variable)

- What is really great about the Arrow algorithm is that it works in a completely asynchronous and concurrent setting (i.e., there can be many find requests at the same time).

Theorem 6.4. *(Arrow, Analysis) In an asynchronous and concurrent setting, a "find" operation terminates with message and time complexity D, where D is the diameter of the spanning tree.*

Before proving Theorem 6.4, we prove the following lemma.

Lemma 6.5. *An edge $\{u, v\}$ of the spanning tree is in one of four states:*

> *1.) Pointer from u to v (no message on edge, no v to u pointer)*
> *2.) Message on the move from u to v (no pointer on the edge)*
> *3.) Pointer from v to u (no message on edge, no u to v pointer)*
> *4.) Message on the move from v to u (no pointer on the edge)*

Proof. W.l.o.g., assume that initially the edge $\{u, v\}$ is in state 1. With a message arrival at u (or if u starts a "find by u" request), the edge goes to state 2. When the message is received at v, v directs its pointer to u and we are therefore in state 3. A new message at v (or a new request initiated by v) then brings the edge back to state 1. $\qquad\square$

Proof of Theorem 6.4. Since the "find" message will only travel on a static tree, it suffices to show that it will not traverse an edge twice. Suppose for the sake of contradiction that there is a first "find" message f that traverses an edge $e = \{u, v\}$ for the second time and assume that e is the first edge that is traversed twice by f. The first time, f traverses e. Assume that e is first traversed from u to v. Since we are on a tree, the second time, e must be traversed from v to u. Because e is the first edge to be traversed twice, f must re-visit e before visiting any other edges. Right before f reaches v, the edge e is in state 2 (f is on the move) and in state 3 (it will immediately return with the pointer from v to u). This is a contradiction to Lemma 6.5. $\qquad\square$

Remarks:

- Finding a good tree is an interesting problem. We would like to have a tree with low stretch, low diameter, low degree, etc.

- It seems that the Arrow algorithm works especially well when lots of "find" operations are initiated concurrently. Most of them will find a "close-by" node, thus having low message/time complexity. For the sake of simplicity we analyze a synchronous system.

Theorem 6.6. *(Arrow, Concurrent Analysis) Let the system be synchronous. Initially, the system is in a quiescent state. At time*

0, a set S of nodes initiates a "find" operation. The message complexity of all "find" operations is $O(\log |S| \cdot m^*)$ where m^* is the message complexity of an optimal (with global knowledge) algorithm on the tree.

Proof Sketch. Let d be the minimum distance of any node in S to the root. There will be a node u_1 at distance d from the root that reaches the root in d time steps, turning all the arrows on the path to the root towards u_1. A node u_2 that finds (is queued behind) u_1 cannot distinguish the system from a system where there was no request u_1, and instead the root was initially located at u_1. The message cost of u_2 is consequentially the distance between u_1 and u_2 on the spanning tree. By induction the total message complexity is exactly as if a collector starts at the root and then "greedily" collects tokens located at the nodes in S (greedily in the sense that the collector always goes towards the closest token). Greedy collecting the tokens is not a good strategy in general because it will traverse the same edge more than twice in the worst case. An asymptotically optimal algorithm can also be translated into a depth-first-search collecting paradigm, traversing each edge at most twice. In another area of computer science, we would call the Arrow algorithm a nearest-neighbor TSP heuristic (without returning to the start/root though), and the optimal algorithm TSP-optimal. It was shown that nearest-neighbor has a logarithmic overhead, which concludes the proof. $\square$

Remarks:

- An average request set S on a not-too-bad tree gives usually a much better bound. However, there is an almost tight $\log |S| / \log \log |S|$ worst-case example.

- It was recently shown that Arrow can do as good in a dynamic setting (where nodes are allowed to initiate requests at any time). In particular the message complexity of the dynamic analysis can be shown to have a $\log D$ overhead only, where D is the diameter of the spanning tree (note that for logarithmic trees, the overhead becomes $\log \log n$).

- What if the spanning tree is a star? Then with Theorem 6.4, each find will terminate in 2 steps! Since also an optimal algorithm has message cost 1, the algorithm is 2-competitive...? Yes, but because of its high degree the star center experiences contention. It can be shown that the contention overhead is at most proportional to the largest degree Δ of the spanning tree, but in a star the degree is linear in the number of nodes.

- Thought experiment: Assume a balanced binary spanning tree—by Theorem 6.4, the message complexity per operation is $2 \log n$. Because a binary tree has maximum degree 3, the contention is at most 3.

- There are better and worse choices for the spanning tree. The stretch of an edge $\{u, v\}$ is defined as distance between u and v in a spanning tree. The maximum stretch of a spanning tree is the maximum stretch over all edges. It was shown how to construct spanning trees that are $O(\log n)$-stretch-competitive.

What if most nodes just want to read the shared object? Then it does not make sense to acquire a lock every time. Instead we can use caching (see Algorithm 6.7).

Algorithm 6.7 Shared Object: Read/Write Caching

- Nodes can either read or write the shared object. For simplicity we first assume that reads or writes do not overlap in time (access to the object is sequential).
- Nodes store three items: a parent pointer pointing to one of the neighbors (as with Arrow), and a cache bit for each edge, plus (potentially) a copy of the object.
- Initially the object is stored at a single node u; all the parent pointers point towards u, all the cache bits are false.
- When initiating a read, a message follows the arrows (this time: without inverting them!) until it reaches a cached version of the object. Then a copy of the object is cached along the path back to the initiating node, and the cache bits on the visited edges are set to true.
- A write at u writes the new value locally (at node u), then searches (follow the parent pointers and reverse them towards u) a first node with a copy. Delete the copy and follow (in parallel, by flooding) all edge that have the cache flag set. Point the parent pointer towards u, and remove the cache flags.

Theorem 6.8. *Algorithm 6.7 is correct. More surprisingly, the message complexity is 3-competitive (at most a factor 3 worse than the optimum).*

Proof. Since the accesses do not overlap by definition, it suffices to show that between two writes, we are 3-competitive. The sequence of accessing nodes is $w_0, r_1, r_2, \ldots, r_k, w_1$. After w_0, the object is stored at w_0 and not cached anywhere else. All reads cost twice the smallest subtree T spanning the write w_0 and all the reads since each read only goes to the first copy. The write w_1 costs T plus the path P from w_1 to T. Since any data management scheme must use an edge in T and P at least once, and our algorithm uses edges in T at most 3 times (and in P at most once), the theorem follows. $\square$

Remarks:

- Concurrent reads are not a problem, also multiple concurrent reads and one write work just fine.

- What about concurrent writes? To achieve consistency writes need to invalidate the caches before writing their value. It is claimed that the strategy then becomes 4-competitive.

- Is the algorithm also time competitive? Well, not really: The optimal algorithm that we compare to is usually offline. This means it knows the whole access sequence in advance. It can then cache the object before the request even appears!

- Algorithms on trees are often simpler, but have the disadvantage that they introduce the extra stretch factor. In a ring, for example, any tree has stretch $n - 1$; so there is always a bad request pattern.

Algorithm 6.9 Shared Object: Pointer Forwarding

Initialization: Object is stored at root r of a precomputed spanning tree T (as in the Arrow algorithm, each node has a parent pointer pointing towards the object).

Accessing Object: (by node u)

1: follow parent pointers to current root r of T
2: send object from r to u
3: r.parent := u; u.parent := u; $\qquad$ // *u is the new root*

6.3 Ivy and Friends

In the following we study algorithms that do not restrict communication to a tree. Of particular interest is the special case of a complete graph (clique). A simple solution for this case is given by Algorithm 6.9.

Remarks:

- If the graph is not complete, routing can be used to find the root.

- Assume that the nodes line up in a linked list. If we always choose the first node of the linked list to acquire the object, we have message/time complexity n. The new topology is again a linear linked list. Pointer forwarding is therefore bad in a worst-case.

- If edges are not FIFO, it can even happen that the number of steps is unbounded for a node having bad luck. An algorithm with such a property is named "not fair," or "not wait-free." (Example: Initially we have the list $4 \rightarrow 3 \rightarrow 2 \rightarrow 1$; 4 starts a find; when the message of 4 passes 3, 3 itself starts a find. The message of 3 may arrive at 2 and then 1 earlier, thus the new end of the list is $2 \rightarrow 1 \rightarrow 3$; once the message of 4 passes 2, the game re-starts.)

There seems to be a natural improvement of the pointer forwarding idea. Instead of simply redirecting the parent pointer from the old root to the new root, we can redirect all the parent pointers of the nodes on the path visited during a find message to the new root. The details are given by Algorithm 6.10. Figure 6.11

Algorithm 6.10 Shared Object: Ivy

Initialization: Object is stored at root r of a precomputed spanning tree T (as before, each node has a parent pointer pointing towards the object). For simplicity, we assume that accesses to the object are sequential.

Start Find Request at Node u:

 1: u sends "find by u" message to parent node
 2: u.parent := u

Upon v receiving "Find by u" Message:

 3: **if** v.parent $= v$ **then**
 4:     send object to u
 5: **else**
 6:     send "find by u" message to v.parent
 7: **end if**
 8: v.parent := u $//$ *u will become the new root*

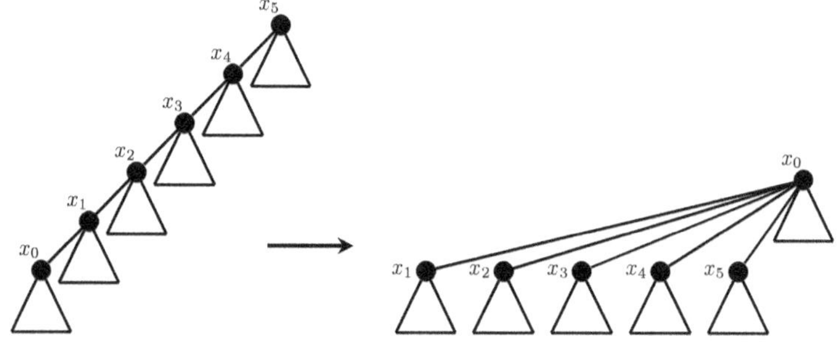

Figure 6.11: Reversal of the path $x_0, x_1, x_2, x_3, x_4, x_5$.

shows how the pointer redirecting affects a given tree (the right tree results from a find request started at node x_0 on the left tree).

Remarks:

- Also with Algorithm 6.10, we might have a bad linked list situation. However, if the start of the list acquires the object, the linked list turns into a star. As the following theorem shows, the search paths are not long on average. Since paths sometimes can be bad, we will need amortized analysis.

Theorem 6.12. *If the initial tree is a star, a find request of Algorithm 6.10 needs at most $\log n$ steps on average, where n is the* *number of processors.*

Proof. All logarithms in the following proof are to base 2. We assume that accesses to the shared object are sequential. We use a potential function argument. Let $s(u)$ be the size of the subtree rooted at node u (the number of nodes in the subtree including u itself). We define the potential Φ of the whole tree T as (V is the set of all nodes)

$$\Phi(T) = \sum_{u \in V} \frac{\log s(u)}{2}.$$

Assume that the path traversed by the ith operation has length k_i, i.e., the ith operation redirects k_i pointers to the new root. Clearly, the number of steps of the ith operation is proportional to k_i. We are interested in the cost of m consecutive operations, $\sum_{i=1}^{m} k_i$.

Let T_0 be the initial tree and let T_i be the tree after the ith operation. Further, let $a_i = k_i - \Phi(T_{i-1}) + \Phi(T_i)$ be the *amortized cost* of the ith operation. We have

$$\sum_{i=1}^{m} a_i = \sum_{i=1}^{m} \left(k_i - \Phi(T_{i-1}) + \Phi(T_i) \right) = \sum_{i=1}^{m} k_i - \Phi(T_0) + \Phi(T_m).$$

For any tree T, we have $\Phi(T) \geq \log(n)/2$. Because we assume that T_0 is a star, we also have $\Phi(T_0) = \log(n)/2$. We therefore get that

$$\sum_{i=1}^{m} a_i \geq \sum_{i=1}^{m} k_i.$$

Hence, it suffices to upper bound the amortized cost of every operation. We thus analyze the amortized cost a_i of the ith operation. Let $x_0, x_1, x_2, \ldots, x_{k_i}$ be the path that is reversed by the operation. Further for $0 \leq j \leq k_i$, let s_j be the size of the subtree rooted at x_j before the reversal. The size of the subtree rooted at x_0 after the reversal is s_{k_i} and the size of the one rooted at x_j after the reversal, for $1 \leq j \leq k_i$, is $s_j - s_{j-1}$ (see Figure 6.11). For all other nodes, the sizes of their subtrees are the same, therefore the corresponding terms cancel out in the ammortized cost a_i. We can thus write a_i as

$$
\begin{aligned}
a_i &= k_i - \left(\sum_{j=0}^{k_i} \frac{1}{2} \log s_j \right) + \left(\frac{1}{2} \log s_{k_i} + \sum_{j=1}^{k_i} \frac{1}{2} \log(s_j - s_{j-1}) \right) \\
&= k_i + \frac{1}{2} \cdot \sum_{j=0}^{k_i-1} \left(\log(s_{j+1} - s_j) - \log s_j \right) \\
&= k_i + \frac{1}{2} \cdot \sum_{j=0}^{k_i-1} \log \left(\frac{s_{j+1} - s_j}{s_j} \right).
\end{aligned}
$$

For $0 \le j \le k_i - 1$, let $\alpha_j = s_{j+1}/s_j$. Note that $s_{j+1} > s_j$ and thus that $\alpha_j > 1$. Further note, that $(s_{j+1} - s_j)/s_j = \alpha_j - 1$. We therefore have that

$$
\begin{aligned}
a_i &= k_i + \frac{1}{2} \cdot \sum_{j=0}^{k_i-1} \log(\alpha_j - 1) \\
&= \sum_{j=0}^{k_i-1} \left(1 + \frac{1}{2} \log(\alpha_j - 1) \right).
\end{aligned}
$$

For $\alpha > 1$, it can be shown that $1 + \log(\alpha - 1)/2 \le \log \alpha$ (see Lemma 6.13). From this inequality, we obtain

$$
\begin{aligned}
a_i &\le \sum_{j=0}^{k_i-1} \log \alpha_j = \sum_{j=0}^{k_i-1} \log \frac{s_{j+1}}{s_j} = \sum_{j=0}^{k_i-1} (\log s_{j+1} - \log s_j) \\
&= \log s_{k_i} - \log s_0 \le \log n,
\end{aligned}
$$

because $s_{k_i} = n$ and $s_0 \ge 1$. This concludes the proof. $\qquad\square$

Lemma 6.13. *For $\alpha > 1$, $1 + \log(\alpha - 1)/2 \le \log \alpha$.*

Proof. The claim can be verified by the following chain of reasoning:

$$
\begin{aligned}
0 &\le (\alpha - 2)^2 \\
0 &\le \alpha^2 - 4\alpha + 4 \\
4(\alpha - 1) &\le \alpha^2 \\
\log_2 \left(4(\alpha - 1) \right) &\le \log_2 \left(\alpha^2 \right) \\
2 + \log_2(\alpha - 1) &\le 2 \log_2 \alpha \\
1 + \frac{1}{2} \log_2(\alpha - 1) &\le \log_2 \alpha.
\end{aligned}
$$

$\qquad\square$

Remarks:

- Systems guys (the algorithm is called Ivy because it was used in a system with the same name) have some fancy heuristics to improve performance even more: For example, the root every now and then broadcasts its name such that paths will be shortened.

- What about concurrent requests? It works with the same argument as in Arrow. Also for Ivy an argument including congestion is missing (and more pressing, since the dynamic topology of a tree cannot be chosen to have low degree and thus low congestion as in Arrow).

- Sometimes the type of accesses allows that several accesses can be combined into one to reduce congestion higher up the tree. Let the tree in Algorithm 6.1 be a balanced binary tree. If the access to a shared variable for example is "add value x to the shared variable", two or more accesses that accidentally meet at a node can be combined into one. Clearly accidental meeting is rare in an asynchronous model. We might be able to use synchronizers (or maybe some other timing tricks) to help meeting a little bit.

Chapter Notes

The Arrow protocol was designed by Raymond [Ray89]. There are real life implementations of the Arrow protocol, such as the Aleph Toolkit [Her99]. The performance of the protocol under high loads was tested in [HW99] and other implementations and variations of the protocol were given in, e.g., [PR99, HTW00].

It has been shown that the find operations of the protocol do not backtrack, i.e., the time and message complexities are $O(D)$ [DH98], and that the Arrow protocol is fault tolerant [HT01]. Given a set of concurrent request, Herlihy et al. [HTW01] showed that the time and message complexities are within factor $\log R$ from the optimal, where R is the number of requests. Later, this analysis was extended to long-lived and asynchronous systems. In particular, Herlihy et al. [HKTW06] showed that the competitive ratio in this asynchronous concurrent setting is $O(\log D)$. Thanks to the lower bound of the greedy TSP heuristic, this is almost tight.

The Ivy system was introduced in [Li88, LH89]. On the theory side, it was shown by Ginat et al. [GST89] that the amortized cost of a single request of the Ivy protocol is $\Theta(\log n)$. Closely related work to the Ivy protocol on the practical side is research on virtual memory and parallel computing on loosely coupled multiprocessors. For example [BB81, LSHL82, FR86] contain studies on variations of the network models, limitations on data sharing between processes and different approaches.

Later, the research focus shifted towards systems where most data operations were read operations, i.e., efficient caching became one of the main objects of study, e.g., [MMVW97].

Arrow and Ivy are designed for trees or cliques, respectively. Arrow and Ivy are combinable, as one can choose whether to point to directly to the source or not – the Arvy protocol is the generalization of Arrow and Ivy [KW19]. Recently, other efficient shared object protocols for general networks have been proposed [SBS12].

Bibliography

[BB81]   Thomas J. Buckholtz and Helen T. Buckholtz. Apollo Domain Architecture. Technical report, Apollo Computer, Inc., 1981.

[DH98]   Michael J. Demmer and Maurice Herlihy. The Arrow Distributed Directory Protocol. In *Proceedings of the 12th International Symposium on Distributed Computing (DISC)*, 1998.

[FR86]   Robert Fitzgerald and Richard F. Rashid. The Integration of Virtual Memory Management and Interprocess Communication in Accent. *ACM Transactions on Computer Systems*, 4(2):147–177, 1986.

[GST89] David Ginat, Daniel Sleator, and Robert Tarjan. A Tight Amortized Bound for Path Reversal. *Information Processing Letters*, 31(1):3–5, 1989.

[Her99] Maurice Herlihy. The Aleph Toolkit: Support for Scalable Distributed Shared Objects. In *Proceedings of the Third International Workshop on Network-Based Parallel Computing: Communication, Architecture, and Applications (CANPC)*, pages 137–149, 1999.

[HKTW06] Maurice Herlihy, Fabian Kuhn, Srikanta Tirthapura, and Roger Wattenhofer. Dynamic Analysis of the Arrow Distributed Protocol. In *Theory of Computing Systems, Volume 39, Number 6*, November 2006.

[HT01] Maurice Herlihy and Srikanta Tirthapura. Self Stabilizing Distributed Queuing. In *Proceedings of the 15th International Conference on Distributed Computing (DISC)*, pages 209–223, 2001.

[HTW00] Maurice Herlihy, Srikanta Tirthapura, and Roger Wattenhofer. Ordered Multicast and Distributed Swap. In *Operating Systems Review, Volume 35/1, 2001. Also in PODC Middleware Symposium, Portland, Oregon*, July 2000.

[HTW01] Maurice Herlihy, Srikanta Tirthapura, and Roger Wattenhofer. Competitive Concurrent Distributed Queuing. In *Twentieth ACM Symposium on Principles of Distributed Computing (PODC)*, August 2001.

[HW99] Maurice Herlihy and Michael Warres. A Tale of Two Directories: Implementing Distributed Shared Objects in Java. In *Proceedings of the ACM 1999 conference on Java Grande (JAVA)*, pages 99–108, 1999.

[KW19] Pankaj Khanchandani and Roger Wattenhofer. The Arvy Distributed Directory Protocol. In *31st ACM Symposium on Parallelism in Algorithms and Architectures (SPAA), Phoenix, AZ, USA*, June 2019.

[LH89] Kai Li and Paul Hudak. Memory Coherence in Shared Virtual Memory Systems. *ACM Transactions on Computer Systems*, 7(4):312–359, November 1989.

[Li88] Kai Li. IVY: Shared Virtual Memory System for Parallel Computing. In *International Conference on Parallel Processing*, 1988.

[LSHL82] Paul J. Leach, Bernard L. Stumpf, James A. Hamilton, and Paul H. Levine. UIDs as Internal Names in a Distributed File System. In *Proceedings of the First ACM SIGACT-SIGOPS Symposium on Principles of Distributed Computing (PODC)*, pages 34–41, 1982.

[MMVW97] B. Maggs, F. Meyer auf der Heide, B. Voecking, and M. Westermann. Exploiting Locality for Data Management in Systems of Limited Bandwidth. In *IEEE Symposium on Foundations of Computer Science (FOCS)*, 1997.

[PR99] David Peleg and Eilon Reshef. A Variant of the Arrow Distributed Directory Protocol with Low Average Complexity. In *Proceedings of the 26th International Colloquium on Automata, Languages and Programming (ICALP)*, pages 615–624, 1999.

[Ray89] Kerry Raymond. A Tree-based Algorithm for Distributed Mutual Exclusion. *ACM Transactions on Computer Systems*, 7:61–77, 1989.

[SBS12] Gokarna Sharma, Costas Busch, and Srivathsan Srinivasagopalan. Distributed Transactional Memory for General Networks. In *26th International Parallel and Distributed Processing Symposium (IPDPS), Shanghai, China*, May 2012.

Chapter 7

Maximal Independent Set

In this chapter we present a highlight of this course, a fast maximal independent set (MIS) algorithm. The algorithm is the first randomized algorithm that we study in this class. In distributed computing, randomization is a powerful and therefore omnipresent concept, as it allows for relatively simple yet efficient algorithms. As such the studied algorithm is archetypal.

A MIS is a basic building block in distributed computing, some other problems pretty much follow directly from the MIS problem. At the end of this chapter, we will give two examples: matching and vertex coloring (see Chapter 1).

7.1 MIS

Definition 7.1 (Independent Set). *Given an undirected Graph $G = (V, E)$ an* **independent set** *is a subset of nodes $U \subseteq V$, such that no two nodes in U are adjacent. An independent set is* **maximal** *if no node can be added without violating independence. An independent set of maximum cardinality is called* **maximum**.

Remarks:

- Computing a maximum independent set (MaxIS) is a notoriously difficult problem. It is equivalent to maximum clique on the complementary graph. Both problems are

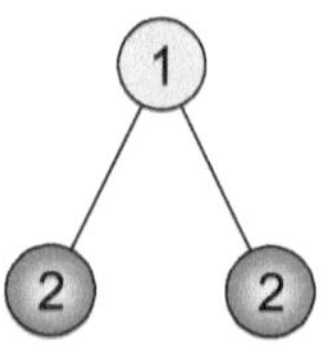

Figure 7.2: Example graph with 1) a maximal independent set (MIS) and 2) a maximum independent set (MaxIS).

NP-hard, in fact not approximable within $n^{\frac{1}{2}-\epsilon}$ within polynomial time.

- In this course we concentrate on the maximal independent set (MIS) problem. Please note that MIS and MaxIS can be quite different, indeed e.g. on a star graph there exists an MIS that is $\Theta(n)$ smaller than the MaxIS (cf. Figure 7.2).

- Computing a MIS sequentially is trivial: Scan the nodes in arbitrary order. If a node u does not violate independence, add u to the MIS. If u violates independence, discard u. So the only question is how to compute a MIS in a distributed way.

Algorithm 7.3 Slow MIS

Require: Node IDs

    Every node v executes the following code:

1: **if** all neighbors of v with larger identifiers have decided not to join the MIS **then**
2:    v decides to join the MIS
3: **end if**

Remarks:

- Not surprisingly the slow algorithm is not better than the sequential algorithm in the worst case, because there might be one single point of activity at any time. Formally:

Theorem 7.4 (Analysis of Algorithm 7.3). *Algorithm 7.3 features a time complexity of $O(n)$ and a message complexity of $O(m)$.*

Remarks:

- This is not very exciting.

- There is a relation between independent sets and node coloring (Chapter 1), since each color class is an independent set, however, not necessarily a MIS. Still, starting with a coloring, one can easily derive a MIS algorithm: In the first round all nodes of the first color join the MIS and notify their neighbors. Then, all nodes of the second color which do not have a neighbor that is already in the MIS join the MIS and inform their neighbors. This process is repeated for all colors. Thus the following corollary holds:

Corollary 7.5. *Given a coloring algorithm that runs in time T and needs C colors, we can construct a MIS in time $T + C$.*

Remarks:

- Using Theorem 1.23 and Corollary 7.5 we get a distributed deterministic MIS algorithm for trees (and for bounded degree graphs) with time complexity $O(\log^* n)$.

- With a lower bound argument one can show that this deterministic MIS algorithm is asymptotically optimal for rings.

- There have been attempts to extend Algorithm 1.17 to more general graphs, however, so far without much success. Below we present a radically different approach that uses randomization.

Algorithm 7.6 Fast MIS

The algorithm operates in synchronous rounds, grouped into phases.

A single phase is as follows:

1) Each node v marks itself with probability $\frac{1}{2d(v)}$, where $d(v)$ is the current degree of v.

2) If no higher degree neighbor of v is also marked, node v joins the MIS. If a higher degree neighbor of v is marked, node v unmarks itself again. (If the neighbors have the same degree, ties are broken arbitrarily, e.g., by identifier).

3) Delete all nodes that joined the MIS and their neighbors, as they cannot join the MIS anymore.

7.2   Original Fast MIS

Remarks:

- Correctness in the sense that the algorithm produces an independent set is relatively simple: Steps 1 and 2 make sure that if a node v joins the MIS, then v's neighbors do not join the MIS at the same time. Step 3 makes sure that v's neighbors will never join the MIS.

- Likewise the algorithm eventually produces a MIS, because the node with the highest degree will mark itself at some point in Step 1.

- So the only remaining question is how fast the algorithm terminates. To understand this, we need to dig a bit deeper.

Lemma 7.7 (Joining MIS). *A node v joins the MIS in Step 2 with probability $p \geq \frac{1}{4d(v)}$.*

Proof: Let M be the set of marked nodes in Step 1 and MIS be the set of nodes that join the MIS in Step 2. Let $H(v)$ be the set of neighbors of v with higher degree, or same degree and higher identifier. Using independence of the random choices of v and nodes in $H(v)$ in Step 1 we get

$$
\begin{aligned}
P\left[v \notin \text{MIS}|v \in M\right] &= P\left[\exists \text{ a node } w \in H(v), w \in M|v \in M\right] \\
&= P\left[\exists \text{ a node } w \in H(v), w \in M\right] \\
&\leq \sum_{w \in H(v)} P\left[w \in M\right] = \sum_{w \in H(v)} \frac{1}{2d(w)} \\
&\leq \sum_{w \in H(v)} \frac{1}{2d(v)} \leq \frac{d(v)}{2d(v)} = \frac{1}{2}.
\end{aligned}
$$

Then

$$
P\left[v \in \text{MIS}\right] = P\left[v \in \text{MIS}|v \in M\right] \cdot P\left[v \in M\right] \geq \frac{1}{2} \cdot \frac{1}{2d(v)}.
$$

$\square$

Lemma 7.8 (Good Nodes). *A node v is called **good** if*

$$
\sum_{w \in N(v)} \frac{1}{2d(w)} \geq \frac{1}{6},
$$

*where $N(v)$ is the set of neighbors of v. Otherwise we call v a **bad** node. A good node will be removed in Step 3 with probability $p \geq \frac{1}{36}$.*

Proof: Let node v be good. Intuitively, good nodes have lots of low-degree neighbors, thus chances are high that one of them goes into the independent set, in which case v will be removed in Step 3 of the algorithm.

If there is a neighbor $w \in N(v)$ with degree at most 2 we are done: With Lemma 7.7 the probability that node w joins the MIS is at least $\frac{1}{8}$, and our good node will be removed in Step 3.

So all we need to worry about is that all neighbors have at least degree 3: For any neighbor w of v we have $\frac{1}{2d(w)} \leq \frac{1}{6}$. Since $\sum_{w \in N(v)} \frac{1}{2d(w)} \geq \frac{1}{6}$ there is a subset of neighbors $S \subseteq N(v)$ such that $\frac{1}{6} \leq \sum_{w \in S} \frac{1}{2d(w)} \leq \frac{1}{3}$

We can now bound the probability that node v will be removed. Let therefore R be the event of v being removed. Again, if a neighbor of v joins the MIS in Step 2, node v will be removed in Step 3.

We have

$$
\begin{aligned}
P[R] \;\geq\;& P[\text{there is a node } u \in S, u \in \text{MIS}] \\
\;\geq\;& \sum_{u \in S} P[u \in \text{MIS}] - \sum_{u,w \in S; u \neq w} P[u \in \text{MIS} \textbf{ and } w \in \text{MIS}].
\end{aligned}
$$

For the last inequality we used the inclusion-exclusion principle truncated after the second order terms. Let M again be the set of marked nodes after Step 1. Using $P[u \in M] \geq P[u \in \text{MIS}]$ we get

$$
\begin{aligned}
P[R] \;\geq\;& \sum_{u \in S} P[u \in \text{MIS}] - \sum_{u,w \in S; u \neq w} P[u \in M \textbf{ and } w \in M] \\
\;\geq\;& \sum_{u \in S} P[u \in \text{MIS}] - \sum_{u \in S}\sum_{w \in S} P[u \in M] \cdot P[w \in M] \\
\;\geq\;& \sum_{u \in S} \frac{1}{4 d(u)} - \sum_{u \in S}\sum_{w \in S} \frac{1}{2 d(u)}\frac{1}{2 d(w)} \\
\;\geq\;& \sum_{u \in S} \frac{1}{2 d(u)} \left(\frac{1}{2} - \sum_{w \in S} \frac{1}{2 d(w)} \right) \geq \frac{1}{6}\left(\frac{1}{2} - \frac{1}{3} \right) = \frac{1}{36}.
\end{aligned}
$$

$\square$

Remarks:

- We would be almost finished if we could prove that many nodes are good in each phase. Unfortunately this is not the case: In a star-graph, for instance, only a single node is good! We need to find a work-around.

Lemma 7.9 (Good Edges). *An edge $e = (u, v)$ is called **bad** if both u and v are bad; else the edge is called **good**. The following holds: At any time at least half of the edges are good.*

Proof: For the proof we construct a directed auxiliary graph: Direct each edge towards the higher degree node (if both nodes have the same degree direct it towards the higher identifier). Now we need a little helper lemma before we can continue with the proof.

Lemma 7.10. *A bad node has outdegree (number of edges pointing away from bad node) at least twice its indegree (number of edges pointing towards bad node).*

Proof: For the sake of contradiction, assume that a bad node v does not have outdegree at least twice its indegree. In other words, at least one third of the neighbor nodes (let's call them S) have degree at most $d(v)$. But then

$$\sum_{w \in N(v)} \frac{1}{2d(w)} \geq \sum_{w \in S} \frac{1}{2d(w)} \geq \sum_{w \in S} \frac{1}{2d(v)} \geq \frac{d(v)}{3} \frac{1}{2d(v)} = \frac{1}{6}$$

which means v is good, a contradiction. $\qquad\square$

Continuing the proof of Lemma 7.9: According to Lemma 7.10 the number of edges directed into bad nodes is at most half the number of edges directed out of bad nodes. Thus, the number of edges directed into bad nodes is at most half the number of edges. Thus, at least half of the edges are directed into good nodes. Since these edges are not bad, they must be good.

Theorem 7.11 (Analysis of Algorithm 7.6). *Algorithm 7.6 terminates in expected time $O(\log n)$.*

Proof: With Lemma 7.8 a good node (and therefore a good edge!) will be deleted with constant probability. Since at least half of the edges are good (Lemma 7.9) a constant fraction of edges will be deleted in each phase.

More formally: With Lemmas 7.8 and 7.9 we know that at least half of the edges will be removed with probability at least $1/36$. Let R be the number of edges to be removed in a certain phase. Using linearity of expectation (cf. Theorem 7.13) we know that $\mathbb{E}[R] \geq m/72$, m being the total number of edges at the start of the phase. Now let $p := P[R \leq \mathbb{E}[R]/2]$. Bounding the expectation yields

$$\begin{aligned}
\mathbb{E}[R] &= \sum_r P[R = r] \cdot r \\
&\leq P[R \leq \mathbb{E}[R]/2] \cdot \mathbb{E}[R]/2 + P[R > \mathbb{E}[R]/2] \cdot m \\
&= p \cdot \mathbb{E}[R]/2 + (1-p) \cdot m.
\end{aligned}$$

Solving for p we get

$$p \leq \frac{m - \mathbb{E}[R]}{m - \mathbb{E}[R]/2} < \frac{m - \mathbb{E}[R]/2}{m} \leq 1 - 1/144.$$

In other words, with probability at least $1/144$ at least $m/144$ edges are removed in a phase. After expected $O(\log m)$ phases all edges are deleted. Since $m \leq n^2$ and thus $O(\log m) = O(\log n)$ the Theorem follows. $\qquad\square$

Remarks:

- With a bit of more math one can even show that Algorithm 7.6 terminates in time $O(\log n)$ "with high probability".

7.3 Fast MIS v2

Algorithm 7.12 Fast MIS 2

The algorithm operates in synchronous rounds, grouped into phases.

A single phase is as follows:

1) Each node v chooses a random value $r(v) \in [0, 1]$ and sends it to its neighbors.

2) If $r(v) < r(w)$ for all neighbors $w \in N(v)$, node v enters the MIS and informs its neighbors.

3) If v or a neighbor of v entered the MIS, v terminates (v and all edges adjacent to v are removed from the graph), otherwise v enters the next phase.

Remarks:

- Correctness in the sense that the algorithm produces an independent set is simple: Steps 1 and 2 make sure that if a node v joins the MIS, then v's neighbors do not join the MIS at the same time. Step 3 makes sure that v's neighbors will never join the MIS.

- Likewise the algorithm eventually produces a MIS, because the node with the globally smallest value will always join the MIS, hence there is progress.

- So the only remaining question is how fast the algorithm terminates. To understand this, we need to dig a bit deeper.

- Our proof will rest on a simple, yet powerful observation about expected values of random variables that *may not be independent*:

Theorem 7.13 (Linearity of Expectation). *Let X_i, $i = 1, \ldots, k$ denote random variables, then*

$$\mathbb{E}\left[\sum_i X_i\right] = \sum_i \mathbb{E}\left[X_i\right].$$

Proof. It is sufficient to prove $\mathbb{E}\left[X + Y\right] = \mathbb{E}\left[X\right] + \mathbb{E}\left[Y\right]$ for two random variables X and Y, because then the statement follows by induction. Since

$$\begin{aligned}
P\left[(X,Y) = (x,y)\right] &= P\left[X = x\right] \cdot P\left[Y = y | X = x\right] \\
&= P\left[Y = y\right] \cdot P\left[X = x | Y = y\right]
\end{aligned}$$

we get that

$$\begin{aligned}
\mathbb{E}\left[X + Y\right] &= \sum_{(X,Y)=(x,y)} P\left[(X,Y) = (x,y)\right] \cdot (x + y) \\
&= \sum_{X=x}\sum_{Y=y} P\left[X = x\right] \cdot P\left[Y = y | X = x\right] \cdot x \\
&+ \sum_{Y=y}\sum_{X=x} P\left[Y = y\right] \cdot P\left[X = x | Y = y\right] \cdot y \\
&= \sum_{X=x} P\left[X = x\right] \cdot x + \sum_{Y=y} P\left[Y = y\right] \cdot y \\
&= \mathbb{E}\left[X\right] + \mathbb{E}\left[Y\right].
\end{aligned}$$

$\square$

Remarks:

- How can we prove that the algorithm only needs $O(\log n)$ phases in expectation? It would be great if this algorithm managed to remove a constant fraction of nodes in each phase. Unfortunately, it does not.

- Instead we will prove that the number of *edges* decreases quickly. Again, it would be great if any single edge was removed with constant probability in Step 3. But again, unfortunately, this is not the case.

- Maybe we can argue about the expected number of edges to be removed in one single phase? Let's see: A node v enters the MIS with probability $1/(d(v)+1)$, where $d(v)$

is the degree of node v. By doing so, not only are v's edges removed, but indeed all the edges of v's neighbors as well – generally these are much more than $d(v)$ edges. So there is hope, but we need to be careful: If we do this the most naive way, we will count the same edge many times.

- How can we fix this? The nice observation is that it is enough to count just some of the removed edges. Given a new MIS node v and a neighbor $w \in N(v)$, we count the edges only if $r(v) < r(x)$ for all $x \in N(w)$. This looks promising. In a star graph, for instance, only the smallest random value can be accounted for removing all the edges of the star.

Lemma 7.14 (Edge Removal). *In a single phase, we remove at least half of the edges in expectation.*

Proof. To simplify the notation, at the start of our phase, the graph is simply $G = (V, E)$. In addition, to ease presentation, we replace each undirected edge $\{v, w\}$ by the two directed edges (v, w) and (w, v).

Suppose that a node v joins the MIS in this phase, i.e., $r(v) < r(w)$ for all neighbors $w \in N(v)$. If in addition we have $r(v) < r(x)$ for all neighbors x of a neighbor w of v, we call this event $(v \to w)$. The probability of event $(v \to w)$ is at least $1/(d(v) + d(w))$, since $d(v) + d(w)$ is the maximum number of nodes adjacent to v or w (or both). As v joins the MIS, all (directed) edges (w, x) with $x \in N(w)$ will be removed; there are $d(w)$ of these edges.

We now count the removed edges. Whether we remove the edges adjacent to w because of event $(v \to w)$ is a random variable $X_{(v \to w)}$. If event $(v \to w)$ occurs, $X_{(v \to w)}$ has the value $d(w)$, if not it has the value 0. For each undirected edge $\{v, w\}$ we have two such variables, $X_{(v \to w)}$ and $X_{(w \to v)}$. Due to Theorem 7.13, the expected value of the sum X of all these random variables is at least

$$\mathbb{E}\left[X\right] = \sum_{\{v,w\}\in E} \mathbb{E}[X_{(v\to w)}] + \mathbb{E}[X_{(w\to v)}]$$

$$= \sum_{\{v,w\}\in E} P\left[\text{Event } (v\to w)\right]\cdot d(w) + P\left[\text{Event } (w\to v)\right]\cdot d(v)$$

$$\geq \sum_{\{v,w\}\in E} \frac{d(w)}{d(v)+d(w)} + \frac{d(v)}{d(w)+d(v)}$$

$$= \sum_{\{v,w\}\in E} 1 = |E|.$$

In other words, in expectation $|E|$ directed edges are removed in a single phase! Note that we did not double count any edge removals, as a directed edge (w,x) can only be removed by an event $(v\to w)$. The event $(v\to w)$ inhibits a concurrent event $(v'\to w)$ since $r(v) < r(v')$ for all $v' \in N(w)$. We may have counted an undirected edge at most twice (once in each direction). So, in expectation at least half of the undirected edges are removed. $\square$

Remarks:

- This enables us to follow a bound on the expected running time of Algorithm 7.12 quite easily.

Theorem 7.15 (Expected running time of Algorithm 7.12). *Algorithm 7.12 terminates after at most $3\log_{4/3} m + 1 \in O(\log n)$ phases in expectation.*

Proof: The probability that in a single phase at least a quarter of all edges are removed is at least $1/3$. For the sake of contradiction, assume not. Then with probability less than $1/3$ we may be lucky and many (potentially all) edges are removed. With probability more than $2/3$ less than $1/4$ of the edges are removed. Hence the expected fraction of removed edges is strictly less than $1/3 \cdot 1 + 2/3 \cdot 1/4 = 1/2$. This contradicts Lemma 7.14.

Hence, in expectation at least every third phase is "good" and removes at least a quarter of the edges. To get rid of all but two edges we need $\log_{4/3} m$ good phases in expectation. The last two edges will certainly be removed in the next phase. Hence a total of $3\log_{4/3} m + 1$ phases are enough in expectation.

Remarks:

- Sometimes one expects a bit more of an algorithm: Not only should the expected time to terminate be good, but the algorithm should *always* terminate quickly. As this is impossible in randomized algorithms (after all, the random choices may be "unlucky" all the time!), researchers often settle for a compromise, and just demand that the probability that the algorithm does not terminate in the specified time can be made absurdly small. For our algorithm, this can be deduced from Lemma 7.14 and another standard tool, namely Chernoff's Bound.

Definition 7.16 (with high probability). *We say that an algorithm terminates $\boldsymbol{w.h.p.}$ (with high probability) within $O(t)$ time if it does so with probability at least $1 - 1/n^c$ for any choice of $c \geq 1$. Here c may affect the constants in the Big-O notation because it is considered a "tunable constant" and usually kept small.*

Definition 7.17 (Chernoff's Bound). *Let $X = \sum_{i=1}^{k} X_i$ be the sum of k independent $0-1$ random variables. Then $\boldsymbol{Chernoff's}$ $\boldsymbol{bound}$ states that w.h.p.*

$$|X - \mathbb{E}[X]| \in O\left(\log n + \sqrt{\mathbb{E}[X] \log n}\right).$$

Corollary 7.18 (Running Time of Algorithm 7.12). *Algorithm 7.12 terminates w.h.p. in $O(\log n)$ time.*

Proof: In Theorem 7.15 we used that *independently* of everything that happened before, in each phase we have a constant probability p that a quarter of the edges are removed. Call such a phase *good*. For some constants C_1 and C_2, let us check after $C_1 \log n + C_2 \in O(\log n)$ phases, in how many phases at least a quarter of the edges have been removed. In expectation, these are at least $p(C_1 \log n + C_2)$ many. Now we look at the random variable $X = \sum_{i=1}^{C_1 \log n + C_2} X_i$, where the X_i are independent $0-1$ variables being one with exactly probability p. Certainly, if X is at least x with some probability, then the probability that we have x good phases can only be larger (if no edges are left, certainly "all" of the remaining edges are removed). To X we can apply Chernoff's bound. If C_1 and C_2 are chosen large enough, they will overcome the constants in the Big-O from Chernoff's bound, i.e., w.h.p. it holds that $|X - \mathbb{E}[X]| \leq \mathbb{E}[X]/2$, implying $X \geq \mathbb{E}[X]/2$. Choosing C_1 large enough, we will have w.h.p. sufficiently many good phases, i.e., the algorithm terminates w.h.p. in $O(\log n)$ phases.

Remarks:

- The algorithm can be improved. Drawing random real numbers in each phase for instance is not necessary. One can achieve the same by sending only a total of $O(\log n)$ random (and as many non-random) bits over each edge.

- One of the main open problems in distributed computing is whether one can beat this logarithmic time, or at least achieve it with a deterministic algorithm.

- Let's turn our attention to applications of MIS next.

7.4 Applications

Definition 7.19 (Matching). *Given a graph $G = (V, E)$ a **matching** is a subset of edges $M \subseteq E$, such that no two edges in M are adjacent (i.e., where no node is adjacent to two edges in the matching). A matching is **maximal** if no edge can be added without violating the above constraint. A matching of maximum cardinality is called **maximum**. A matching is called **perfect** if each node is adjacent to an edge in the matching.*

Remarks:

- In contrast to MaxIS, a maximum matching can be found in polynomial time, and is also easy to approximate, since any maximal matching is a 2-approximation.

- An independent set algorithm is also a matching algorithm: Let $G = (V, E)$ be the graph for which we want to construct the matching. The so-called line graph G' is defined as follows: for every edge in G there is a node in G'; two nodes in G' are connected by an edge if their respective edges in G are adjacent. A (maximal) independent set in the line graph G' is a (maximal) matching in the original graph G, and vice versa. Using Algorithm 7.12 directly produces a $O(\log n)$ bound for maximal matching.

- More importantly, our MIS algorithm can also be used for vertex coloring (Problem 1.1):

Algorithm 7.20 General Graph Coloring

1: Given a graph $G = (V, E)$ we virtually build a graph $G' = (V', E')$ as follows:
2: Every node $v \in V$ clones itself $d(v) + 1$ times $(v_0, \ldots, v_{d(v)} \in V')$, $d(v)$ being the degree of v in G.
3: The edge set E' of G' is as follows:
4: First all clones are in a clique: $(v_i, v_j) \in E'$, for all $v \in V$ and all $0 \leq i < j \leq d(v)$
5: Second all i^{th} clones of neighbors in the original graph G are connected: $(u_i, v_i) \in E'$, for all $(u, v) \in E$ and all $0 \leq i \leq \min(d(u), d(v))$.
6: Now we simply run (simulate) the fast MIS Algorithm 7.12 on G'.
7: If node v_i is in the MIS in G', then node v gets color i.

Theorem 7.21 (Analysis of Algorithm 7.20). *Algorithm 7.20 ($\Delta + 1$)-colors an arbitrary graph in $O(\log n)$ time, with high probability, Δ being the largest degree in the graph.*

Proof: Thanks to the clique among the clones at most one clone is in the MIS. And because of the $d(v) + 1$ clones of node v every node will get a free color! The running time remains logarithmic since G' has $O\left(n^2\right)$ nodes and the exponent becomes a constant factor when applying the logarithm.

Remarks:

- This solves our open problem from Chapter 1.1!

- Together with Corollary 7.5 we get quite close ties between ($\Delta + 1$)-coloring and the MIS problem.

- Computing a MIS also solves another graph problem on graphs of bounded independence.

Definition 7.22 (Bounded Independence). *$G = (V, E)$ is of **bounded independence**, if for every node $v \in V$ the largest independent set in the neighborhood $N(v)$ is bounded by a constant.*

Definition 7.23 ((Minimum) Dominating Sets). *A **dominating set** is a subset of the nodes such that each node is in the set or adjacent to a node in the set. A **minimum dominating set** is a dominating set containing the least possible number of nodes.*

Remarks:

- In general, finding a dominating set less than factor $\log n$ larger than an minimum dominating set is NP-hard.

- Any MIS is a dominating set: if a node was not covered, it could join the independent set.

- In general a MIS and a minimum dominating sets have not much in common (think of a star). For graphs of bounded independence, this is different.

Corollary 7.24. *On graphs of bounded independence, a constant-factor approximation to a minimum dominating set can be found in time $O(\log n)$ w.h.p.*

Proof: Denote by M a minimum dominating set and by I a MIS. Since M is a dominating set, each node from I is in M or adjacent to a node in M. Since the graph is of bounded independence, no node in M is adjacent to more than constantly many nodes from I. Thus, $|I| \in O(|M|)$. Therefore, we can compute a MIS with Algorithm 7.12 and output it as the dominating set, which takes $O(\log n)$ rounds w.h.p.

Chapter Notes

As we have seen, a MIS can be used in versatile ways. Indeed, it was once argued that the cells of a fly compute a MIS to decide where to grow hair [AAB+11]. The fast MIS algorithm is a simplified version of an algorithm by Luby [Lub86]. Around the same time there have been a number of other papers dealing with the same or related problems, for instance by Alon, Babai, and Itai [ABI86], or by Israeli and Itai [II86]. The analysis presented in Section 7.2 takes elements of all these papers, and from other papers on distributed weighted matching [WW04]. The analysis in the book [Pel00] by David Peleg is different, and only achieves $O(\log^2 n)$ time. The new MIS variant (with the simpler analysis) of Section 7.3 is by Métivier, Robson, Saheb-Djahromi and Zemmari [MRSDZ11]. With some adaptations, the algorithms [Lub86, MRSDZ11] only need to exchange a total of $O(\log n)$ bits per node, which is asymptotically optimum, even on unoriented trees [KSOS06]. However, the distributed time complexity for MIS is still somewhat open, as the strongest lower bounds are $\Omega(\sqrt{\log n})$ or $\Omega(\log \Delta)$ [KMW04]. Recent research regarding the MIS problem focused on improving the $O(\log n)$ time complexity for special graph classes, for instances growth-bounded graphs [SW08] or trees [LW11]. There are also results that depend on the degree of the graph [BE09, Kuh09]. Deterministic MIS algorithms are still far from the lower bounds, as the best deterministic MIS algorithm takes $2^{O(\sqrt{\log n})}$ time [PS96]. The maximum matching algorithm mentioned in the remarks is the blossom algorithm by Jack Edmonds.

Bibliography

[AAB⁺11] Yehuda Afek, Noga Alon, Omer Barad, Eran Hornstein, Naama Barkai, and Ziv Bar-Joseph. A Biological Solution to a Fundamental Distributed Computing Problem. volume 331, pages 183–185. American Association for the Advancement of Science, January 2011.

[ABI86] Noga Alon, László Babai, and Alon Itai. A Fast and Simple Randomized Parallel Algorithm for the Maximal Independent Set Problem. *J. Algorithms*, 7(4):567–583, 1986.

[BE09] Leonid Barenboim and Michael Elkin. Distributed (delta+1)-coloring in linear (in delta) time. In *41st ACM Symposium On Theory of Computing (STOC)*, 2009.

[II86] Amos Israeli and Alon Itai. A Fast and Simple Randomized Parallel Algorithm for Maximal Matching. *Inf. Process. Lett.*, 22(2):77–80, 1986.

[KMW04] F. Kuhn, T. Moscibroda, and R. Wattenhofer. What Cannot Be Computed Locally! In *Proceedings of the 23rd ACM Symposium on Principles of Distributed Computing (PODC)*, July 2004.

[KSOS06] Kishore Kothapalli, Christian Scheideler, Melih Onus, and Christian Schindelhauer. Distributed coloring in

$O(\sqrt{\log n})$ Bit Rounds. In *20th international conference on Parallel and Distributed Processing (IPDPS)*, 2006.

[Kuh09] Fabian Kuhn. Weak graph colorings: distributed algorithms and applications. In *21st ACM Symposium on Parallelism in Algorithms and Architectures (SPAA)*, 2009.

[Lub86] Michael Luby. A Simple Parallel Algorithm for the Maximal Independent Set Problem. *SIAM J. Comput.*, 15(4):1036–1053, 1986.

[LW11] Christoph Lenzen and Roger Wattenhofer. MIS on trees. In *PODC*, pages 41–48, 2011.

[MRSDZ11] Yves Métivier, John Michael Robson, Nasser Saheb-Djahromi, and Akka Zemmari. An optimal bit complexity randomized distributed MIS algorithm. *Distributed Computing*, 23(5-6):331–340, 2011.

[Pel00] David Peleg. *Distributed Computing: a Locality-Sensitive Approach*. Society for Industrial and Applied Mathematics, Philadelphia, PA, USA, 2000.

[PS96] Alessandro Panconesi and Aravind Srinivasan. On the Complexity of Distributed Network Decomposition. *J. Algorithms*, 20(2):356–374, 1996.

[SW08] Johannes Schneider and Roger Wattenhofer. A Log-Star Distributed Maximal Independent Set Algorithm for Growth-Bounded Graphs. In *27th ACM Symposium on Principles of Distributed Computing (PODC), Toronto, Canada*, August 2008.

[WW04] Mirjam Wattenhofer and Roger Wattenhofer. Distributed Weighted Matching. In *18th Annual Conference on Distributed Computing (DISC), Amsterdam, Netherlands*, October 2004.

Chapter 8

Locality Lower Bounds

In Chapter 1, we looked at distributed algorithms for coloring. In particular, we saw that rings and rooted trees can be colored with 3 colors in $\log^* n + O(1)$ rounds.

8.1 Model

In this chapter, we will reconsider the distributed coloring problem. We will look at a classic lower bound that shows that the result of Chapter 1 is tight: Coloring rings (and rooted trees) indeed requires $\Omega(\log^* n)$ rounds. In particular, we will prove a lower bound for coloring in the following setting:

- We consider deterministic, synchronous algorithms.

- Message size and local computations are unbounded.

- We assume that the network is a directed ring with n nodes.

- Nodes have unique labels (identifiers) from 1 to n.

Remarks:

- A generalization of the lower bound to randomized algorithms is possible.

- Except for restricting to deterministic algorithms, all the conditions above make a lower bound stronger: Any lower bound for synchronous algorithms certainly also holds for

---

Algorithm 8.1 Synchronous Algorithm: Canonical Form

1: In r rounds: **send** complete initial state to nodes at distance
   at most r
2:             *// do all the communication first*
3: Compute output based on complete information about r-
   neighborhood
4:           *// do all the computation in the end*

---

asynchronous ones. A lower bound that is true if message
size and local computations are not restricted is clearly
also valid if we require a bound on the maximal message
size or the amount of local computations. Similarly, assuming that the ring is directed and that node labels are
from 1 to n (instead of choosing IDs from a more general
domain) also strengthens the lower bound.

- Instead of directly proving that 3-coloring a ring needs
  $\Omega(\log^* n)$ rounds, we will prove a slightly more general
  statement. We will consider deterministic algorithms with
  time complexity r (for arbitrary r) and derive a lower
  bound on the number of colors that are needed if we
  want to properly color an n-node ring with an r-round
  algorithm. A 3-coloring lower bound can then be derived
  by taking the smallest r for which an r-round algorithm
  needs 3 or fewer colors.

8.2 Locality

Let us for a moment look at distributed algorithms more generally (i.e., not only at coloring and not only at rings). Assume
that initially, all nodes only know their own label (identifier) and
potentially some additional input. As information needs at least
r rounds to travel r hops, after r rounds, a node v can only learn
about other nodes at distance at most r. If message size and local
computations are not restricted, it is in fact not hard to see, that in
r rounds, a node v can exactly learn all the node labels and inputs
up to distance r. As shown by the following lemma, this allows to
transform every deterministic r-round synchronous algorithm into
a simple canonical form.

Lemma 8.2. *If message size and local computations are not bounded, every deterministic, synchronous r-round algorithm can be transformed into an algorithm of the form given by Algorithm 8.1 (i.e., it is possible to first communicate for r rounds and then do all the computations in the end).*

Proof. Consider some r-round algorithm $\mathcal{A}$. We want to show that $\mathcal{A}$ can be brought to the canonical form given by Algorithm 8.1. First, we let the nodes communicate for r rounds. Assume that in every round, every node sends its complete state to all of its neighbors (remember that there is no restriction on the maximal message size). By induction, after i rounds, every node knows the initial state of all other nodes at distance at most i. Hence, after r rounds, a node v has the combined initial knowledge of all the nodes in its r-neighborhood. We want to show that this suffices to locally (at node v) simulate enough of Algorithm $\mathcal{A}$ to compute all the messages that v receives in the r communication rounds of a regular execution of Algorithm $\mathcal{A}$.

Concretely, we prove the following statement by induction on i. For all nodes at distance at most $r - i + 1$ from v, node v can compute all messages of the first i rounds of a regular execution of $\mathcal{A}$. Note that this implies that v can compute all the messages it receives from its neighbors during all r rounds. Because v knows the initial state of all nodes in the r-neighborhood, v can clearly compute all messages of the first round (i.e., the statement is true for $i = 1$). Let us now consider the induction step from i to $i + 1$. By the induction hypothesis, v can compute the messages of the first i rounds of all nodes in its $(r - i + 1)$-neighborhood. It can therefore compute all messages that are received by nodes in the $(r - i)$-neighborhood in the first i rounds. This is of course exactly what is needed to compute the messages of round $i + 1$ of nodes in the $(r - i)$-neighborhood. $\qquad\square$

Remarks:

- It is straightforward to generalize the canonical form to randomized algorithms: Every node first computes all the random bits it needs throughout the algorithm. The random bits are then part of the initial state of a node.

Definition 8.3 (r-hop view). *We call the collection of the initial states of all nodes in the r-neighborhood of a node v, the r-hop view of v.*

Remarks:

- Assume that initially, every node knows its degree, its label (identifier) and potentially some additional input. The r-hop view of a node v then includes the complete topology of the r-neighborhood (excluding edges between nodes at distance r) and the labels and additional inputs of all nodes in the r-neighborhood.

Based on the definition of an r-hop view, we can state the following corollary of Lemma 8.2.

Corollary 8.4. *A deterministic r-round algorithm $\mathcal{A}$ is a function that maps every possible r-hop view to the set of possible outputs.*

Proof. By Lemma 8.2, we know that we can transform Algorithm $\mathcal{A}$ to the canonical form given by Algorithm 8.1. After r communication rounds, every node v knows exactly its r-hop view. This information suffices to compute the output of node v. $\qquad\square$

Remarks:

- Note that the above corollary implies that two nodes with equal r-hop views have to compute the same output in every r-round algorithm.

- For coloring algorithms, the only input of a node v is its label. The r-hop view of a node therefore is its labeled r-neighborhood.

- If we only consider rings, r-hop neighborhoods are particularly simple. The labeled r-neighborhood of a node v (and hence its r-hop view) in an oriented ring is simply a $(2r+1)$-tuple $(\ell_{-r}, \ell_{-r+1}, \ldots, \ell_0, \ldots, \ell_r)$ of distinct node labels where ℓ_0 is the label of v. Assume that for $i > 0$, ℓ_i is the label of the ith clockwise neighbor of v and ℓ_{-i} is the label of the ith counterclockwise neighbor of v. A deterministic coloring algorithm for oriented rings therefore is a function that maps $(2r+1)$-tuples of node labels to colors.

- Consider two r-hop views $\mathcal{V}_r = (\ell_{-r}, \ldots, \ell_r)$ and $\mathcal{V}'_r = (\ell'_{-r}, \ldots, \ell'_r)$. If $\ell'_i = \ell_{i+1}$ for $-r \leq i \leq r-1$ and if $\ell'_r \neq \ell_i$ for $-r \leq i \leq r$, the r-hop view $\mathcal{V}'_r$ can be the r-hop view of a clockwise neighbor of a node with r-hop view $\mathcal{V}_r$. Therefore, every algorithm $\mathcal{A}$ that computes a valid coloring needs to assign different colors to $\mathcal{V}_r$ and $\mathcal{V}'_r$. Otherwise, there is a ring labeling for which $\mathcal{A}$ assigns the same color to two adjacent nodes.

8.3 The Neighborhood Graph

We will now make the above observations concerning colorings of rings a bit more formal. Instead of thinking of an r-round coloring algorithm as a function from all possible r-hop views to colors, we will use a slightly different perspective. Interestingly, the problem of understanding distributed coloring algorithms can itself be seen as a classical graph coloring problem.

Definition 8.5 (Neighborhood Graph). *For a given family of network graphs $\mathcal{G}$, the r-neighborhood graph $\mathcal{N}_r(\mathcal{G})$ is defined as follows. The node set of $\mathcal{N}_r(\mathcal{G})$ is the set of all possible labeled r-neighborhoods (i.e., all possible r-hop views). There is an edge between two labeled r-neighborhoods $\mathcal{V}_r$ and $\mathcal{V}'_r$ if $\mathcal{V}_r$ and $\mathcal{V}'_r$ are the r-hop views of two adjacent nodes in any graph in $\mathcal{G}$.*

Example 8.6. *Figure 8.7 shows a family of graphs $\mathcal{G}$, and Figure 8.8 shows the corresponding 1-neighborhood graph $\mathcal{N}_1(\mathcal{G})$.*

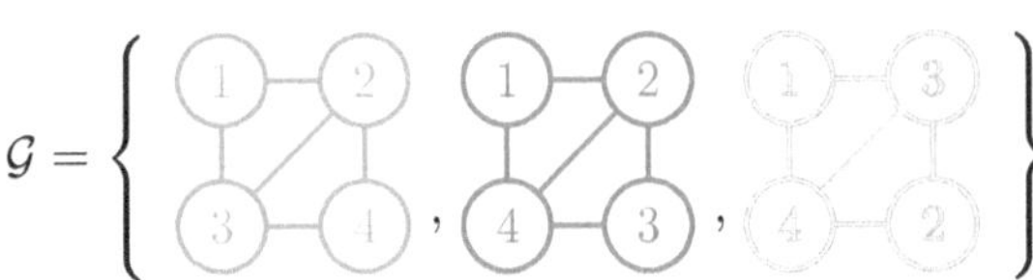

Figure 8.7: A family $\mathcal{G}$ consisting of three graphs. Notice the different labels.

Lemma 8.9. *For a given family of network graphs $\mathcal{G}$, there is an r-round algorithm that colors graphs of $\mathcal{G}$ with c colors iff the chromatic number of the neighborhood graph is $\chi(\mathcal{N}_r(\mathcal{G})) \leq c$.*

Proof. We have seen that a coloring algorithm is a function that maps every possible r-hop view to a color. Hence, a coloring algorithm assigns a color to every node of the neighborhood graph $\mathcal{N}_r(\mathcal{G})$. If two r-hop views $\mathcal{V}_r$ and $\mathcal{V}'_r$ are the r-hop views of two

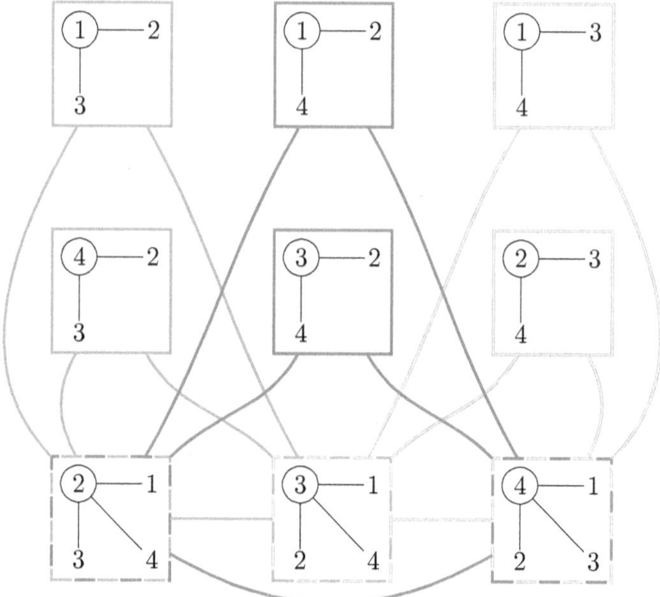

Figure 8.8: 1-neighborhood graph $\mathcal{N}_1(\mathcal{G})$ of the family in Figure 8.7. The colors of 1-hop views indicate which graphs in $\mathcal{G}$ they can be found in. The colors of edges indicate which graphs in $\mathcal{G}$ contain neighboring nodes that have the connected 1-hop views.

adjacent nodes u and v (for some labeled graph in $\mathcal{G}$), every correct coloring algorithm must assign different colors to $\mathcal{V}_r$ and $\mathcal{V}'_r$. Thus, specifying an r-round coloring algorithm for a family of network graphs $\mathcal{G}$ is equivalent to coloring the respective neighborhood graph $\mathcal{N}_r(\mathcal{G})$. $\qquad\square$

Instead of directly defining the neighborhood graph for directed rings, we define directed graphs $\mathcal{B}_k$ that are closely related to the neighborhood graph. The node set of $\mathcal{B}_k$ contains all k-tuples of increasing node labels ($[n] = \{1, \ldots, n\}$):

$$V[\mathcal{B}_k] \;=\; \big\{(\alpha_1, \ldots, \alpha_k) : \alpha_i \in [n], i < j \to \alpha_i < \alpha_j\big\} \tag{8.1}$$

For $\underline{\alpha} = (\alpha_1, \ldots, \alpha_k)$ and $\underline{\beta} = (\beta_1, \ldots, \beta_k)$ there is a directed edge from $\underline{\alpha}$ to $\underline{\beta}$ iff

$$\forall i \in \{1, \ldots, k-1\} : \beta_i = \alpha_{i+1}. \tag{8.2}$$

Lemma 8.10. *Viewed as an undirected graph, the graph $\mathcal{B}_{2r+1}$ is a subgraph of the r-neighborhood graph of directed n-node rings with node labels from $[n]$.*

Proof. The claim follows directly from the observations regarding r-hop views of nodes in a directed ring from Section 8.2. The set of k-tuples of increasing node labels is a subset of the set of k-tuples of distinct node labels. Two nodes of $\mathcal{B}_{2r+1}$ are connected by a directed edge iff the two corresponding r-hop views are connected by a directed edge in the neighborhood graph. Note that if there is an edge between $\underline{\alpha}$ and $\underline{\beta}$ in $\mathcal{B}_k$, $\alpha_1 \neq \beta_k$ because the node labels in $\underline{\alpha}$ and $\underline{\beta}$ are increasing. $\qquad\square$

To determine a lower bound on the number of colors an r-round algorithm needs for directed n-node rings, it therefore suffices to determine a lower bound on the chromatic number of $\mathcal{B}_{2r+1}$. To obtain such a lower bound, we need the following definition.

Definition 8.11 (Diline Graph). *The directed line graph (diline graph) $\mathcal{DL}(G)$ of a directed graph $G = (V, E)$ is defined as follows. The node set of $\mathcal{DL}(G)$ is $V[\mathcal{DL}(G)] = E$. There is a directed edge $\big((w, x), (y, z)\big)$ between $(w, x) \in E$ and $(y, z) \in E$ iff $x = y$, i.e., if the first edge ends where the second one starts.*

Lemma 8.12. *If $n > k$, the graph $\mathcal{B}_{k+1}$ can be defined recursively as follows:*

$$\mathcal{B}_{k+1} = \mathcal{DL}(\mathcal{B}_k).$$

Proof. The edges of $\mathcal{B}_k$ are pairs of k-tuples $\underline{\alpha} = (\alpha_1, \ldots, \alpha_k)$ and $\underline{\beta} = (\beta_1, \ldots, \beta_k)$ that satisfy Conditions (8.1) and (8.2). Because the last $k-1$ labels in $\underline{\alpha}$ are equal to the first $k-1$ labels in $\underline{\beta}$, the pair $(\underline{\alpha}, \underline{\beta})$ can be represented by a $(k+1)$-tuple $\underline{\gamma} = (\gamma_1, \ldots, \gamma_{k+1})$ with $\gamma_1 = \alpha_1$, $\gamma_i = \beta_{i-1} = \alpha_i$ for $2 \leq i \leq k$, and $\gamma_{k+1} = \beta_k$. Because the labels in $\underline{\alpha}$ and the labels in $\underline{\beta}$ are increasing, the labels in $\underline{\gamma}$ are increasing as well. The two graphs $\mathcal{B}_{k+1}$ and $\mathcal{DL}(\mathcal{B}_k)$ therefore have the same node sets. There is an edge between two nodes $(\underline{\alpha}_1, \underline{\beta}_1)$ and $(\underline{\alpha}_2, \underline{\beta}_2)$ of $\mathcal{DL}(\mathcal{B}_k)$ if $\underline{\beta}_1 = \underline{\alpha}_2$. This is equivalent to requiring that the two corresponding $(k+1)$-tuples $\underline{\gamma}_1$ and $\underline{\gamma}_2$ are neighbors in $\mathcal{B}_{k+1}$, i.e., that the last k labels of $\underline{\gamma}_1$ are equal to the first k labels of $\underline{\gamma}_2$. $\qquad\square$

The following lemma establishes a useful connection between the chromatic numbers of a directed graph G and its diline graph $\mathcal{DL}(G)$.

Lemma 8.13. *For the chromatic numbers $\chi(G)$ and $\chi(\mathcal{DL}(G))$ of a directed graph G and its diline graph, it holds that*

$$\chi(\mathcal{DL}(G)) \geq \log_2\left(\chi(G)\right).$$

Proof. Given a c-coloring of $\mathcal{DL}(G)$, we show how to construct a 2^c coloring of G. The claim of the lemma then follows because this implies that $\chi(G) \leq 2^{\chi(\mathcal{DL}(G))}$.

Assume that we are given a c-coloring of $\mathcal{DL}(G)$. A c-coloring of the diline graph $\mathcal{DL}(G)$ can be seen as a coloring of the edges of G such that no two adjacent edges have the same color. For a node v of G, let S_v be the set of colors of its outgoing edges. Let u and v be two nodes such that G contains a directed edge (u, v) from u to v and let x be the color of (u, v). Clearly, $x \in S_u$ because (u, v) is an outgoing edge of u. Because adjacent edges have different colors, no outgoing edge (v, w) of v can have color x. Therefore $x \notin S_v$. This implies that $S_u \neq S_v$. We can therefore use these color sets to obtain a vertex coloring of G, i.e., the color of u is S_u and the color of v is S_v. Because the number of possible subsets of $[c]$ is 2^c, this yields a 2^c-coloring of G. $\qquad\square$

Let $\log^{(i)} x$ be the i-fold application of the base-2 logarithm to x:

$$\log^{(1)} x = \log_2 x, \quad \log^{(i+1)} x = \log_2(\log^{(i)} x).$$

Remember from Chapter 1 that

$$\log^* x = 1 \text{ if } x \leq 2, \quad \log^* x = 1 + \min\{i : \log^{(i)} x \leq 2\}.$$

For the chromatic number of $\mathcal{B}_k$, we obtain

Lemma 8.14. *For all $n \geq 1$, $\chi(\mathcal{B}_1) = n$. Further, for $n \geq k \geq 2$, $\chi(\mathcal{B}_k) \geq \log^{(k-1)} n$.*

Proof. For $k = 1$, $\mathcal{B}_k$ is the complete graph on n nodes with a directed edge from node i to node j iff $i < j$. Therefore, $\chi(\mathcal{B}_1) = n$. For $k > 2$, the claim follows by induction and Lemmas 8.12 and 8.13. $\qquad\square$

This finally allows us to state a lower bound on the number of rounds needed to color a directed ring with 3 colors.

Theorem 8.15. *Every deterministic, distributed algorithm to color a directed ring with 3 or less colors needs at least $(\log^* n)/2 - 1$ rounds.*

Proof. Using the connection between $\mathcal{B}_k$ and the neighborhood graph for directed rings, it suffices to show that $\chi(\mathcal{B}_{2r+1}) > 3$ for all $r < (\log^* n)/2 - 1$. From Lemma 8.14, we know that $\chi(\mathcal{B}_{2r+1}) \geq \log^{(2r)} n$. To obtain $\log^{(2r)} n \leq 2$, we need $r \geq (\log^* n)/2 - 1$. Because $\log_2 3 < 2$, we therefore have $\log^{(2r)} n > 3$ if $r < \log^* n/2 - 1$. $\qquad\square$

Corollary 8.16. *Every deterministic, distributed algorithm to compute an MIS of a directed ring needs at least* $\log^* n/2 - O(1)$ *rounds.*

Remarks:

- It is straightforward to see that also for a constant $c > 3$, the number of rounds needed to color a ring with c or less colors is $\log^* n/2 - O(1)$.

- There basically (up to additive constants) is a gap of a factor of 2 between the $\log^* n + O(1)$ upper bound of Chapter 1 and the $\log^* n/2 - O(1)$ lower bound of this chapter. It is possible to show that the lower bound is tight, even for undirected rings (for directed rings, this will be part of the exercises).

- Alternatively, the lower bound can also be presented as an application of Ramsey's theory. Ramsey's theory is best introduced with an example: Assume you host a party, and you want to invite people such that there are no three people who mutually know each other, and no three people which are mutual strangers. How many people can you invite? This is an example of Ramsey's theorem, which says that for any given integer c, and any given integers $n_1, \ldots, n_c$, there is a Ramsey number $R(n_1, \ldots, n_c)$, such that if the edges of a complete graph with $R(n_1, \ldots, n_c)$ nodes are colored with c different colors, then for some color i the graph contains some complete subgraph of color i of size n_i. The special case in the party example is looking for $R(3,3)$.

- Ramsey theory is more general, as it deals with hyperedges. A normal edge is essentially a subset of two nodes; a hyperedge is a subset of k nodes. The party example can be explained in this context: We have (hyper)edges of the form $\{i, j\}$, with $1 \leq i, j \leq n$. Choosing n sufficiently large, coloring the edges with two colors must exhibit a set S of 3 edges $\{i, j\} \subset \{v_1, v_2, v_3\}$, such that all edges in S have the same color. To prove our coloring lower bound using Ramsey theory, we form all hyperedges of size $k = 2r+1$, and color them with 3 colors. Choosing n sufficiently large, there must be a set $S = \{v_1, \ldots, v_{k+1}\}$ of $k + 1$ identifiers, such that all $k + 1$ hyperedges consisting of k nodes from S have the same color. Note that both $\{v_1, \ldots, v_k\}$ and $\{v_2, \ldots, v_{k+1}\}$ are in the set S, hence there will be two neighboring views with the same color. Ramsey theory shows that in this case n will grow as a power tower (tetration) in k. Thus, if n is so large that k is smaller than some function growing like $\log^* n$, the coloring algorithm cannot be correct.

- The neighborhood graph concept can be used more generally to study distributed graph coloring. It can for instance be used to show that with a single round (every node sends its identifier to all neighbors) it is possible to color a graph with $(1 + o(1))\Delta^2 \ln n$ colors, and that every one-round algorithm needs at least $\Omega(\Delta^2 / \log^2 \Delta + \log \log n)$ colors.

- One may also extend the proof to other problems, for instance one may show that a constant approximation of the minimum dominating set problem on unit disk graphs costs at least log-star time.

- Using r-hop views and the fact that nodes with equal r-hop views have to make the same decisions is the basic principle behind almost all locality lower bounds (in fact, we are not aware of a locality lower bound that does not use this principle). Using this basic technique (but a completely different proof otherwise), it is for instance possible to show that computing an MIS (and many other problems) in a general graph requires at least $\Omega(\sqrt{\log n / \log \log n})$ and $\Omega(\log \Delta / \log \log \Delta)$ rounds.

Chapter Notes

The lower bound proof in this chapter is by Linial [Lin92], proving asymptotic optimality of the technique of Chapter 1. This proof can also be found in Chapter 7.5 of [Pel00]. An alternative proof that omits the neighborhood graph construction is presented in [LS14]. The lower bound is also true for randomized algorithms [Nao91]. Recently, this lower bound technique was adapted to other problems [CHW08, LW08]. In some sense, Linial's seminal work raised the question of what can be computed in $O(1)$ time [NS93], essentially starting distributed complexity theory.

More recently, using a different argument, Kuhn et al. [KMW04, KMW16] managed to show more substantial lower bounds for a number of combinatorial problems including minimum vertex cover (MVC), minimum dominating set (MDS), maximal matching, or maximal independent set (MIS). More concretely, Kuhn et al. showed that all these problems need polylogarithmic time (for a polylogarithmic approximation, in case of approximation problems such as MVC and MDS). Some of these bounds are tight, e.g. the MVC $\Omega(\log \Delta / \log \log \Delta)$ lower bound is surprisingly tight [BYCHS16]. For recent surveys regarding locality lower bounds we refer to e.g. [Suo12, KMW16].

Ramsey theory was started by Frank P. Ramsey with his 1930 article called "On a problem of formal logic" [Ram30]. For an introduction to Ramsey theory we refer to e.g. [NR90, LR03].

Bibliography

[BYCHS16] Reuven Bar-Yehuda, Keren Censor-Hillel, and Gregory Schwartzman. A distributed $(2+\epsilon)$-approximation for vertex cover in $o(\log\delta/\epsilon \log \log \delta)$ rounds. pages 3–8, 2016.

[CHW08] A. Czygrinow, M. Hańćkowiak, and W. Wawrzyniak. Fast Distributed Approximations in Planar Graphs. In *Proceedings of the 22nd International Symposium on Distributed Computing (DISC)*, 2008.

[KMW04] F. Kuhn, T. Moscibroda, and R. Wattenhofer. What Cannot Be Computed Locally! In *Proceedings of the 23rd ACM Symposium on Principles of Distributed Computing (PODC)*, July 2004.

[KMW16] Fabian Kuhn, Thomas Moscibroda, and Roger Wattenhofer. Local Computation: Lower and Upper Bounds. In *Journal of the ACM (JACM)*, 2016.

[Lin92] N. Linial. Locality in Distributed Graph Algorithms. *SIAM Journal on Computing*, 21(1)(1):193–201, February 1992.

[LR03] Bruce M. Landman and Aaron Robertson. *Ramsey Theory on the Integers*. American Mathematical Society, 2003.

[LS14] Juhana Laurinharju and Jukka Suomela. Brief Announcement: Linial's Lower Bound Made Easy. In *Proceedings of the 2014 ACM Symposium on Principles of Distributed Computing*, PODC '14, pages 377–378, New York, NY, USA, 2014. ACM.

[LW08] Christoph Lenzen and Roger Wattenhofer. Leveraging Linial's Locality Limit. In *22nd International Symposium on Distributed Computing (DISC)*, Arcachon, France, September 2008.

[Nao91] Moni Naor. A Lower Bound on Probabilistic Algorithms for Distributive Ring Coloring. *SIAM J. Discrete Math.*, 4(3):409–412, 1991.

[NR90] Jaroslav Nesetril and Vojtech Rodl, editors. *Mathematics of Ramsey Theory*. Springer Berlin Heidelberg, 1990.

[NS93] Moni Naor and Larry Stockmeyer. What can be Computed Locally? In *Proceedings of the twenty-fifth annual ACM symposium on Theory of computing*, STOC '93, pages 184–193, New York, NY, USA, 1993. ACM.

[Pel00] David Peleg. *Distributed Computing: a Locality-Sensitive Approach*. Society for Industrial and Applied Mathematics, Philadelphia, PA, USA, 2000.

[Ram30] F. P. Ramsey. On a Problem of Formal Logic. *Proc. London Math. Soc. (3)*, 30:264–286, 1930.

[Suo12] Jukka Suomela. Survey of Local Algorithms. http://www.cs.helsinki.fi/local-survey/, 2012.

Chapter 9

Global Problems

This chapter is on "hard" problems in distributed computing. In sequential computing, there are NP-hard problems which are conjectured to take exponential time. Is there something similar in distributed computing? Using flooding/echo (Algorithms 2.9, 2.10) from Chapter 2, everything so far was solvable basically in $O(D)$ time, where D is the diameter of the network.

9.1   Diameter & APSP

But how do we compute the diameter itself!?! With flooding/echo, of course!

Algorithm 9.1 Naive Diameter Construction

1: all nodes compute their radius by synchronous flooding/echo
2: all nodes flood their radius on the constructed BFS tree
3: the maximum radius a node sees is the diameter

Remarks:

- Since all these phases only take $O(D)$ time, nodes know the diameter in $O(D)$ time, which is asymptotically optimal.

- However, there is a problem! Nodes are now involved in n parallel flooding/echo operations, thus a node may have to handle many and big messages in one single time step. Although this is not strictly illegal in the message passing model, it still feels like cheating! A natural question is whether we can do the same by just sending short messages in each round.

- In Definition 1.8 of Chapter 1 we postulated that nodes should send only messages of "reasonable" size. In this chapter we strengthen the definition a bit, and require that each message should have at most $O(\log n)$ bits. This is generally enough to communicate a constant number of ID's or values to neighbors, but not enough to communicate everything a node knows!

- A simple way to avoid large messages is to split them into small messages that are sent using several rounds. This can cause that messages are getting delayed in some nodes but not in others. The flooding might not use edges of a BFS tree anymore! These floodings might not compute correct distances anymore! On the other hand we know that the maximal message size in Algorithm 9.1 is $O(n \log n)$. So we could just simulate each of these "big message" rounds by n "small message" rounds using small messages. This yields a runtime of $O(nD)$ which is not desirable. A third possible approach is "starting each flooding/echo one after each other" and results in $O(nD)$ in the worst case as well.

- So let us fix the above algorithm! The key idea is to arrange the flooding-echo processes in a more organized way: Start the flooding processes in a certain order and prove that at any time, each node is only involved in one flooding. This is realized in Algorithm 9.3.

Definition 9.2. *(BFS_v) Performing a breadth first search at node v produces spanning tree BFS_v (see Chapter 2). This takes time $O(D)$ using small messages.*

Remarks:

- A spanning tree of a graph G can be traversed in time $O(n)$ by sending a pebble over an edge in each time slot.

- This can be done using, e.g., a depth first search (DFS): Start at the root of a tree, recursively visit all nodes in the following way. If the current node still has an unvisited child, then the pebble always visits that child first. Return to the parent only when all children have been visited.

- Algorithm 9.3 works as follows: Given a graph G, first a leader l computes its BFS tree BFS_l. Then we send a pebble P to traverse tree BFS_l. Each time pebble P enters a node v for the first time, P waits one time slot, and then starts a breadth first search (BFS) – using edges in G – from v with the aim of computing the distances from v to all other nodes. Since we start a BFS_v from every node v, each node u learns its distance to all these nodes v during the according execution of BFS_v. There is no need for an echo-process at the end of BFS_u.

Algorithm 9.3 Computes APSP on G.

1: Assume we have a leader node l (if not, compute one first)
2: **compute** BFS_l of leader l
3: **send** a pebble P to traverse BFS_l in a DFS way;
4: **while** P traverses BFS_l **do**
5:     **if** P visits a new node v **then**
6:         immediately **start** BFS_v from node v;   // compute all distances to v
7:         pebble P **waits** one time slot;   // avoid congestion
8:     **end if**
9: **end while**

Remarks:

- The depth of node u in BFS_v is $d(u, v)$

- Having all distances is nice, but how do we get the diameter? Well, as before, each node could just flood its radius (its maximum distance) into the network. However, messages are small now and we need to modify this slightly. In each round a node only sends the maximal distance that it is aware of to its neighbors. After D rounds each node will know the maximum distance among all nodes.

Lemma 9.4. *In Algorithm 9.3, at no time a node w is simultaneously active for both BFS_u and BFS_v.*

Proof. Assume a BFS_u is started at time t_u at node u. Then node w will be involved in BFS_u at time $t_u + d(u, w)$. Now, consider a node v whose BFS_v is started at time $t_v > t_u$. According to the algorithm this implies that the pebble visits v after u and took some time to travel from u to v. In particular, the time to get from u to v is at least $d(u, v)$. In addition the pebble waited one time slot at node u after starting BFS_u, and we have $t_v \geq t_u + d(u, v) + 1$. Using this and the triangle inequality, we get that node w is involved in BFS_v strictly after being involved in BFS_u since $t_v + d(v, w) \geq (t_u + d(u, v) + 1) + d(v, w) \geq t_u + d(u, w) + 1 > t_u + d(u, w)$. $\square$

Theorem 9.5. *Algorithm 9.3 computes APSP (all pairs shortest path) in time $O(n)$.*

Proof. Since the previous lemma holds for any pair of vertices, no two BFS "interfere" with each other, i.e. all messages can be sent on time without congestion. Hence, all BFS stop at most D time slots after they were started. We conclude that the runtime of the algorithm is determined by the time $O(D)$ we need to build tree BFS_l, plus the time $O(n)$ that P needs to traverse BFS_l, plus the time $O(D)$ needed by the last BFS that P initiated. Since $D \leq n$, this is all in $O(n)$. $\square$

Remarks:

- All of a sudden our algorithm needs $O(n)$ time, and possibly $n \gg D$. We should be able to do better, right?!

- Unfortunately not! One can show that computing the diameter of a network needs $\Omega(n/\log n)$ time.

- Note that one can check whether a graph has diameter 1 by exchanging some specific information such as degree with the neighbors. However, already checking diameter 2 is difficult.

9.2   Lower Bound Graphs

We define a family $\mathcal{G}$ of graphs that we use to prove a lower bound on the rounds needed to compute the diameter. To simplify our analysis, we assume that $(n - 2)$ can be divided by 8. We start by defining four sets of nodes, each consisting of $q = q(n) := (n - 2)/4$ nodes. Throughout this chapter we write $[q]$ as a short version of $\{1, \ldots, q\}$ and define:

$$
\begin{aligned}
\mathbf{L_0} &:= \{l_i \mid i \in [q]\} & // \text{ upper left in Figure 9.6} \\
\mathbf{L_1} &:= \{l_i' \mid i \in [q]\} & // \text{ lower left} \\
\mathbf{R_0} &:= \{r_i \mid i \in [q]\} & // \text{ upper right} \\
\mathbf{R_1} &:= \{r_i' \mid i \in [q]\} & // \text{ lower right}
\end{aligned}
$$

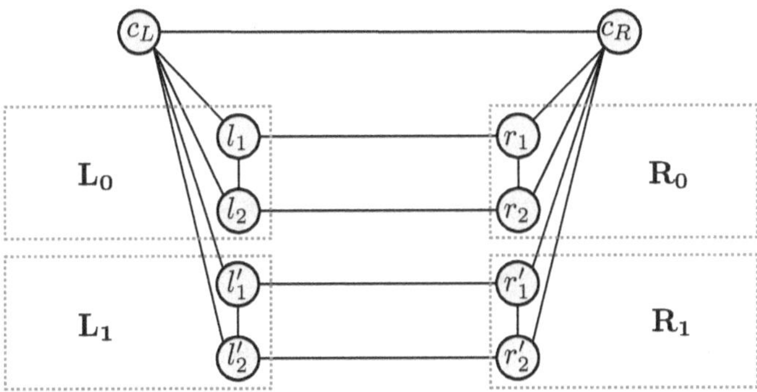

Figure 9.6: The above skeleton G' contains $n = 10$ nodes, such that $q = 2$.

We add node c_L and connect it to all nodes in $\mathbf{L_0}$ and $\mathbf{L_1}$. Then we add node c_R, connected to all nodes in $\mathbf{R_0}$ and $\mathbf{R_1}$. Furthermore, nodes c_L and c_R are connected by an edge. For $i \in [q]$ we connect l_i to r_i and l_i' to r_i'. Also we add edges such that nodes in $\mathbf{L_0}$ are a clique, nodes in $\mathbf{L_1}$ are a clique, nodes in $\mathbf{R_0}$ are a clique, and nodes in $\mathbf{R_1}$ are a clique. The resulting graph is called G'. Graph G' is the skeleton of any graph in family $\mathcal{G}$.

More formally skeleton $G' = (V', E')$ is:

$$V' := \mathbf{L_0} \ \cup \ \mathbf{L_1} \ \cup \ \mathbf{R_0} \ \cup \ \mathbf{R_1} \ \cup \ \{c_L, c_R\}$$

$$
\begin{aligned}
E' := \ &\bigcup_{v \in \mathbf{L_0} \cup \mathbf{L_1}} \{(v, c_L)\} && //\text{connections to } c_L \\
\cup \ &\bigcup_{v \in \mathbf{R_0} \cup \mathbf{R_1}} \{(v, c_R)\} && //\text{connections to } c_R \\
\cup \ &\bigcup_{i \in [q]} \{(l_i, r_i), (l_i', r_i')\} \cup \{(c_L, c_R)\} && //\text{connects left to right} \\
\cup \ &\bigcup_{S \in \{\mathbf{L_0}, \mathbf{L_1}, \mathbf{R_0}, \mathbf{R_1}\}} \ \bigcup_{u \neq v \in S} \{(u, v)\} && //\text{clique edges}
\end{aligned}
$$

To simplify our arguments, we partition G' into two parts: **Part L** is the subgraph induced by nodes $\mathbf{L_0} \cup \mathbf{L_1} \cup \{c_L\}$. **Part R** is the subgraph induced by nodes $\mathbf{R_0} \cup \mathbf{R_1} \cup \{c_R\}$.

Family $\mathcal{G}$ contains any graph G that is derived from G' by adding any combination of edges of the form (l_i, l_j') resp. (r_i, r_j') with $l_i \in \mathbf{L_0}$, $l_j' \in \mathbf{L_1}$, $r_i \in \mathbf{R_0}$, and $r_j' \in \mathbf{R_1}$.

Lemma 9.8. *The diameter of a graph $G = (V, E) \in \mathcal{G}$ is 2 if and only if: For each tuple (i, j) with $i, j \in [q]$, there is either edge (l_i, l_j') or edge (r_i, r_j') (or both edges) in E.*

Proof. Note that the distance between most pairs of nodes is at most 2. In particular, the radius of c_L resp. c_R is 2. Thanks to c_L resp. c_R the distance between, any two nodes within **Part L** resp. within **Part R** is at most 2. Because of the cliques $\mathbf{L_0}, \mathbf{L_1}, \mathbf{R_0}, \mathbf{R_1}$, distances between l_i and r_j resp. l_i' and r_j' is at most 2.

The only interesting case is between a node $l_i \in \mathbf{L_0}$ and node $r_j' \in \mathbf{R_1}$ (or, symmetrically, between $l_j' \in \mathbf{L_1}$ and node $r_i \in \mathbf{R_0}$). If either edge (l_i, l_j') or edge (r_i, r_j') is present, then this distance is 2, since the path (l_i, l_j', r_j') or the path (l_i, r_i, r_j') exists. If neither of the two edges exist, then the neighborhood of l_i consists of $\{c_L, r_i\}$, all nodes in $\mathbf{L_0}$, and some nodes in $\mathbf{L_1} \setminus \{l_j'\}$, and the neighborhood of r_j' consists of $\{c_R, l_j'\}$, all nodes in $\mathbf{R_1}$, and some nodes in $\mathbf{R_0} \setminus \{r_i\}$ (see for example Figure 9.9 with $i = 2$ and $j = 2$.) Since the two neighborhoods do not share a common node, the distance between l_i and r_j' is (at least) 3. $\qquad \square$

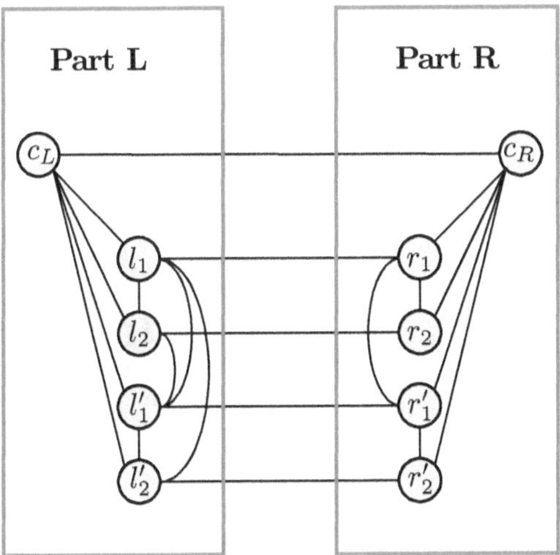

Figure 9.7: The above graph G has $n = 10$ and is a member of family $\mathcal{G}$. What is the diameter of G?

Remarks:

- Each part contains up to $q^2 \in \Theta(n^2)$ edges not belonging to the skeleton.

- There are $2q+1 \in \Theta(n)$ edges connecting the left and the right part. Since in each round we can transmit $O(\log n)$ bits over each edge (in each direction), the bandwidth between **Part L** and **Part R** is $O(n \log n)$.

- If we transmit the information of the $\Theta(n^2)$ edges in a naive way with a bandwidth of $O(n \log n)$, we need $\Omega(n/\log n)$ time. But maybe we can do better?!? Can an algorithm be smarter and only send the information that is really necessary to tell whether the diameter is 2?

- It turns out that any algorithm needs $\Omega(n/\log n)$ rounds, since the information that is really necessary to tell that the diameter is larger than 2 contains basically $\Theta(n^2)$ bits.

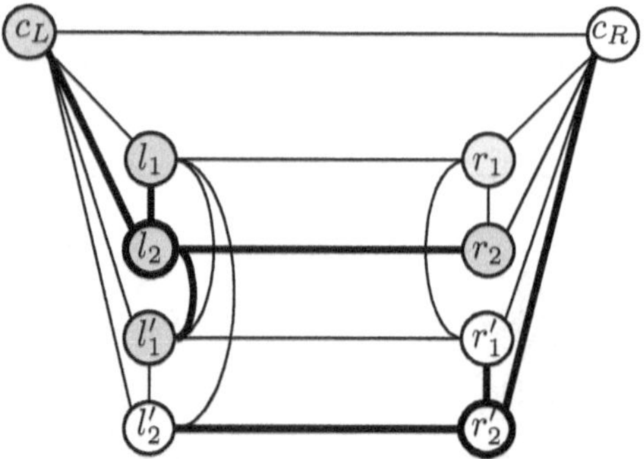

Figure 9.9: Nodes in the neighborhood of l_2 are cyan, the neighborhood of r_2' is white. Since these neighborhoods do not intersect, the distance of these two nodes is $\mathrm{d}(l_2, r_2') > 2$. If edge (l_2, l_2') was included, their distance would be 2.

9.3   Communication Complexity

To prove the last remark formally, we can use arguments from two-party communication complexity. This area essentially deals with a basic version of distributed computation: two parties are given some input each and want to solve a task on this input.

We consider two students (Alice and Bob) at two different universities connected by a communication channel (e.g., via email) and we assume this channel to be reliable. Now Alice and Bob want to check whether they received the same problem set for homework (we assume their professors are lazy and wrote it on the black board instead of putting a nicely prepared document online.) Do Alice and Bob really need to type the whole problem set into their emails? In a more formal way: Alice receives an k-bit string x and Bob another k-bit string y, and the goal is for both of them to compute the equality function.

Definition 9.10 (Equality). *We define the equality function $\boldsymbol{EQ}$ to be:*

$$\boldsymbol{EQ}(x,y) := \begin{cases} 1 & : x = y \\ 0 & : x \neq y \,. \end{cases}$$

Remarks:

- In a more general setting, Alice and Bob are interested in computing a certain function $f : \{0,1\}^k \times \{0,1\}^k \to \{0,1\}$ with the least amount of communication between them. Of course they can always succeed by having Alice send her whole k-bit string to Bob, who then computes the function, but the idea here is to find clever ways of calculating f with less than k bits of communication. We measure how clever they can be as follows:

Definition 9.11. *(Communication complexity CC.) The communication complexity of protocol A for function f is $CC(A, f) :=$ minimum number of bits exchanged between Alice and Bob in the worst case when using A. The communication complexity of f is $CC(f) := \min\{CC(A, f) \mid A \text{ solves } f\}$. That is the minimal number of bits that the best protocol needs to send in the worst case.*

Definition 9.12. *For a given function f, we define a $2^k \times 2^k$ matrix M^f representing f. That is $M^f_{x,y} := f(x, y)$.*

Example 9.13. *For EQ, in case $k = 3$, matrix M^{EQ} looks like this:*

$$
\begin{pmatrix}
\begin{array}{c|cccccccc}
EQ & 000 & 001 & 010 & 011 & 100 & 101 & 110 & 111 & \leftarrow x \\
\hline
000 & 1 & 0 & 0 & 0 & 0 & 0 & 0 & 0 \\
001 & 0 & 1 & 0 & 0 & 0 & 0 & 0 & 0 \\
010 & 0 & 0 & 1 & 0 & 0 & 0 & 0 & 0 \\
011 & 0 & 0 & 0 & 1 & 0 & 0 & 0 & 0 \\
100 & 0 & 0 & 0 & 0 & 1 & 0 & 0 & 0 \\
101 & 0 & 0 & 0 & 0 & 0 & 1 & 0 & 0 \\
110 & 0 & 0 & 0 & 0 & 0 & 0 & 1 & 0 \\
111 & 0 & 0 & 0 & 0 & 0 & 0 & 0 & 1 \\
\uparrow y
\end{array}
\end{pmatrix}
$$

As a next step we define a (combinatorial) monochromatic rectangle. These are "submatrices" of M^f which contain the same entry.

Definition 9.14 (Monochromatic Rectangle). *A set $R \subseteq \{0,1\}^k \times \{0,1\}^k$ is called a monochromatic rectangle, if*

- *whenever $(x_1, y_1) \in R$ and $(x_2, y_2) \in R$ then $(x_1, y_2) \in R$.*

- *there is a fixed z such that $f(x, y) = z$ for all $(x, y) \in R$.*

Example 9.15. *The first three of the following rectangles are monochromatic, the last one is not:*

		Rectangle	Example 9.13
R_1	$=$	$\{011\} \times \{011\}$	*light gray*
R_2	$=$	$\{011, 100, 101, 110\} \times \{000, 001\}$	*gray*
R_3	$=$	$\{000, 001, 101\} \times \{011, 100, 110, 111\}$	*dark gray*
R_4	$=$	$\{000, 001\} \times \{000, 001\}$	*boxed*

Each time Alice and Bob exchange a bit, they can eliminate columns/rows of the matrix M^f and a combinatorial rectangle is left. They can stop communicating when this remaining rectangle is monochromatic. However, maybe there is a more efficient way to exchange information about a given bit string than just naively transmitting contained bits? In order to cover all possible ways of communication, we need the following definition:

Definition 9.16 (Fooling Set). *A set $S \subset \{0,1\}^k \times \{0,1\}^k$ fools f if there is a fixed z such that*

- *$f(x,y) = z$ for each $(x,y) \in S$*

- *For any $(x_1, y_1) \neq (x_2, y_2) \in S$, the rectangle $\{x_1, x_2\} \times \{y_1, y_2\}$ is not monochromatic: Either $f(x_1, y_2) \neq z$, $f(x_2, y_1) \neq z$ or both $\neq z$.*

Example 9.17. *Consider $S = \{(000, 000), (001, 001)\}$. Take a look at the non-monochromatic rectangle R_4 in Example 9.15. Verify that S is indeed a fooling set for **EQ**!*

Remarks:

- Can you find a larger fooling set for EQ?

- We assume that Alice and Bob take turns in sending a bit. This results in 2 possible actions (send 0/1) per round and in 2^t *action patterns* during a sequence of t rounds.

Lemma 9.18. *If S is a fooling set for f, then $CC(f) = \Omega(\log |S|)$.*

Proof. We prove the statement via contradiction: fix a protocol A and assume that it needs $t < \log(|S|)$ rounds in the worst case. Then there are 2^t possible action patterns, with $2^t < |S|$. Hence for at least two elements of S, let us call them $(x_1, y_1), (x_2, y_2)$, protocol A produces the same action pattern P. Naturally, the action pattern on the alternative inputs $(x_1, y_2), (x_2, y_1)$ will be P as well: in the first round Alice and Bob have no information on the other party's string and send the same bit that was sent in P. Based on this, they determine the second bit to be exchanged, which will be the same as the second one in P since they cannot distinguish the cases. This continues for all t rounds. We conclude that after t rounds, Alice does not know whether Bob's input is y_1 or y_2 and Bob does not know whether Alice's input is x_1 or x_2. By the definition of fooling sets, either

- $f(x_1, y_2) \neq f(x_1, y_1)$ in which case Alice (with input x_1) does not know the solution yet,

or

- $f(x_2, y_1) \neq f(x_1, y_1)$ in which case Bob (with input y_1) does not know the solution yet.

This contradicts the assumption that A leads to a correct decision for all inputs after t rounds. Therefore at least $\log(|S|)$ rounds are necessary. $\qquad\square$

Theorem 9.19. $CC(\boldsymbol{EQ}) = \Omega(k)$.

Proof. The set $S := \{(x, x) \mid x \in \{0, 1\}^k\}$ fools EQ and has size 2^k. Now apply Lemma 9.18. $\qquad\square$

Definition 9.20. *Denote the negation of a string z by $\overline{z}$ and by $x \circ y$ the concatenation of strings x and y.*

Lemma 9.21. *Let x, y be k-bit strings. Then $x \neq y$ if and only if there is an index $i \in [2k]$ such that the ith bit of $x \circ \overline{x}$ and the ith bit of $\overline{y} \circ y$ are both 0.*

Proof. If $x \neq y$, there is an $j \in [k]$ such that x and y differ in the jth bit. Therefore either the jth bit of both x and $\overline{y}$ is 0, or the jth bit of $\overline{x}$ and y is 0. For this reason, there is an $i \in [2k]$ such that $x \circ \overline{x}$ and $\overline{y} \circ y$ are both 0 at position i.

If $x = y$, then for any $i \in [2k]$ it is always the case that either the ith bit of $x \circ \overline{x}$ is 1 or the ith bit of $\overline{y} \circ y$ (which is the negation of $x \circ \overline{x}$ in this case) is 1. $\qquad\square$

Remarks:

- With these insights we get back to the problem of computing the diameter of a graph and relate this problem to *EQ*.

Definition 9.22. *Using the parameter q defined before, we define a bijective map between all pairs x, y of q^2-bit strings and the graphs in $\mathcal{G}$: each pair of strings x, y is mapped to graph $G_{x,y} \in \mathcal{G}$ that is derived from skeleton G' by adding*

- *edge (l_i, l'_j) to **Part L** if and only if the $(j + q \cdot (i-1))^{th}$ bit of x is 1.*

- *edge (r_i, r'_j) to **Part R** if and only if the $(j + q \cdot (i-1))^{th}$ bit of y is 1.*

Remarks:

- Clearly, **Part L** of $G_{x,y}$ depends on x only and **Part R** depends on y only.

Lemma 9.23. *Let x and y be $\frac{q^2}{2}$-bit strings given to Alice and Bob.[1] Then graph $G := G_{x \circ \bar{x}, \bar{y} \circ y} \in \mathcal{G}$ has diameter 2 if and only if $x = y$.*

Proof. By Lemma 9.21 and the construction of G, there is neither edge (l_i, l'_j) nor edge (r_i, r'_j) in $E(G)$ for some (i, j) if and only if $x \neq y$. Applying Lemma 9.8 yields: G has diameter 2 if and only if $x = y$. $\qquad\square$

Theorem 9.24. *Any distributed algorithm A that decides whether a graph G has diameter D needs $\Omega\left(\frac{n}{\log n} + D\right)$ time.*

Proof. Computing D for sure needs time $\Omega(D)$. It remains to prove $\Omega\left(\frac{n}{\log n}\right)$. To prove this term of the lower bound, it suffices to study $D = 2$. Assume there is a distributed algorithm A that decides whether the diameter of a graph is 2 in time $o(n/\log n)$. When Alice and Bob are given $\frac{q^2}{2}$-bit inputs x and y, they can simulate A to decide whether $x = y$ as follows: Alice constructs **Part L** of $G_{x \circ \bar{x}, \bar{y} \circ y}$ and Bob constructs **Part R**. As we remarked, both parts are independent of each other such that **Part L** can be constructed

---

[1] Thats why we need that $n - 2$ can be divided by 8.

by Alice without knowing y and **Part R** can be constructed by Bob without knowing x. Furthermore, $G_{x\circ\bar{x},\bar{y}\circ y}$ has diameter 2 if and only if $x = y$ (Lemma 9.23.)

Now Alice and Bob simulate the distributed algorithm A round by round: In the first round, they determine which messages the nodes in their part of G would send. Then they use their communication channel to exchange all $2(2q + 1) \in \Theta(n)$ messages that would be sent over edges between **Part L** and **Part R** in this round while executing A on G. Based on this Alice and Bob determine which messages would be sent in round two and so on. For each round simulated by Alice and Bob, they only need to communicate $O(n \log n)$ bits: $O(\log n)$ bits for each of $O(n)$ messages. Since A makes a decision after $o(n/\log n)$ rounds, this yields a total communication of $o(n^2)$ bits. On the other hand, Lemma 9.19 states that to decide whether x equals y, Alice and Bob need to communicate at least $\Omega\left(\frac{q^2}{2}\right) = \Omega(n^2)$ bits. A contradiction. $\quad\square$

Remarks:

- Until now we only considered deterministic algorithms. Can one do better using randomness?

Algorithm 9.25 Randomized evaluation of *EQ*.

1: Alice and Bob use public randomness. That is they both have access to the same random bit string $z \in \{0, 1\}^k$
2: Alice sends bit $a := \sum_{i \in [k]} x_i \cdot z_i \mod 2$ to Bob
3: Bob sends bit $b := \sum_{i \in [k]} y_i \cdot z_i \mod 2$ to Alice
4: **if** $a \neq b$ **then**
5:     we know $x \neq y$
6: **end if**

Lemma 9.26. *If $x \neq y$, Algorithm 9.25 discovers $x \neq y$ with probability at least $1/2$.*

Proof. Note that if $x = y$ we have $a = b$ for sure.

If $x \neq y$, Algorithm 9.25 may not reveal inequality. For instance, for $k = 2$, if $x = 01$, $y = 10$ and $z = 11$ we get $a = b = 1$. In general, let I be the set of indices where $x_i \neq y_i$, i.e. $I := \{i \in [k] \mid x_i \neq y_i\}$. Since $x \neq y$, we know that $|I| > 0$. We have

$$|a - b| \equiv \sum_{i \in I} z_i \pmod 2,$$

and since all z_i with $i \in I$ are random, we get that $a \neq b$ with probability at least $1/2$. $\square$

Remarks:

- By excluding the vector $z = 0^k$ we can even get a discovery probability strictly larger than $1/2$.

- Repeating the Algorithm 9.25 with different random strings z, the error probability can be reduced arbitrarily.

- Does this imply that there is a fast randomized algorithm to determine the diameter? Unfortunately not!

- Sometimes public randomness is not available, but private randomness is. Here Alice has her own random string and Bob has his own random string. A modified version of Algorithm 9.25 also works with private randomness at the cost of the runtime.

- One can prove an $\Omega(n/\log n)$ lower bound for any randomized distributed algorithm that computes the diameter. To do so one considers the disjointness function *DISJ* instead of equality. Here, Alice is given a subset $X \subseteq [k]$ and and Bob is given a subset $Y \subseteq [k]$ and they need to determine whether $Y \cap X = \emptyset$. (X and Y can be represented by k-bit strings x, y.) The reduction is similar as the one presented above but uses graph $G_{\overline{x},\overline{y}}$ instead of $G_{x \circ \overline{x}, \overline{y} \circ y}$. However, the lower bound for the randomized communication complexity of *DISJ* is more involved than the lower bound for $CC(EQ)$.

- Since one can compute the diameter given a solution for APSP, an $\Omega(n/\log n)$ lower bound for APSP is implied. As such, our simple Algorithm 9.3 is almost optimal!

- Many prominent functions allow for a low communication complexity. For instance, $CC(PARITY) = 2$. What is the Hamming distance (number of different entries) of two strings? It is known that $CC(HAM \geq d) = \Omega(d)$. Also, $CC($decide whether "$HAM \geq k/2 + \sqrt{k}$" or "$HAM \leq k/2 - \sqrt{k}$"$) = \Omega(k)$, even when using randomness. This problem is known as the Gap-Hamming-Distance.

- Lower bounds in communication complexity have many applications. Apart from getting lower bounds in distributed computing, one can also get lower bounds regarding circuit depth or query times for static data structures.

- In the distributed setting with limited bandwidth we showed that computing the diameter has about the same complexity as computing all pairs shortest paths. In contrast, in sequential computing, it is a major open problem whether the diameter can be computed faster than all pairs shortest paths. No nontrivial lower bounds are known, only that $\Omega(n^2)$ steps are needed – partly due to the fact that there can be n^2 edges/distances in a graph. On the other hand the currently best algorithm uses fast matrix multiplication and terminates after $O(n^{2.3727})$ steps.

9.4 Distributed Complexity Theory

We conclude this chapter with a short overview on the main complexity classes of distributed message passing algorithms. Given a network with n nodes and diameter D, we managed to establish a rich selection of upper and lower bounds regarding how much time it takes to solve or approximate a problem. Currently we know five main distributed complexity classes:

- Strictly *local* problems can be solved in constant $O(1)$ time, e.g., a constant approximation of a dominating set in a planar graph.

- Just a little bit slower are problems that can be solved in *log-star* $O(\log^* n)$ time, e.g., many combinatorial optimization problems in special graph classes such as growth bounded graphs. 3-coloring a ring takes $O(\log^* n)$.

- A large body of problems is *polylogarithmic* (or *pseudo-local*), in the sense that they seem to be strictly local but are not, as they need $O(\text{polylog } n)$ time, e.g., the maximal independent set problem.

- There are problems which are *global* and need $O(D)$ time, e.g., to count the number of nodes in the network.

- Finally there are problems which need *polynomial* $O(\text{poly } n)$ time, even if the diameter D is a constant, e.g., computing the diameter of the network.

Chapter Notes

The linear time algorithm for computing the diameter was discovered independently by [HW12, PRT12]. The presented matching lower bound is by Frischknecht et al. [FHW12], extending techniques by [DHK$^+$11].

Due to its importance in network design, shortest path-problems in general and the APSP problem in particular were among the earliest studied problems in distributed computing. Developed algorithms were immediately used, e.g., as early as in 1969 in the ARPANET (see [Lyn96], p.506). Routing messages via shortest paths were extensively discussed to be beneficial in [Taj77, MS79, MRR80, SS80, CM82] and in many other papers. It is not surprising that there is plenty of literature dealing with algorithms for distributed APSP, but most of them focused on secondary targets such as trading time for message complexity. E.g., papers [AR78, Tou80, Che82] obtain a communication complexity of roughly $O(n \cdot m)$ bits/messages and still require superlinear runtime. Also a lot of effort was spent to obtain fast sequential algorithms for various versions of computing APSP or related problems such as the diameter problem, e.g., [CW90, AGM91, AMGN92, Sei95, SZ99, BVW08]. These algorithms are based on fast matrix multiplication such that currently the best runtime is $O(n^{2.3727})$ due to [Wil12].

The problem sets in which one needs to distinguish diameter 2 from 4 are inspired by a combinatorial $(\times, 3/2)$-approximation in a sequential setting by Aingworth et. al. [ACIM99]. The main idea behind this approximation is to distinguish diameter 2 from 4. This part was transferred to the distributed setting in [HW12].

Two-party communication complexity was introduced by Andy Yao in [Yao79]. Later, Yao received the Turing Award. A nice introduction to communication complexity covering techniques such as fooling-sets is the book by Nisan and Kushilevitz [KN97].

Bibliography

[ACIM99] D. Aingworth, C. Chekuri, P. Indyk, and R. Motwani. Fast Estimation of Diameter and Shortest Paths

(Without Matrix Multiplication). *SIAM Journal on Computing (SICOMP)*, 28(4):1167–1181, 1999.

[AGM91] N. Alon, Z. Galil, and O. Margalit. On the exponent of the all pairs shortest path problem. In *Proceedings of the 32nd Annual IEEE Symposium on Foundations of Computer Science (FOCS)*, pages 569–575, 1991.

[AMGN92] N. Alon, O. Margalit, Z. Galilt, and M. Naor. Witnesses for Boolean Matrix Multiplication and for Shortest Paths. In *Proceedings of the 33rd Annual Symposium on Foundations of Computer Science (FOCS)*, pages 417–426. IEEE Computer Society, 1992.

[AR78] J.M. Abram and IB Rhodes. A decentralized shortest path algorithm. In *Proceedings of the 16th Allerton Conference on Communication, Control and Computing (Allerton)*, pages 271–277, 1978.

[BVW08] G.E. Blelloch, V. Vassilevska, and R. Williams. A New Combinatorial Approach for Sparse Graph Problems. In *Proceedings of the 35th international colloquium on Automata, Languages and Programming, Part I (ICALP)*, pages 108–120. Springer-Verlag, 2008.

[Che82] C.C. Chen. A distributed algorithm for shortest paths. *IEEE Transactions on Computers (TC)*, 100(9):898–899, 1982.

[CM82] K.M. Chandy and J. Misra. Distributed computation on graphs: Shortest path algorithms. *Communications of the ACM (CACM)*, 25(11):833–837, 1982.

[CW90] D. Coppersmith and S. Winograd. Matrix multiplication via arithmetic progressions. *Journal of symbolic computation (JSC)*, 9(3):251–280, 1990.

[DHK+11] A. Das Sarma, S. Holzer, L. Kor, A. Korman, D. Nanongkai, G. Pandurangan, D. Peleg, and R. Wattenhofer. Distributed Verification and Hardness of Distributed Approximation. *Proceedings of the 43rd annual ACM Symposium on Theory of Computing (STOC)*, 2011.

[FHW12] S. Frischknecht, S. Holzer, and R. Wattenhofer. Networks Cannot Compute Their Diameter in Sublinear Time. In *Proceedings of the 23rd annual ACM-SIAM Symposium on Discrete Algorithms (SODA)*, pages 1150–1162, January 2012.

[HW12] Stephan Holzer and Roger Wattenhofer. Optimal Distributed All Pairs Shortest Paths and Applications. In *PODC*, page to appear, 2012.

[KN97] E. Kushilevitz and N. Nisan. *Communication complexity*. Cambridge University Press, 1997.

[Lyn96] Nancy A. Lynch. *Distributed Algorithms*. Morgan Kaufmann Publishers Inc., San Francisco, CA, USA, 1996.

[MRR80] J. McQuillan, I. Richer, and E. Rosen. The new routing algorithm for the ARPANET. *IEEE Transactions on Communications (TC)*, 28(5):711–719, 1980.

[MS79] P. Merlin and A. Segall. A failsafe distributed routing protocol. *IEEE Transactions on Communications (TC)*, 27(9):1280–1287, 1979.

[PRT12] David Peleg, Liam Roditty, and Elad Tal. Distributed Algorithms for Network Diameter and Girth. In *ICALP*, page to appear, 2012.

[Sei95] R. Seidel. On the all-pairs-shortest-path problem in unweighted undirected graphs. *Journal of Computer and System Sciences (JCSS)*, 51(3):400–403, 1995.

[SS80] M. Schwartz and T. Stern. Routing techniques used in computer communication networks. *IEEE Transactions on Communications (TC)*, 28(4):539–552, 1980.

[SZ99] A. Shoshan and U. Zwick. All pairs shortest paths in undirected graphs with integer weights. In *Proceedings of the 40th Annual IEEE Symposium on Foundations of Computer Science (FOCS)*, pages 605–614. IEEE, 1999.

[Taj77] W.D. Tajibnapis. A correctness proof of a topology information maintenance protocol for a distributed computer network. *Communications of the ACM (CACM)*, 20(7):477–485, 1977.

[Tou80] S. Toueg. An all-pairs shortest-paths distributed algorithm. *Tech. Rep. RC 8327, IBM TJ Watson Research Center, Yorktown Heights, NY 10598, USA*, 1980.

[Wil12] V.V. Williams. Multiplying Matrices Faster Than Coppersmith-Winograd. *Proceedings of the 44th annual ACM Symposium on Theory of Computing (STOC)*, 2012.

[Yao79] A.C.C. Yao. Some complexity questions related to distributive computing. In *Proceedings of the 11th annual ACM symposium on Theory of computing (STOC)*, pages 209–213. ACM, 1979.

Chapter 10

Synchronization

So far, we have mainly studied synchronous algorithms. Generally, asynchronous algorithms are more difficult to obtain. Also it is substantially harder to reason about asynchronous algorithms than about synchronous ones. For instance, computing a BFS tree (Chapter 2) efficiently requires much more work in an asynchronous system. However, many real systems are not synchronous, and we therefore have to design asynchronous algorithms. In this chapter, we will look at general simulation techniques, called *synchronizers*, that allow running synchronous algorithms in asynchronous environments.

10.1 Basics

A synchronizer generates sequences of *clock pulses* at each node of the network satisfying the condition given by the following definition.

Definition 10.1 (valid clock pulse). *We call a clock pulse generated at a node v **valid** if it is generated after v received all the messages of the synchronous algorithm sent to v by its neighbors in the previous pulses.*

Given a mechanism that generates the clock pulses, a synchronous algorithm is turned into an asynchronous algorithm in an obvious way: As soon as the ith clock pulse is generated at node

v, v performs all the actions (local computations and sending of messages) of round i of the synchronous algorithm.

Theorem 10.2. *If all generated clock pulses are valid according to Definition 10.1, the above method provides an asynchronous algorithm that behaves exactly the same way as the given synchronous algorithm.*

Proof. When the ith pulse is generated at a node v, v has sent and received exactly the same messages and performed the same local computations as in the first $i - 1$ rounds of the synchronous algorithm. $\qquad\square$

The main problem when generating the clock pulses at a node v is that v cannot know what messages its neighbors are sending to it in a given synchronous round. Because there are no bounds on link delays, v cannot simply wait "long enough" before generating the next pulse. In order satisfy Definition 10.1, nodes have to send additional messages for the purpose of synchronization. The total complexity of the resulting asynchronous algorithm depends on the overhead introduced by the synchronizer. For a synchronizer $\mathcal{S}$, let $T(\mathcal{S})$ and $M(\mathcal{S})$ be the time and message complexities of $\mathcal{S}$ for each generated clock pulse. As we will see, some of the synchronizers need an initialization phase. We denote the time and message complexities of the initialization by $T_{\text{init}}(\mathcal{S})$ and $M_{\text{init}}(\mathcal{S})$, respectively. If $T(\mathcal{A})$ and $M(\mathcal{A})$ are the time and message complexities of the given synchronous algorithm $\mathcal{A}$, the total time and message complexities T_{tot} and M_{tot} of the resulting asynchronous algorithm then become

$$\begin{aligned} T_{tot} &= T_{\text{init}}(\mathcal{S}) + T(\mathcal{A}) \cdot (1 + T(\mathcal{S})) \quad \text{and} \\ M_{tot} &= M_{\text{init}}(\mathcal{S}) + M(\mathcal{A}) + T(\mathcal{A}) \cdot M(\mathcal{S}), \end{aligned}$$

respectively.

Remarks:

- Because the initialization only needs to be done once for each network, we will mostly be interested in the overheads $T(\mathcal{S})$ and $M(\mathcal{S})$ per round of the synchronous algorithm.

Definition 10.3 (Safe Node)**.** *A node v is **safe** with respect to a certain clock pulse if all messages of the synchronous algorithm sent by v in that pulse have already arrived at their destinations.*

Lemma 10.4. *If all neighbors of a node v are safe with respect to the current clock pulse of v, the next pulse can be generated for v.*

Proof. If all neighbors of v are safe with respect to a certain pulse, v has received all messages of the given pulse. Node v therefore satisfies the condition of Definition 10.1 for generating a valid next pulse. $\qquad\square$

Remarks:

- In order to detect safety, we require that all algorithms send acknowledgements for all received messages. As soon as a node v has received an acknowledgement for each message that it has sent in a certain pulse, it knows that it is safe with respect to that pulse. Note that sending acknowledgements does not increase the asymptotic time and message complexities.

10.2 The Local Synchronizer α

Algorithm 10.5 Synchronizer α (at node v)

1: **wait** until v is safe
2: **send** SAFE to all neighbors
3: **wait** until v receives SAFE messages from all neighbors
4: start new pulse

Synchronizer α is very simple. It does not need an initialization. Using acknowledgements, each node eventually detects that it is safe. It then reports this fact directly to all its neighbors. Whenever a node learns that all its neighbors are safe, a new pulse is generated. Algorithm 10.5 formally describes the synchronizer α.

Theorem 10.6. *The time and message complexities of synchronizer α per synchronous round are*

$$T(\alpha) \;=\; O(1) \quad and \quad M(\alpha) \;=\; O(m).$$

Proof. Communication is only between neighbors. As soon as all neighbors of a node v become safe, v knows of this fact after one additional time unit. For every clock pulse, synchronizer α sends at most four additional messages over every edge: Each of the nodes may have to acknowledge a message and reports safety. $\qquad\square$

Remarks:

- Synchronizer α was presented in a framework, mostly set up to have a common standard to discuss different synchronizers. Without the framework, synchronizer α can be explained more easily:

  1. Send message to all neighbors, include round information i and actual data of round i (if any).

  2. Wait for message of round i from all neighbors, and go to next round.

- Although synchronizer α allows for simple and fast synchronization, it produces awfully many messages. Can we do better? Yes.

10.3   The Global Synchronizer β

Algorithm 10.7 Synchronizer β (at node v)

1: **wait** until v is safe
2: **wait** until v receives SAFE messages from all its children in T

3: **if** $v \neq \ell$ **then**
4:    **send** SAFE message to parent in T
5:    **wait** until PULSE message received from parent in T
6: **end if**
7: **send** PULSE message to children in T
8: start new pulse

Synchronizer β needs an initialization that computes a leader node ℓ and a spanning tree T rooted at ℓ. As soon as all nodes are safe, this information is propagated to ℓ by a convergecast. The leader then broadcasts this information to all nodes. The details of synchronizer β are given in Algorithm 10.7.

Theorem 10.8. *The time and message complexities of synchronizer β per synchronous round are*

$$T(\beta) \;=\; O(\text{diameter}(T)) \;\leq\; O(n) \quad and \quad M(\beta) \;=\; O(n).$$

The time and message complexities for the initialization are

$$T_{\text{init}}(\beta) \;=\; O(n) \quad and \quad M_{\text{init}}(\beta) \;=\; O(m + n \log n).$$

Proof. Because the diameter of T is at most $n-1$, the convergecast and the broadcast together take at most $2n - 2$ time units. Per clock pulse, the synchronizer sends at most $2n - 2$ synchronization messages (one in each direction over each edge of T).

With the improved variant of the GHS algorithm (Algorithm 2.18) mentioned in Chapter 2, it is possible to construct an MST in time $O(n)$ with $O(m + n \log n)$ messages in an asynchronous environment. Once the tree is computed, the tree can be made rooted in time $O(n)$ with $O(n)$ messages. $\qquad\square$

Remarks:

- We now got a time-efficient synchronizer (α) and a message-efficient synchronizer (β), it is only natural to ask whether we can have the best of both worlds. And, indeed, we can. How is that synchronizer called? Quite obviously: γ.

10.4 The Hybrid Synchronizer γ

Synchronizer γ can be seen as a combination of synchronizers α and β. In the initialization phase, the network is partitioned into clusters of small diameter. In each cluster, a leader node is chosen and a BFS tree rooted at this leader node is computed. These trees are called the *intracluster trees*. Two clusters C_1 and C_2 are called neighboring if there are nodes $u \in C_1$ and $v \in C_2$ for which $(u, v) \in E$. For every two neighboring clusters, an *intercluster edge* is chosen, which will serve for communication between these clusters. Figure 10.9 illustrates this partitioning into clusters. We will discuss the details of how to construct such a partition in the next section. We say that a cluster is safe if all its nodes are safe.

Synchronizer γ works in two phases. In a first phase, synchronizer β is applied separately in each cluster by using the intracluster trees. Whenever the leader of a cluster learns that its cluster is safe, it reports this fact to all the nodes in the clusters as well as to the

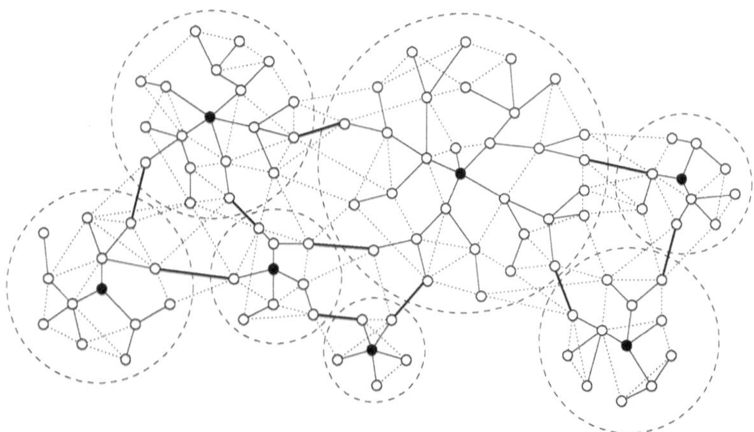

Figure 10.9: A cluster partition of a network: The dashed cycles specify the clusters, cluster leaders are black, the solid edges are the edges of the intracluster trees, and the bold solid edges are the intercluster edges

leaders of the neighboring clusters. Now, the nodes of the cluster enter the second phase where they wait until all the neighboring clusters are known to be safe and then generate the next pulse. Hence, we essentially apply synchronizer α between clusters. A detailed description is given by Algorithm 10.10.

Theorem 10.11. *Let m_C be the number of intercluster edges and let k be the maximum cluster radius (i.e., the maximum distance of a leaf to its cluster leader). The time and message complexities of synchronizer γ are*

$$T(\gamma) \;=\; O(k) \quad and \quad M(\gamma) \;=\; O(n + m_C).$$

Proof. We ignore acknowledgements, as they do not affect the asymptotic complexities. Let us first look at the number of messages. Over every intracluster tree edge, exactly one SAFE message, one CLUSTERSAFE message, one NEIGHBORSAFE message, and one PULSE message is sent. Further, one NEIGHBOR-SAFE message is sent over every intercluster edge. Because there are less than n intracluster tree edges, the total message complexity therefore is at most $4n + 2m_C = O(n + m_C)$.

For the time complexity, note that the depth of each intracluster tree is at most k. On each intracluster tree, two convergecasts

---

Algorithm 10.10 Synchronizer γ (at node v)

1: **wait** until v is safe
2: **wait** until v receives SAFE messages from all children in intracluster tree
3: **if** v is not cluster leader **then**
4:    **send** SAFE message to parent in intracluster tree
5:    **wait** until CLUSTERSAFE message received from parent
6: **end if**
7: **send** CLUSTERSAFE message to all children in intracluster tree
8: **send** NEIGHBORSAFE message over all intercluster edges of v
9: **wait** until v receives NEIGHBORSAFE messages from all adjacent intercluster edges and all children in intracluster tree

10: **if** v is not cluster leader **then**
11:    **send** NEIGHBORSAFE message to parent in intracluster tree
12:    **wait** until PULSE message received from parent
13: **end if**
14: **send** PULSE message to children in intracluster tree
15: start new pulse

(the SAFE and NEIGHBORSAFE messages) and two broadcasts (the CLUSTERSAFE and PULSE messages) are performed. The time complexity for this is at most $4k$. There is one more time unit needed to send the NEIGHBORSAFE messages over the intercluster edges. The total time complexity therefore is at most $4k + 1 = O(k)$. $\qquad\square$

10.5 Network Partition

We will now look at the initialization phase of synchronizer γ. Algorithm 10.12 describes how to construct a partition into clusters that can be used for synchronizer γ. In Algorithm 10.12, $B(v, r)$ denotes the ball of radius r around v, i.e., $B(v, r) = \{u \in V : d(u, v) \leq r\}$ where $d(u, v)$ is the hop distance between u and v. The algorithm has a parameter $\rho > 1$. The clusters are constructed sequentially. Each cluster is started at an arbitrary node that has not been included in a cluster. Then the cluster radius is grown as long as the cluster grows by a factor more than ρ.

Algorithm 10.12 Cluster construction

1: **while** unprocessed nodes **do**
2:     select an arbitrary unprocessed node v;
3:     $r := 0$;
4:     **while** $|B(v, r + 1)| > \rho|B(v, r)|$ **do**
5:         $r := r + 1$
6:     **end while**
7:     makeCluster($B(v, r)$) $//$ all nodes in $B(v, r)$ are now processed
8: **end while**

Remarks:

- The algorithm allows a trade-off between the cluster diameter k (and thus the time complexity) and the number of intercluster edges m_C (and thus the message complexity). We will quantify the possibilities in the next section.

- Two very simple partitions would be to make a cluster out of every single node or to make one big cluster that contains the whole graph. We then get synchronizers α and β as special cases of synchronizer γ.

Theorem 10.13. *Algorithm 10.12 computes a partition of the network graph into clusters of radius at most $\log_\rho n$. The number of intercluster edges is at most $(\rho - 1) \cdot n$.*

Proof. The radius of a cluster is initially 0 and does only grow as long as it grows by a factor larger than ρ. Since there are only n nodes in the graph, this can happen at most $\log_\rho n$ times.

To count the number of intercluster edges, observe that an edge can only become an intercluster edge if it connects a node at the boundary of a cluster with a node outside a cluster. Consider a cluster C of size $|C|$. We know that $C = B(v, r)$ for some $v \in V$ and $r \geq 0$. Further, we know that $|B(v, r + 1)| \leq \rho \cdot |B(v, r)|$. The number of nodes adjacent to cluster C is therefore at most $|B(v, r + 1) \setminus B(v, r)| \leq \rho \cdot |C| - |C|$. Because there is only one intercluster edge connecting two clusters by definition, the number of intercluster edges adjacent to C is at most $(\rho - 1) \cdot |C|$. Summing over all clusters, we get that the total number of intercluster edges is at most $(\rho - 1) \cdot n$. $\square$

Corollary 10.14. *Using $\rho = 2$, Algorithm 10.12 computes a clustering with cluster radius at most $\log_2 n$ and with at most n intercluster edges.*

Corollary 10.15. *Using $\rho = n^{1/k}$, Algorithm 10.12 computes a clustering with cluster radius at most k and at most $O(n^{1+1/k})$ intercluster edges.*

Remarks:

- Algorithm 10.12 describes a centralized construction of the partitioning of the graph. For $\rho \geq 2$, the clustering can be computed by an asynchronous distributed algorithm in time $O(n)$ with $O(m+n\log n)$ (reasonably sized) messages (showing this will be part of the exercises).

- It can be shown that the trade-off between cluster radius and number of intercluster edges of Algorithm 10.12 is asymptotically optimal. There are graphs for which every clustering into clusters of radius at most k requires $n^{1+c/k}$ intercluster edges for some constant c.

The above remarks lead to a complete characterization of the complexity of synchronizer γ.

Corollary 10.16. *The time and message complexities of synchronizer γ per synchronous round are*

$$T(\gamma) \;=\; O(k) \quad and \quad M(\gamma) \;=\; O(n^{1+1/k}).$$

The time and message complexities for the initialization are

$$T_{\text{init}}(\gamma) \;=\; O(n) \quad and \quad M_{\text{init}}(\gamma) \;=\; O(m + n\log n).$$

Remarks:

- In Chapter 2, you have seen that by using flooding, there is a very simple synchronous algorithm to compute a BFS tree in time $O(D)$ with message complexity $O(m)$. If we use synchronizer γ to make this algorithm asynchronous, we get an algorithm with time complexity $O(n + D\log n)$ and message complexity $O(m + n\log n + D \cdot n)$ (including initialization).

- The synchronizers α, β, and γ achieve global synchronization, i.e. every node generates every clock pulse. The disadvantage of this is that nodes that do not participate in a computation also have to participate in the synchronization. In many computations (e.g. in a BFS construction), many nodes only participate for a few synchronous rounds. In such scenarios, it is possible to achieve time and message complexity $O(\log^3 n)$ per synchronous round (without initialization).

- It can be shown that if all nodes in the network need to generate all pulses, the trade-off of synchronizer γ is asymptotically optimal.

- Partitions of networks into clusters of small diameter and coverings of networks with clusters of small diameters come in many variations and have various applications in distributed computations. In particular, apart from synchronizers, algorithms for routing, the construction of sparse spanning subgraphs, distributed data structures, and even computations of local structures such as a MIS or a dominating set are based on some kind of network partitions or covers.

10.6   Clock Synchronization

"A man with one clock knows what time it is – a man with two is never sure."

Synchronizers can directly be used to give nodes in an asynchronous network a common notion of time. In wireless networks, for instance, many basic protocols need an accurate time. Sometimes a common time in the whole network is needed, often it is enough to synchronize neighbors. The purpose of the time division multiple access (TDMA) protocol is to use the common wireless channel as efficiently as possible, i.e., interfering nodes should never transmit at the same time (on the same frequency). If we use synchronizer β to give the nodes a common notion of time, every single clock cycle costs D time units!

Often, each (wireless) node is equipped with an internal clock. Using this clock, it should be possible to divide time into slots, and make each node send (or listen, or sleep, respectively) in the appropriate slots according to the media access control (MAC) layer protocol used.

However, as it turns out, synchronizing clocks in a network is not trivial. As nodes' internal clocks are not perfect, they will run at speeds that are time-dependent. For instance, variations in temperature or supply voltage will affect this *clock drift*. For standard clocks, the drift is in the order of parts per million, i.e., within a second, it will accumulate to a couple of microseconds. Wireless TDMA protocols account for this by introducing *guard times*. Whenever a node knows that it is about to receive a message from a neighbor, it powers up its radio a little bit earlier to make sure that it does not miss the message even when clocks are not perfectly synchronized. If nodes are badly synchronized, messages of different slots might collide.

In the *clock synchronization* problem, we are given a network (graph) with n nodes. The goal for each node is to have a logical clock such that the logical clock values are well synchronized, and close to real time. Each node is equipped with a hardware clock, that ticks more or less in real time, i.e., the time between two pulses is arbitrary between $[1 - \epsilon, 1 + \epsilon]$, for a constant $\epsilon \ll 1$. Similarly as in our asynchronous model, we assume that messages sent over the edges of the graph have a delivery time between $[0, 1]$. In other words, we have a bounded but variable drift on the hardware clocks and an arbitrary jitter in the delivery times. The goal is to design a message-passing algorithm that ensures that the logical clock skew of adjacent nodes is as small as possible at all times.

Theorem 10.17. *The global clock skew (the logical clock difference between any two nodes in the graph) is $\Omega(D)$, where D is the diameter of the graph.*

Proof. For a node u, let t_u be the logical time of u and let $(u \to v)$ denote a message sent from u to a node v. Let $t(m)$ be the time delay of a message m and let u and v be neighboring nodes. First consider a case where the message delays between u and v are $1/2$. Then all the messages sent by u and v at time i according to the clock of the sender arrive at time $i + 1/2$ according to the clock of the receiver.

Then consider the following cases

- $t_u = t_v + 1/2,\ t(u \to v) = 1,\ t(v \to u) = 0$

- $t_u = t_v - 1/2,\ t(u \to v) = 0,\ t(v \to u) = 1,$

where the message delivery time is always fast for one node and slow for the other and the logical clocks are off by $1/2$. In both scenarios, the messages sent at time i according to the clock of the sender arrive at time $i + 1/2$ according to the logical clock of the receiver. Therefore, for nodes u and v, both cases with clock drift seem the same as the case with perfectly synchronized clocks. Furthermore, in a linked list of D nodes, the left- and rightmost nodes l, r cannot distinguish $t_l = t_r + D/2$ from $t_l = t_r - D/2$. $\square$

Remarks:

- From Theorem 10.17, it directly follows that all the clock synchronization algorithms we studied have a global skew of $\Omega(D)$.

- Many natural algorithms manage to achieve a global clock skew of $O(D)$.

As both the message jitter and hardware clock drift are bounded by constants, it feels like we should be able to get a constant drift between neighboring nodes. As synchronizer α pays most attention to the local synchronization, we take a look at a protocol inspired by the synchronizer α. A pseudo-code representation for the clock synchronization protocol α is given in Algorithm 10.18.

Algorithm 10.18 Clock synchronization α (at node v)

1: **repeat**
2:    **send** logical time t_v to all neighbors
3:    **if** Receive logical time t_u, where $t_u > t_v$, from any neighbor u **then**
4:       $t_v := t_u$
5:    **end if**
6: **until** done

Lemma 10.19. *The clock synchronization protocol α has a local skew of $\Omega(n)$.*

Proof. Let the graph be a linked list of D nodes. We denote the nodes by $v_1, v_2, \ldots, v_D$ from left to right and the logical clock of node v_i by t_i. Apart from the left-most node v_1 all hardware clocks run with speed 1 (real time). Node v_1 runs at maximum speed, i.e. the time between two pulses is not 1 but $1 - \epsilon$. Assume that initially all message delays are 1. After some time, node v_1 will start to speed up v_2, and after some more time v_2 will speed up v_3, and so on. At some point of time, we will have a clock skew of 1 between any two neighbors. In particular $t_1 = t_D + D - 1$.

Now we start playing around with the message delays. Let $t_1 = T$. First we set the delay between the v_1 and v_2 to 0. Now node v_2 immediately adjusts its logical clock to T. After this event (which is instantaneous in our model) we set the delay between v_2 and v_3 to 0, which results in v_3 setting its logical clock to T as well. We perform this successively to all pairs of nodes until v_{D-2} and v_{D-1}. Now node v_{D-1} sets its logical clock to T, which indicates that the difference between the logical clocks of v_{D-1} and v_D is $T - (T - (D - 1)) = D - 1$. $\qquad\square$

Remarks:

- The introduced examples may seem cooked-up, but examples like this exist in all networks, and for all algorithms. Indeed, it was shown that any natural clock synchronization algorithm must have a bad local skew. In particular, a protocol that averages between all neighbors is even worse than the introduced α algorithm. This algorithm has a clock skew of $\Omega(D^2)$ in the linked list, at all times.

- It was shown that the local clock skew is $\Theta(\log D)$, i.e., there is a protocol that achieves this bound, and there is a proof that no algorithm can be better than this bound!

- Note that these are worst-case bounds. In practice, clock drift and message delays may not be the worst possible, typically the speed of hardware clocks changes at a comparatively slow pace and the message transmission times follow a benign probability distribution. If we assume this, better protocols do exist.

Chapter Notes

The idea behind synchronizers is quite intuitive and as such, synchronizers α and β were implicitly used in various asynchronous algorithms [Gal76, Cha79, CL85] before being proposed as separate entities. The general idea of applying synchronizers to run synchronous algorithms in asynchronous networks was first introduced by Awerbuch [Awe85a]. His work also formally introduced the synchronizers α and β. Improved synchronizers that exploit inactive nodes or hypercube networks were presented in [AP90, PU87].

Naturally, as synchronizers are motivated by practical difficulties with local clocks, there are plenty of real life applications. Studies regarding applications can be found in, e.g., [SM86, Awe85b, LTC89, AP90, PU87]. Synchronizers in the presence of network failures have been discussed in [AP88, HS94].

It has been known for a long time that the global clock skew is $\Theta(D)$ [LL84, ST87]. The problem of synchronizing the clocks of nearby nodes was introduced by Fan and Lynch in [LF04]; they proved a surprising lower bound of $\Omega(\log D / \log \log D)$ for the local skew. The first algorithm providing a non-trivial local skew of $O(\sqrt{D})$ was given in [LW06]. Later, matching upper and lower bounds of $\Theta(\log D)$ were given in [LLW10]. The problem has also been studied in a dynamic setting [KLO09, KLLO10].

Clock synchronization is a well-studied problem in practice, for instance regarding the global clock skew in sensor networks, e.g. [EGE02, GKS03, MKSL04, PSJ04]. One more recent line of work is focussing on the problem of minimizing the local clock skew [BvRW07, SW09, LSW09, FW10, FZTS11].

Bibliography

[AP88] Baruch Awerbuch and David Peleg. Adapting to Asynchronous Dynamic Networks with Polylogarithmic Overhead. In *24th ACM Symposium on Foundations of Computer Science (FOCS)*, pages 206–220, 1988.

[AP90] Baruch Awerbuch and David Peleg. Network Synchronization with Polylogarithmic Overhead. In *Proceedings of the 31st IEEE Symposium on Foundations of Computer Science (FOCS)*, 1990.

[Awe85a] Baruch Awerbuch. Complexity of Network Synchronization. *Journal of the ACM (JACM)*, 32(4):804–823, October 1985.

[Awe85b] Baruch Awerbuch. Reducing Complexities of the Distributed Max-flow and Breadth-first-search Algorithms by Means of Network Synchronization. *Networks*, 15:425–437, 1985.

[BvRW07] Nicolas Burri, Pascal von Rickenbach, and Roger Wattenhofer. Dozer: Ultra-Low Power Data Gathering in Sensor Networks. In *International Conference on Information Processing in Sensor Networks (IPSN), Cambridge, Massachusetts, USA*, April 2007.

[Cha79] E.J.H. Chang. *Decentralized Algorithms in Distributed Systems*. PhD thesis, University of Toronto, 1979.

[CL85] K. Mani Chandy and Leslie Lamport. Distributed Snapshots: Determining Global States of Distributed Systems. *ACM Transactions on Computer Systems*, 1:63–75, 1985.

[EGE02] Jeremy Elson, Lewis Girod, and Deborah Estrin. Fine-grained Network Time Synchronization Using Reference Broadcasts. *ACM SIGOPS Operating Systems Review*, 36:147–163, 2002.

[FW10] Roland Flury and Roger Wattenhofer. Slotted Programming for Sensor Networks. In *International Conference on Information Processing in Sensor Networks (IPSN), Stockholm, Sweden*, April 2010.

[FZTS11] Federico Ferrari, Marco Zimmerling, Lothar Thiele, and Olga Saukh. Efficient Network Flooding and Time Synchronization with Glossy. In *Proceedings of the 10th International Conference on Information Processing in Sensor Networks (IPSN)*, pages 73–84, 2011.

[Gal76] Robert Gallager. Distributed Minimum Hop Algorithms. Technical report, Lab. for Information and Decision Systems, 1976.

[GKS03] Saurabh Ganeriwal, Ram Kumar, and Mani B. Srivastava. Timing-sync Protocol for Sensor Networks. In *Proceedings of the 1st international conference on Embedded Networked Sensor Systems (SenSys)*, 2003.

[HS94] M. Harrington and A. K. Somani. Synchronizing Hypercube Networks in the Presence of Faults. *IEEE Transactions on Computers*, 43(10):1175–1183, 1994.

[KLLO10] Fabian Kuhn, Christoph Lenzen, Thomas Locher, and Rotem Oshman. Optimal Gradient Clock Synchronization in Dynamic Networks. In *29th Symposium on*

Principles of Distributed Computing (PODC), Zurich, Switzerland, July 2010.

[KLO09] Fabian Kuhn, Thomas Locher, and Rotem Oshman. Gradient Clock Synchronization in Dynamic Networks. In *21st ACM Symposium on Parallelism in Algorithms and Architectures (SPAA), Calgary, Canada*, August 2009.

[LF04] Nancy Lynch and Rui Fan. Gradient Clock Synchronization. In *Proceedings of the 23rd Annual ACM Symposium on Principles of Distributed Computing (PODC)*, 2004.

[LL84] Jennifer Lundelius and Nancy Lynch. An Upper and Lower Bound for Clock Synchronization. *Information and Control*, 62:190–204, 1984.

[LLW10] Christoph Lenzen, Thomas Locher, and Roger Wattenhofer. Tight Bounds for Clock Synchronization. In *Journal of the ACM, Volume 57, Number 2*, January 2010.

[LSW09] Christoph Lenzen, Philipp Sommer, and Roger Wattenhofer. Optimal Clock Synchronization in Networks. In *7th ACM Conference on Embedded Networked Sensor Systems (SenSys), Berkeley, California, USA*, November 2009.

[LTC89] K. B. Lakshmanan, K. Thulasiraman, and M. A. Comeau. An Efficient Distributed Protocol for Finding Shortest Paths in Networks with Negative Weights. *IEEE Trans. Softw. Eng.*, 15:639–644, 1989.

[LW06] Thomas Locher and Roger Wattenhofer. Oblivious Gradient Clock Synchronization. In *20th International Symposium on Distributed Computing (DISC), Stockholm, Sweden*, September 2006.

[MKSL04] Miklós Maróti, Branislav Kusy, Gyula Simon, and Ákos Lédeczi. The Flooding Time Synchronization Protocol. In *Proceedings of the 2nd international Conference on Embedded Networked Sensor Systems*, SenSys '04, 2004.

[PSJ04] Santashil PalChaudhuri, Amit Kumar Saha, and David B. Johnson. Adaptive Clock Synchronization in Sensor Networks. In *Proceedings of the 3rd International Symposium on Information Processing in Sensor Networks*, IPSN '04, 2004.

[PU87] David Peleg and Jeffrey D. Ullman. An Optimal Synchronizer for the Hypercube. In *Proceedings of the sixth annual ACM Symposium on Principles of Distributed Computing*, PODC '87, pages 77–85, 1987.

[SM86] Baruch Shieber and Shlomo Moran. Slowing Sequential Algorithms for Obtaining Fast Distributed and Parallel Algorithms: Maximum Matchings. In *Proceedings of the fifth annual ACM Symposium on Principles of Distributed Computing*, PODC '86, pages 282–292, 1986.

[ST87] T. K. Srikanth and S. Toueg. Optimal Clock Synchronization. *Journal of the ACM*, 34:626–645, 1987.

[SW09] Philipp Sommer and Roger Wattenhofer. Gradient Clock Synchronization in Wireless Sensor Networks. In *8th ACM/IEEE International Conference on Information Processing in Sensor Networks (IPSN), San Francisco, USA*, April 2009.

Chapter 11

Stabilization

A large branch of research in distributed computing deals with fault-tolerance. Being able to tolerate a considerable fraction of failing or even maliciously behaving ("Byzantine") nodes while trying to reach *consensus* (on e.g. the output of a function) among the nodes that work properly is crucial for building reliable systems. However, consensus protocols require that a majority of the nodes remains non-faulty all the time.

Can we design a distributed system that survives transient (short-lived) failures, even if *all* nodes are temporarily failing? In other words, can we build a distributed system that *repairs itself*?

11.1 Self-Stabilization

Definition 11.1 (Self-Stabilization). *A distributed system is **self-stabilizing** if, starting from an arbitrary state, it is guaranteed to converge to a legitimate state. If the system is in a legitimate state, it is guaranteed to remain there, provided that no further faults happen. A state is **legitimate** if the state satisfies the specifications of the distributed system.*

Remarks:

- What kind of transient failures can we tolerate? An adversary can crash nodes, or make nodes behave Byzantine. Indeed, temporarily an adversary can do harm in even worse ways, e.g. by corrupting the volatile memory of a node (without the node noticing – not unlike the movie Memento), or by corrupting messages on the fly (without anybody noticing). However, as all failures are transient, eventually all nodes must work correctly again, that is, crashed nodes get resurrected, Byzantine nodes stop being malicious, messages are being delivered reliably, and the memory of the nodes is secure.

- Clearly, the read only memory (ROM) must be taboo at all times for the adversary. No system can repair itself if the program code itself or constants are corrupted. The adversary can only corrupt the variables in the volatile random access memory (RAM).

Definition 11.2 (Time Complexity). *The time complexity of a self-stabilizing system is the time that passed after the last (transient) failure until the system has converged to a legitimate state again, staying legitimate.*

Remarks:

- Self-stabilization enables a distributed system to recover from a transient fault regardless of its nature. A self-stabilizing system does not have to be initialized as it eventually (after convergence) will behave correctly.

- One of the first self-stabilizing algorithms was Dijkstra's token ring network. A token ring is an early form of a local area network where nodes are arranged in a ring, communicating by a token. The system is correct if there is exactly one token in the ring. Let's have a look at a simple solution. Given an oriented ring, we simply call the clockwise neighbor parent (p), and the counterclockwise neighbor child (c). Also, there is a leader node v_0. Every node v is in a state $S(v) \in \{0, 1, \ldots, n\}$, perpetually informing its child about its state. The token is implicitly passed on by nodes switching state. Upon noticing a change of the parent state $S(p)$, node v executes the following code:

Theorem 11.4. *Algorithm 11.3 stabilizes correctly.*

Algorithm 11.3 Self-stabilizing Token Ring

1: **if** $v = v_0$ **then**
2:    **if** $S(v) = S(p)$ **then**
3:       $S(v) := S(v) + 1 \ (\text{mod } n)$
4:    **end if**
5: **else**
6:    $S(v) := S(p)$
7: **end if**

Proof: As long as some nodes or edges are faulty, anything can happen. In self-stabilization, we only consider the system after all faults already have happened (at time t_0, however starting in an arbitrary state).

Every node apart from leader v_0 will always attain the state of its parent. It may happen that one node after the other will learn the current state of the leader. In this case the system stabilizes after the leader increases its state at most n time units after time t_0. It may however be that the leader increases its state even if the system is not stable, e.g. because its parent or parent's parent accidentally had the same state at time t_0.

The leader will increase its state possibly multiple times without reaching stability, however, at some point the leader will reach state s, a state that no other node had at time t_0. (Since there are n nodes and n states, this will eventually happen.) At this point the system must stabilize because the leader cannot push for $s + 1$ $(\text{mod } n)$ until every node (including its parent) has s.

After stabilization, there will always be only one node changing its state, i.e., the system remains in a legitimate state.

$\square$

Remarks:

- Although one might think the time complexity of the algorithm is quite bad, it is asymptotically optimal.

- It can be a lot of fun designing self-stabilizing algorithms. Let us try to build a system, where the nodes organize themselves as a maximal independent set (MIS, Chapter 7):

Algorithm 11.5 Self-stabilizing MIS

Require: Node IDs

    Every node v executes the following code:

1: **loop**
2:    Leave MIS if a neighbor with a larger ID is in the MIS
3:    Join MIS if no neighbor with larger ID joins MIS
4:    Send (node ID, MIS or not MIS) to all neighbors
5: **end loop**

Remarks:

- Note that the main idea of Algorithm 11.5 is from Algorithm 7.3, Chapter 7.

- As long as some nodes are faulty, anything can happen: Faulty nodes may for instance decide to join the MIS, but report to their neighbors that they did not join the MIS. Similarly messages may be corrupted during transport. As soon as the system (nodes, messages) is correct, however, the system will converge to a MIS. (The arguments are the same as in Chapter 7).

- Self-stabilizing algorithms always run in an infinite loop, because transient failures can hit the system at any time. Without the infinite loop, an adversary can always corrupt the solution "after" the algorithm terminated.

- The problem of Algorithm 11.5 is its time complexity, which may be linear in the number of nodes. This is not very exciting. We need something better! Since Algorithm 11.5 was just the self-stabilizing variant of the slow MIS Algorithm 7.3, maybe we can hope to "self-stabilize" some of our fast algorithms from Chapter 7?

- Yes, we can! Indeed there is a general transformation that takes any local algorithm (efficient but not fault-tolerant) and turns it into a self-stabilizing algorithm, keeping the same level of efficiency and efficacy. We present the general transformation below.

Theorem 11.6 (Transformation). *We are given a deterministic local algorithm $\mathcal{A}$ that computes a solution of a given problem in k synchronous communication rounds. Using our transformation, we* *get a self-stabilizing system with time complexity k. In other words, if the adversary does not corrupt the system for k time units, the solution is stable. In addition, if the adversary does not corrupt any node or message closer than distance k from a node u, node u will be stable.*

Proof: In the proof, we present the transformation. First, however, we need to be more formal about the deterministic local algorithm $\mathcal{A}$. In $\mathcal{A}$, each node of the network computes its decision in k phases. In phase i, node u computes its local variables according to its local variables and received messages of the earlier phases. Then node u sends its messages of phase i to its neighbors. Finally node u receives the messages of phase i from its neighbors. The set of local variables of node u in phase i is given by L_u^i. (In the very first phase, node u initializes its local variables with L_u^1.) The message sent from node u to node v in phase i is denoted by $m_{u,v}^i$. Since the algorithm $\mathcal{A}$ is deterministic, node u can compute its local variables L_u^i and messages $m_{u,*}^i$ of phase i from its state of earlier phases, by simply applying functions f_L and f_m. In particular,

$$L_u^i \;=\; f_L(u, L_u^{i-1}, m_{*,u}^{i-1}), \text{ for } i > 1, \text{ and} \qquad (11.1)$$

$$m_{u,v}^i \;=\; f_m(u, v, L_u^i), \text{ for } i \geq 1. \qquad (11.2)$$

The self-stabilizing algorithm needs to simulate all the k phases of the local algorithm $\mathcal{A}$ in parallel. Each node u stores its local variables $L_u^1, \ldots, L_u^k$ as well as all messages received $m_{*,u}^1, \ldots, m_{*,u}^k$ in two tables in RAM. For simplicity, each node u also stores all the sent messages $m_{u,*}^1, \ldots, m_{u,*}^k$ in a third table. If a message or a local variable for a particular phase is unknown, the entry in the table will be marked with a special value $\perp$ ("unknown"). Initially, all entries in the table are $\perp$.

Clearly, in the self-stabilizing model, an adversary can choose to change table values at all times, and even reset these values to $\perp$. Our self-stabilizing algorithm needs to constantly work against this adversary. In particular, each node u runs these two procedures constantly:

- For all neighbors: Send each neighbor v a message containing the complete row of messages of algorithm $\mathcal{A}$, that is, send the vector $(m_{u,v}^1, \ldots, m_{u,v}^k)$ to neighbor v. Similarly, if neighbor u receives such a vector from neighbor v, then neighbor u

replaces neighbor v's row in the table of incoming messages by the received vector $(m_{v,u}^1, \ldots, m_{v,u}^k)$.

- Because of the adversary, node u must constantly recompute its local variables (including the initialization) and outgoing message vectors using Functions (11.1) and (11.2) respectively.

The proof is by induction. Let $N^i(u)$ be the i-neighborhood of node u (that is, all nodes within distance i of node u). We assume that the adversary has not corrupted any node in $N^k(u)$ since time t_0. At time t_0 all nodes in $N^k(u)$ will check and correct their initialization. Following Equation (11.2), at time t_0 all nodes in $N^k(u)$ will send the correct message entry for the first round $(m_{*,*}^1)$ to all neighbors. Asynchronous messages take at most 1 time unit to be received at a destination. Hence, using the induction with Equations (11.1) and (11.2) it follows that at time $t_0 + i$, all nodes in $N^{k-i}(u)$ have received the correct messages $m_{*,*}^1, \ldots, m_{*,*}^i$. Consequently, at time $t_0 + k$ node u has received all messages of local algorithm $\mathcal{A}$ correctly, and will compute the same result value as in $\mathcal{A}$. $\qquad\square$

Remarks:

- Using our transformation (also known as "local checking"), designing self-stabilizing algorithms just turned from art to craft.

- As we have seen, many local algorithms are randomized. This brings two additional problems. Firstly, one may not exactly know how long the algorithm will take. This is not really a problem since we can simply send around all the messages needed, until the algorithm is finished. The transformation of Theorem 11.6 works also if nodes just send all messages that are not $\perp$. Secondly, we must be careful about the adversary. In particular we need to restrict the adversary such that a node can produce a reproducible sufficiently long string of random bits. This can be achieved by storing the sufficiently long string along with the program code in the read only memory (ROM). Alternatively, the algorithm might not store the random bit string in its ROM, but only the seed for a random bit generator. We need this in order to keep the adversary from reshuffling random bits until the bits become "bad", and the expected (or with high probability) efficacy or efficiency guarantees of the original local algorithm $\mathcal{A}$ cannot be guaranteed anymore.

- Since most local algorithms have only a few communication rounds, and only exchange small messages, the memory overhead of the transformation is usually bearable. In addition, information can often be compressed in a suitable way so that for many algorithms message size will remain polylogarithmic. For example, the information of the fast MIS algorithm (Algorithm 7.12) consists of a series of random values (one for each round), plus two boolean values per round. These boolean values represent whether the node joins the MIS, or whether a neighbor of the node joins the MIS. The order of the values tells in which round a decision is made. Indeed, the series of random bits can even be compressed just into the random seed value, and the neighbors can compute the random values of each round themselves.

- There is hope that our transformation as well gives good algorithms for mobile networks, that is for networks where the topology of the network may change. Indeed, for deterministic local approximation algorithms, this is true: If the adversary does not change the topology of a node's k-neighborhood in time k, the solution will locally be stable again.

- For randomized local approximation algorithms however, this is not that simple. Assume for example, that we have a randomized local algorithm for the dominating set problem. An adversary can constantly switch the topology of the network, until it finds a topology for which the random bits (which are not really random because these random bits are in ROM) give a solution with a bad approximation ratio. By defining a weaker adversarial model, we can fix this problem. Essentially, the adversary needs to be oblivious, in the sense that it cannot see the solution. Then it will not be possible for the adversary to restart the random computation if the solution is "too good".

- Self-stabilization is the original approach, and self-organization may be the general theme, but new buzzwords pop up every now and then, e.g. self-configuration, self-management, self-regulation, self-repairing, self-healing, self-optimization, self-adaptivity, or self-protection. Generally all these are summarized as "self-*". One computing giant coined the term "autonomic computing" to reflect the trend of self-managing distributed systems.

11.2   Advanced Stabilization

We finish the chapter with a non-trivial example beyond self-stabilization, showing the beauty and potential of the area: In a small town, every evening each citizen calls all his (or her) friends, asking them whether they will vote for the Democratic or the Republican party at the next election.[1] In our town citizens listen to their friends, and everybody re-chooses his or her affiliation according to the majority of friends.[2] Is this process going to "stabilize" (in one way or another)?

Remarks:

- Is eventually everybody voting for the same party? No.

- Will each citizen eventually stay with the same party? No.

- Will citizens that stayed with the same party for some time, stay with that party forever? No.

- And if their friends also constantly root for the same party? No.

- Will this beast stabilize at all?!? Yes!

Eventually every citizen will either stay with the same party for the rest of her life, or switch her opinion every day.

Theorem 11.7 (Dems & Reps). *Eventually every citizen is rooting for the same party every other day.*

---

[1]We are in the US, and as we know from The Simpsons, you "throw your vote away" if you vote for somebody else. As a consequence our example has two parties only.

[2]Assume for the sake of simplicity that everybody has an odd number of friends.

Proof: To prove that the opinions eventually become fixed or cycle every other day, think of each friendship as a pair of (directed) edges, one in each direction. Let us say an edge is currently *bad* if the party of the *advising* friend differs from the next-day's party of the *advised* friend. In other words, the edge is bad if the advised friend did not follow the advisor's opinion (which means that the advisor was in the minority). An edge that is not bad, is *good.*

Consider the out-edges of citizen u on day t, during which (say) u roots for the Democrats. Assume that on day t, g out-edges of u are good, and b out-edges are bad. Note that $g + b$ is the degree of u. Since g out-edges are good, g friends of u root for the Democrats on day $t + 1$. Likewise, b friends of u root for the Republicans on day $t + 1$. In other words, on the evening of day $t + 1$ citizen u will receive g recommendations for Democrats, and b for Republicans. We distinguish two cases:

- $g > b$: In this case, citizen u will again root for the Democrats on day $t + 2$. Note that this means, on day $t + 1$, exactly g in-edges of u are good, and exactly b in-edges are bad. In other words, the number of bad out-edges on day t is exactly the number of bad in-edges on day $t + 1$.

- $g < b$: In this case, citizen u will root for the Republicans on day $t + 2$. Please note that on day $t + 1$, exactly b in-edges of u are good, and exactly g in-edges are bad. In other words, the number of bad out-edges on day t was exactly the number of good in-edges on day $t + 1$ (and vice versa). This means that the number of bad out-edges on day t is strictly larger than the number of bad in-edges on day $t + 1$.

We can summarize these two cases by the following observation. If a citizen u votes for the same party on day t as on day $t + 2$, the number of her bad out-edges on day t is the same as the number of her bad in-edges on day $t + 1$. If a citizen u votes for different parties on the days t and $t + 2$, the number of her bad out-edges on day t is strictly larger than the number of her bad in-edges on day $t + 1$.

We now account for the total number of bad edges. We denote the total number of bad out-edges on day t with BO_t and by the total number of bad in-edges on day t with BI_t. Using the analysis of the two cases, and summing up for all citizens, we know that $BO_t \geq BI_{t+1}$. Moreover, each out-edge of a citizen is an in-edge for another citizen, hence $BO_t = BI_t$. In fact, if any citizen switches its party from day t to $t + 2$, we know that the total number of bad edges strictly decreases, i.e., $BO_{t+1} = BI_{t+1} < BO_t$. But BO cannot decrease forever. Once $BO_{t+1} = BO_t$, every citizen u votes for the same party on day $t+2$ as u voted on day t, and the system stabilizes in the sense that every citizen will either stick with his or her party forever or flip-flop every day. $\qquad\square$

Remarks:

- The model can be generalized considerably by, for example, adding weights to vertices (meaning some citizens' opinions are more important than others), adding weights to edges (meaning the influence between some citizens is stronger than between others), allowing loops (citizens who consider their own current opinions as well), allowing tie-breaking mechanisms, and even allowing different thresholds for party changes.

- How long does it take until the system stabilizes?

- Some may be reminded of Conway's Game of Life: We are given an infinite two-dimensional grid of cells, each of which is in one of two possible states, *dead* or *alive*. Every cell interacts with its eight neighbors. In each round, the following transitions occur: Any live cell with fewer than two live neighbors dies, as if caused by loneliness. Any live cell with more than three live neighbors dies, as if by overcrowding. Any live cell with two or three live neighbors lives on to the next generation. Any dead cell with exactly three live neighbors is "born" and becomes a live cell. The initial pattern constitutes the "seed" of the system. The first generation is created by applying the above rules simultaneously to every cell in the seed, births and deaths happen simultaneously, and the discrete moment at which this happens is sometimes called a tick. (In other words, each generation is a pure function of the one before.) The rules continue to be applied repeatedly to create further generations. John Conway figured that these rules were enough to generate interesting situations, including "breeders" with create "guns" which in turn create "gliders". As such Life in some sense answers an old question by John von Neumann, whether there can be a simple machine that can build copies of itself. In fact Life is Turing complete, that is, as powerful as any computer.

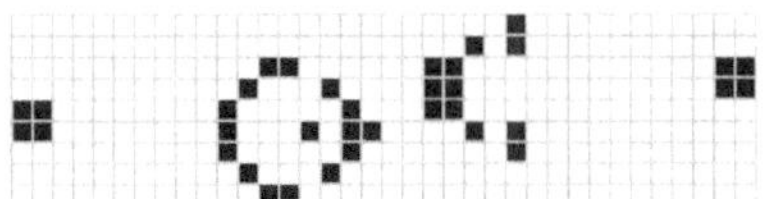

Figure 11.8: A "glider gun"...

Figure 11.9: ...in action.

Chapter Notes

Self-stabilization was first introduced in a paper by Edsger W. Dijkstra in 1974 [Dij74], in the context of a token ring network. It was shown that the ring stabilizes in time $\Theta(n)$. For his work Dijkstra received the 2002 ACM PODC Influential Paper Award. Shortly after receiving the award he passed away. With Dijkstra being such an eminent person in distributed computing (e.g. concurrency, semaphores,mutual exclusion, deadlock, finding shortest paths in graphs, fault-tolerance, self-stabilization), the award was renamed Edsger W. Dijkstra Prize in Distributed Computing. In 1991 Awerbuch et al. showed that any algorithm can be modified into a self-stabilizing algorithm that stabilizes in the same time that is needed to compute the solution from scratch [APSV91].

The Republicans vs. Democrats problem was popularized by Peter Winkler, in his column "Puzzled" [Win08]. Goles et al. already proved in [GO80] that any configuration of any such system with symmetric edge weights will end up in a situation where each citizen votes for the same party every second day. Winkler additionally proved that the time such a system takes to stabilize is bounded by $O(n^2)$. Frischknecht et al. constructed a worst case graph which takes $\Omega(n^2/\log^2 n)$ rounds to stabilize [FKW13]. Keller et al. generalized this results in [KPW14], showing that a graph with symmetric edge weights stabilizes in $O(W(G))$, where $W(G)$ is the sum of edge weights in graph G. They also constructed a weighted graph with exponential stabilization time. Closely related to this puzzle is the well known Game of Life which was described by the mathematician John Conway and made popular by Martin Gardner [Gar70]. In the Game of Life cells can be either dead or alive and change their states according to the number of alive neighbors.

Bibliography

[APSV91] Baruch Awerbuch, Boaz Patt-Shamir, and George Varghese. Self-Stabilization By Local Checking and Correction. In *In Proceedings of IEEE Symposium on Foundations of Computer Science (FOCS)*, 1991.

[Dij74] Edsger W. Dijkstra. Self-stabilizing systems in spite of distributed control. *Communications of the ACM*, 17(11):943–644, November 1974.

[FKW13] Silvio Frischknecht, Barbara Keller, and Roger Wattenhofer. Convergence in (Social) Influence Networks. In *27th International Symposium on Distributed Computing (DISC), Jerusalem, Israel*, October 2013.

[Gar70] M. Gardner. Mathematical Games: The fantastic combinations of John Conway's new solitaire game Life. *Scientific American*, 223:120–123, October 1970.

[GO80] E. Goles and J. Olivos. Periodic behavior of generalized threshold functions. *Discrete Mathematics*, 30:187–189, 1980.

[KPW14] Barbara Keller, David Peleg, and Roger Wattenhofer. How even Tiny Influence can have a Big Impact! In *7th International Conference on Fun with Algorithms (FUN), Lipari Island, Italy*, July 2014.

[Win08] P. Winkler. Puzzled. *Communications of the ACM*, 51(9):103–103, August 2008.

Chapter 12

Social Networks

Distributed computing is applicable in various contexts. This lecture exemplarily studies one of these contexts, social networks, an area of study whose origins date back a century. To give you a first impression, consider Figure 12.1.

12.1 Small World Networks

Back in 1929, Frigyes Karinthy published a volume of short stories that postulated that the world was "shrinking" because human beings were connected more and more. Some claim that he was inspired by radio network pioneer Guglielmo Marconi's 1909 Nobel Prize speech. Despite physical distance, the growing density of human "networks" renders the actual social distance smaller and smaller. As a result, it is believed that any two individuals can be connected through at most five (or so) acquaintances, i.e., within six hops.

The topic was hot in the 1960s. For instance, in 1964, Marshall McLuhan coined the metaphor "Global Village". He wrote: "As electrically contracted, the globe is no more than a village". He argues that due to the almost instantaneous reaction times of new ("electric") technologies, each individual inevitably feels the consequences of his actions and thus automatically deeply participates in the global society. McLuhan understood what we now can directly observe – real and virtual world are moving together. He realized that the transmission medium, rather than the transmitted information is at the core of change, as expressed by his famous phrase

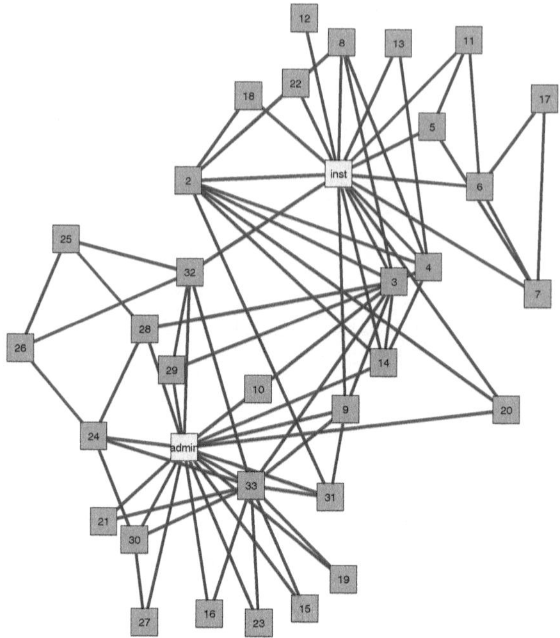

Figure 12.1: This graph shows the social relations between the members of a karate club, studied by anthropologist Wayne Zachary in the 1970s. Two people (nodes) stand out, the instructor and the administrator of the club, both happen to have many friends among club members. At some point, a dispute caused the club to split into two. Can you predict how the club partitioned? (If not, just search the Internet for Zachary and Karate.)

"the medium is the message".

This idea has been followed ardently in the 1960s by several sociologists, first by Michael Gurevich, later by Stanley Milgram. Milgram wanted to know the average path length between two "random" humans, by using various experiments, generally using randomly chosen individuals from the US Midwest as starting points, and a stockbroker living in a suburb of Boston as target. The starting points were given name, address, occupation, plus some personal information about the target. They were asked to send a letter to the target. However, they were not allowed to *directly* send the letter, rather, they had to pass it to somebody they knew on first-name basis and that they thought to have a higher probability to know the target person. This process was repeated, until somebody knew the target person, and could deliver the letter. Shortly after starting the experiment, letters have been received. Most letters were lost during the process, but if they arrived, the average path length was about 5.5. The observation that the entire population is connected by short acquaintance chains got later popularized by the terms "six degrees of separation" and "small world".

Statisticians tried to explain Milgram's experiments, by essentially giving network models that allowed for short diameters, i.e., each node is connected to each other node by only a few hops. Until today there is a thriving research community in statistical physics that tries to understand network properties that allow for "small world" effects.

The world is often fascinated by graphs with a small radius. For example, movie fanatics study the who-acted-with-whom-in-the-same-movie graph. For this graph it has long been believed that the actor Kevin Bacon has a particularly small radius. The number of hops from Bacon even got a name, the Bacon Number. In the meantime, however, it has been shown that there are "better" centers in the Hollywood universe, such as Sean Connery, Christopher Lee, Rod Steiger, Gene Hackman, or Michael Caine. The center of other social networks has also been explored, Paul Erdös for instance is well known in the math community.

One of the keywords in this area are power-law graphs, networks where node degrees are distributed according to a power-law distribution, i.e., the number of nodes with degree δ is proportional to $\delta^{-\alpha}$, for some $\alpha > 1$. Such power-law graphs have been witnessed in many application areas, apart from social networks also in the web, or in biology or physics.

Obviously, two power-law graphs might look and behave completely differently, even if α and the number of edges is exactly the same.

One well-known model towards this end is the Watts-Strogatz model. Watts and Strogatz argued that social networks should be modeled by a combination of two networks: As the basis we take a network that has a large cluster coefficient ...

Definition 12.2. *The cluster coefficient of a network is defined by the probability that two friends of a node are likely to be friends as well, averaged over all the nodes.*

..., then we augment such a graph with random links, every

node for instance points to a constant number of other nodes, chosen uniformly at random. This augmentation represents acquaintances that connect nodes to parts of the network that would otherwise be far away.

Remarks:

- Without further information, knowing the cluster coefficient is of questionable value: Assume we arrange the nodes in a grid. Technically, if we connect each node to its four closest neighbors, the graph has cluster coefficient 0, since there are no triangles; if we instead connect each node with its eight closest neighbors, the cluster coefficient is $3/7$. The cluster coefficient is quite different, even though both networks have similar characteristics.

This is interesting, but not enough to really understand what is going on. For Milgram's experiments to work, it is not sufficient to connect the nodes in a certain way. In addition, the nodes *themselves* need to know how to forward a message to one of their neighbors, even though they cannot know whether that neighbor is really closer to the target. In other words, nodes are not just following physical laws, but they make decisions themselves.

Let us consider an artificial network with nodes on a grid topology, plus some additional random links per node. In a quantitative study it was shown that the random links need a specific distance distribution to allow for efficient greedy routing. This distribution marks the sweet spot for any navigable network.

Definition 12.4 (Augmented Grid). *We take $n = m^2$ nodes $(i, j) \in V = \{1, \ldots, m\}^2$ that are identified with the lattice points on an $m \times m$ grid. We define the distance between two nodes (i, j) and (k, ℓ) as $d((i, j), (k, \ell)) = |k-i|+|\ell-j|$ as the distance between them on the $m \times m$ lattice. The network is modeled using a parameter $\alpha \geq 0$. Each node u has a directed edge to every lattice neighbor. These are the **local contacts** of a node. In addition, each node also has an additional random link (the **long-range contact**). For all u and v, the long-range contact of u points to node v with probability proportional to $d(u, v)^{-\alpha}$, i.e., with probability $d(u, v)^{-\alpha} / \sum_{w \in V \setminus \{u\}} d(u, w)^{-\alpha}$. Figure 12.3 illustrates the model.*

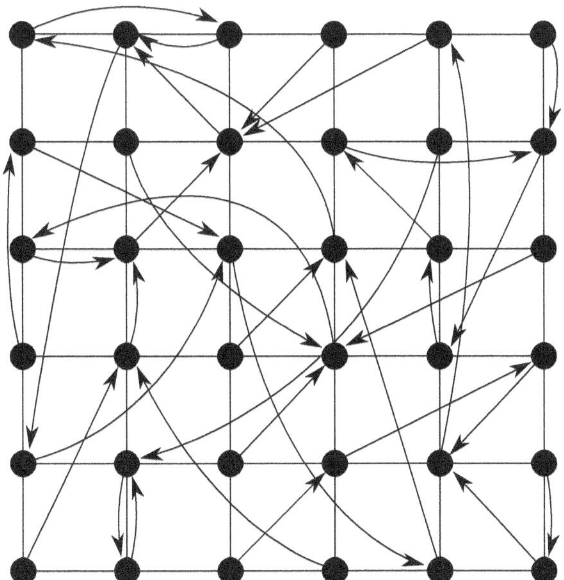

Figure 12.3: Augmented grid with $m = 6$

Remarks:

- The network model has the following geographic interpretation: nodes (individuals) live on a grid and know their neighbors on the grid. Further, each node has some additional acquaintances throughout the network.

- The parameter α controls how the additional neighbors are distributed across the grid. If $\alpha = 0$, long-range contacts are chosen uniformly at random (as in the Watts-Strogatz model). As α increases, long-range contacts become shorter on average. In the extreme case, if $\alpha \to \infty$, all long-range contacts are to immediate neighbors on the grid.

- It can be shown that as long as $\alpha \leq 2$, the diameter of the resulting graph is polylogarithmic in n (polynomial in $\log n$) with high probability. In particular, if the long-range contacts are chosen uniformly at random ($\alpha = 0$), the diameter is $O(\log n)$.

Since the augmented grid contains random links, we do not know anything for sure about how the random links are distributed. In theory, all links could point to the same node! However, this is almost certainly not the case. Formally this is captured by the term *with high probability* that we have already seen in Definition 7.16.

Definition 12.5 (With High Probability). *Some probabilistic event is said to occur **with high probability (w.h.p.)**, if it happens with a probability $p \geq 1 - 1/n^c$, where c is a constant. The constant c may be chosen arbitrarily, but it is considered constant with respect to Big-O notation.*

Remarks:

- For instance, a running time bound of $c \log n$ or $e^{c!} \log n +$ $5000c$ with probability at least $1 - 1/n^c$ would be $O(\log n)$ w.h.p., but a running time of n^c would not be $O(n)$ w.h.p. since c might also be 50.

- This definition is very powerful, as any polynomial (in n) number of statements that hold w.h.p. also holds w.h.p. at the same time, regardless of any dependencies between random variables!

Theorem 12.6. *The diameter of the augmented grid with $\alpha = 0$ is $O(\log n)$ with high probability.*

Proof Sketch. For simplicity, we will only show that we can reach a target node t starting from some source node s. However, it can be shown that (essentially) each of the intermediate claims holds with high probability, which then by means of the union bound yields that *all* of the claims hold simultaneously with high probability for *all* pairs of nodes (see exercises).

Let N_s be the $\lceil \log n \rceil$-hop neighborhood of source s on the grid, containing $\Omega(\log^2 n)$ nodes. Each of the nodes in N_s has a random link, probably leading to distant parts of the graph. As long as we have reached only $o(n)$ nodes, any new random link will with probability $1 - o(1)$ lead to a node for which none of its grid neighbors has been visited yet. Thus, in expectation we find almost $|N_s|$ new nodes whose neighbors are "fresh". Using their grid links, we will reach $(4 - o(1))|N_s|$ more nodes within one more hop. If bad luck strikes, it could still happen that many of these links lead to a few nodes, already visited nodes, or nodes that are very close to each other. But that is very unlikely, as we have lots of random choices! Indeed, it can be shown that not only in expectation, but with high probability $(5 - o(1))|N_s|$ many nodes are reached this way (see exercises).

Because all the new nodes have (so far unused) random links, we can repeat this reasoning inductively, implying that the number of nodes grows by (at least) a constant factor for every two hops. Thus, after $O(\log n)$ hops, we will have reached $n/\log n$ nodes (which is still small compared to n). Finally, consider the expected number of links from these nodes that enter the $(\log n)$-neighborhood of some target node t with respect to the grid. Since this neighborhood consists of $\Omega(\log^2 n)$ nodes, in expectation $\Omega(\log n)$ links come close enough to target t. This is large enough to almost guarantee that this happens (see exercises). Summing everything up, we still used merely $O(\log n)$ hops in total to get from s to t.

$\square$

This shows that for $\alpha = 0$ (and in fact for all $\alpha \leq 2$), the resulting network has a small diameter. Recall however that we also wanted the network to be navigable. For this, we consider a simple greedy routing strategy (Algorithm 12.7).

Algorithm 12.7 Greedy Routing

1: **while** not at destination **do**
2:     go to a neighbor which is closest to destination (considering grid distance only)
3: **end while**

Lemma 12.8. *In the augmented grid, Algorithm 12.7 finds a routing path of length at most $2(m - 1) \in O(\sqrt{n})$.*

Proof. Because of the grid, there is always a neighbor which is closer to the destination. Since with each hop we reduce the distance to the target at least by one in one of the two grid dimensions, we will reach the destination within $2(m - 1)$ steps. $\square$

This is not really what Milgram's experiment promises. We want to know how much the additional random links speed up the process. To this end, we first need to understand how likely it is that the random link of node u points to node v, in terms of their grid distance $d(u, v)$, the number of nodes n, and the constant parameter α.

Lemma 12.9. *Node u's random link points to a node v with probability*

- $\Theta(1/(d(u,v)^\alpha m^{2-\alpha}))$ *if $\alpha < 2$.*

- $\Theta(1/(d(u,v)^2 \log n))$ *if $\alpha = 2$,*

- $\Theta(1/d(u,v)^\alpha)$ *if $\alpha > 2$.*

Moreover, if $\alpha > 2$, the probability to see a link of length at least d is in $\Theta(1/d^{\alpha-2})$.

Proof. For a constant $\alpha \neq 2$, we have that

$$\sum_{w \in V \setminus \{u\}} \frac{1}{d(u,w)^\alpha} \in \sum_{r=1}^{m} \frac{\Theta(r)}{r^\alpha} = \Theta\left(\int_{r=1}^{m} \frac{1}{r^{\alpha-1}}\, dr\right)$$

$$= \Theta\left(\left[\frac{r^{2-\alpha}}{2-\alpha}\right]_1^m\right).$$

If $\alpha < 2$, this gives $\Theta(m^{2-\alpha})$, if $\alpha > 2$, it is in $\Theta(1)$. If $\alpha = 2$, we get

$$\sum_{w \in V \setminus \{u\}} \frac{1}{d(u,w)^\alpha} \in \sum_{r=1}^{m} \frac{\Theta(r)}{r^2} = \Theta(1)\cdot\sum_{r=1}^{m} \frac{1}{r} = \Theta(\log m) = \Theta(\log n).$$

Multiplying with $d(u,v)^\alpha$ yields the first three bounds. For the last statement, compute

$$\sum_{\substack{v \in V \\ d(u,v) \geq d}} \Theta(1/d(u,v)^\alpha) = \Theta\left(\int_{r=d}^{m} \frac{r}{r^\alpha}\, dr\right)$$

$$= \Theta\left(\left[\frac{r^{2-\alpha}}{2-\alpha}\right]_d^m\right) = \Theta(1/d^{\alpha-2}).$$

$\square$

Remarks:

- If $\alpha > 2$, according to the lemma, the probability to see a random link of length at least $d = m^{1/(\alpha-1)}$ is $\Theta(1/d^{\alpha-2}) = \Theta(1/m^{(\alpha-2)/(\alpha-1)})$. In expectation we have to take $\Theta(m^{(\alpha-2)/(\alpha-1)})$ hops until we see a random link of length at least d. When just following links of length less than d, it takes more than $m/d = m/m^{1/(\alpha-1)} = m^{(\alpha-2)/(\alpha-1)}$ hops. In other words, in expectation, either way we need at least $m^{(\alpha-2)/(\alpha-1)} = m^{\Omega(1)}$ hops to the destination.

- If $\alpha < 2$, there is a (slightly more complicated) argument. First we draw a border around the nodes in distance $m^{(2-\alpha)/3}$ to the target. Within this border there are about $m^{2(2-\alpha)/3}$ many nodes in the target area. Assume that the source is outside the target area. Starting at the source, the probability to find a random link that leads directly inside the target area is according to the lemma at most $m^{2(2-\alpha)/3} \cdot \Theta(1/m^{2-\alpha})) = \Theta(1/m^{(2-\alpha)/3})$. In other words, until we find a random link that leads into the target area, in expectation, we have to do $\Theta(m^{(2-\alpha)/3})$ hops. This is too slow, and our greedy strategy is probably faster, as thanks to having $\alpha < 2$ there are many long-range links. However, it means that we will probably enter the border of the target area on a regular grid link. Once inside the target area, again the probability of short-cutting our trip by a random long-range link is $\Theta(1/m^{(2-\alpha)/3})$, so we probably just follow grid links, $m^{(2-\alpha)/3} = m^{\Omega(1)}$ many of them.

- In summary, if $\alpha \neq 2$, our greedy routing algorithm takes $m^{\Omega(1)} = n^{\Omega(1)}$ expected hops to reach the destination. This is polynomial in the number of nodes n, and the social network can hardly be called a "small world".

- Maybe we can get a polylogarithmic bound on n if we set $\alpha = 2$?

Definition 12.10 (Phase). *Consider routing from source s to target t and assume that we are at some intermediate node w. We say that we are in phase j at node w if the lattice distance $d(w, t)$ to the target node t is between $2^j < d(w, t) \leq 2^{j+1}$.*

Remarks:

- Enumerating the phases in decreasing order is useful, as notation becomes less cumbersome.

- There are $\lceil \log m \rceil \in O(\log n)$ phases.

Lemma 12.11. *Assume that we are in phase j at node w when routing from s to t. The probability for getting (at least) to phase $j - 1$ in one step is at least $\Omega(1/\log n)$.*

Proof. Let B_j be the set of nodes x with $d(x, t) \leq 2^j$. We get from phase j to (at least) phase $j - 1$ if the long-range contact of node w points to some node in B_j. Note that we always make progress while following the greedy routing path. Therefore, we have not seen node w before and the long-range contact of w points to a random node that is independent of anything seen on the path from s to w.

For all nodes $x \in B_j$, we have $d(w, x) \leq d(w, t) + d(x, t) \leq 2^{j+1} + 2^j < 2^{j+2}$. Hence, for each node $x \in B_j$, the probability that the long-range contact of w points to x is $\Omega(1/2^{2j+4} \log n)$. Further, the number of nodes in B_j is at least $(2^j)^2/2 = 2^{2j-1}$. Hence, the probability that some node in B_j is the long range contact of w is at least

$$\Omega\left(|B_j| \cdot \frac{1}{2^{2j+4} \log n}\right) = \Omega\left(\frac{2^{2j-1}}{2^{2j+4} \log n}\right) = \Omega\left(\frac{1}{\log n}\right). \qquad \square$$

Theorem 12.12. *Consider the greedy routing path from a node s to a node t on an augmented grid with parameter $\alpha = 2$. The expected length of the path is $O(\log^2 n)$.*

Proof. We already observed that the total number of phases is $O(\log n)$ (the distance to the target is halved when we go from phase j to phase $j - 1$). At each point during the routing process, the probability of proceeding to the next phase is at least $\Omega(1/\log n)$. Let X_j be the number of steps in phase j. Because the probability for ending the phase is $\Omega(1/\log n)$ in each step, in expectation we need $O(\log n)$ steps to proceed to the next phase, i.e., $\mathbb{E}[X_j] \in O(\log n)$. Let $X = \sum_j X_j$ be the total number of steps of the routing process. By linearity of expectation, we have

$$\mathbb{E}[X] = \sum_j \mathbb{E}[X_j] \in O(\log^2 n). \qquad \square$$

Remarks:

- One can show that the $O(\log^2 n)$ result also holds w.h.p.

- In real world social networks, the parameter α was evaluated experimentally. The assumption is that you are connected to the geographically closest nodes, and then have some random long-range contacts. For Facebook grandpa LiveJournal it was shown that α is not really 2, but rather around 1.25.

12.2 Propagation Studies

In networks, nodes may influence each other's behavior and decisions. There are many applications where nodes influence their neighbors, e.g., they may impact their opinions, or they may bias what products they buy, or they may pass on a disease.

On a beach (modeled as a line segment), it is best to place an ice cream stand right in the middle of the segment, because you will be able to "control" the beach most easily. What about the second stand, where should it settle? The answer generally depends on the model, but assuming that people will buy ice cream from the stand that is closer, it should go right next to the first stand.

Rumors can spread surprisingly fast through social networks. Traditionally this happens by word of mouth, but with the emergence of the Internet and its possibilities new ways of rumor propagation are available. People write email, use instant messengers or publish their thoughts in a blog. Many factors influence the dissemination of rumors. It is especially important where in a network a rumor is initiated and how convincing it is. Furthermore the underlying network structure decides how fast the information can spread and how many people are reached. More generally, we can speak of diffusion of information in networks. The analysis of these diffusion processes can be useful for viral marketing, e.g., to target a few influential people to initiate marketing campaigns. A company may wish to distribute the rumor of a new product via the most influential individuals in popular social networks such as Facebook. A second company might want to introduce a competing product and has hence to select where to seed the information to be disseminated. Rumor spreading is quite similar to our ice cream stand problem.

More formally, we may study propagation problems in graphs. Given a graph, and two players. Let the first player choose a seed node u_1; afterwards let the second player choose a seed node u_2, with $u_2 \neq u_1$. The goal of the game is to maximize the number of nodes that are closer to one's own seed node.

In many graphs it is an advantage to choose first. In a star graph for instance the first player can choose the center node of the star, controlling all but one node. In some other graphs, the second player can at least score even. But is there a graph where the second player has an advantage?

Theorem 12.13. *In a two player rumor game where both players select one node to initiate their rumor in the graph, the first player does not always win.*

Proof. See Figure 12.14 for an example where the second player will always win, regardless of the decision the first player. If the first player chooses the node x_0 in the center, the second player can select x_1. Choice x_1 will be outwitted by x_2, and x_2 itself can be answered by z_1. All other strategies are either symmetric, or even less promising for the first player. $\square$

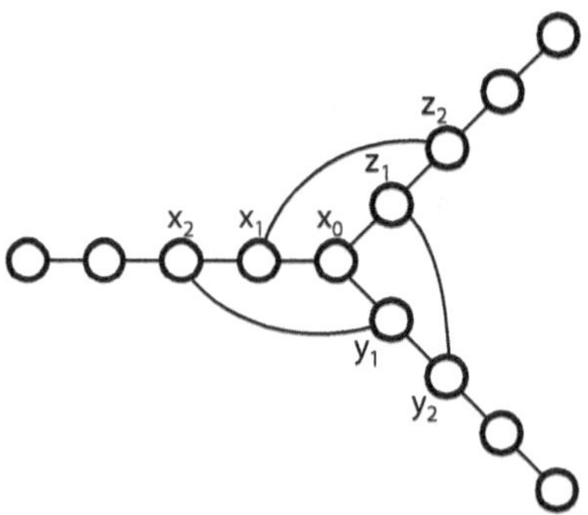

Figure 12.14: Counter example.

Chapter Notes

A simple form of a social network is the famous stable marriage problem [DS62] in which a stable matching bipartite graph has to be found. There exists a great many of variations which are based on this initial problem, e.g., [KC82, KMV94, EO06, FKPS10, Hoe11]. Social networks like Facebook, Twitter and others have grown very fast in the last years and hence spurred interest to research them. How users influence other users has been studied both from a theoretical point of view [KKT03] and in practice [CHBG10]. The structure of these networks can be measured and studied [MMG+07]. More than half of the users in social networks share more information than they expect to [LGKM11].

The small world phenomenon that we presented in this chapter is analyzed by Kleinberg [Kle00]. A general overview is in [DJ10].

Bibliography

[CHBG10] Meeyoung Cha, Hamed Haddadi, Fabrício Benevenuto, and P. Krishna Gummadi. Measuring User Influence in Twitter: The Million Follower Fallacy. In *ICWSM*, 2010.

[DJ10] Easley David and Kleinberg Jon. *Networks, Crowds, and Markets: Reasoning About a Highly Connected World*. Cambridge University Press, New York, NY, USA, 2010.

[DS62] D. Gale and L.S. Shapley. College Admission and the Stability of Marriage. *American Mathematical Monthly*, 69(1):9–15, 1962.

[EO06] Federico Echenique and Jorge Oviedo. A theory of stability in many-to-many matching markets. *Theoretical Economics*, 1(2):233–273, 2006.

[FKPS10] Patrik Floréen, Petteri Kaski, Valentin Polishchuk, and Jukka Suomela. Almost Stable Matchings by Truncating the Gale-Shapley Algorithm. *Algorithmica*, 58(1):102–118, 2010.

[Hoe11] Martin Hoefer. Local Matching Dynamics in Social Networks. *Automata Languages and Programming*, pages 113–124, 2011.

[Kar29] Frigyes Karinthy. Chain-Links, 1929.

[KC82] Alexander S. Kelso and Vincent P. Crawford. Job Matching, Coalition Formation, and Gross Substitutes. *Econometrica*, 50(6):1483–1504, 1982.

[KKT03] David Kempe, Jon M. Kleinberg, and Éva Tardos. Maximizing the spread of influence through a social network. In *KDD*, 2003.

[Kle00] Jon M. Kleinberg. The small-world phenomenon: an algorithm perspective. In *STOC*, 2000.

[KMV94] Samir Khuller, Stephen G. Mitchell, and Vijay V. Vazirani. On-line algorithms for weighted bipartite matching and stable marriages. *Theoretical Computer Science*, 127:255–267, May 1994.

[LGKM11] Yabing Liu, Krishna P. Gummadi, Balanchander Krishnamurthy, and Alan Mislove. Analyzing Facebook privacy settings: User expectations vs. reality. In *Proceedings of the 11th ACM/USENIX Internet Measurement Conference (IMC'11)*, Berlin, Germany, November 2011.

[McL64] Marshall McLuhan. *Understanding media: The extensions of man*. McGraw-Hill, New York, 1964.

[Mil67] Stanley Milgram. The Small World Problem. *Psychology Today*, 2:60–67, 1967.

[MMG+07] Alan Mislove, Massimiliano Marcon, P. Krishna Gummadi, Peter Druschel, and Bobby Bhattacharjee. Measurement and analysis of online social networks. In *Internet Measurement Comference*, 2007.

[WS98] Duncan J. Watts and Steven H. Strogatz. Collective dynamics of "small-world" networks. *Nature*, 393(6684):440–442, Jun 1998.

[Zac77] W W Zachary. An information flow model for conflict and fission in small groups. *Journal of Anthropological Research*, 33(4):452–473, 1977.

Chapter 13

Wireless Protocols

Wireless communication was one of the major success stories of the last decades. Today, different wireless standards such as wireless local area networks (WLAN) are omnipresent. In some sense, from a distributed computing viewpoint wireless networks are quite simple, as they cannot form arbitrary network topologies. Simplistic models of wireless networks include geometric graph models such as the so-called unit disk graph. Modern models are more robust: The network graph is restricted, e.g., the total number of neighbors of a node which are not adjacent is likely to be small. This observation is hard to capture with purely geometric models, and motivates more advanced network connectivity models such as bounded growth or bounded independence.

However, on the other hand, wireless communication is also more difficult than standard message passing, as for instance nodes are not able to transmit a different message to each neighbor at the same time. And if two neighbors are transmitting at the same time, they interfere, and a node may not be able to decipher anything.

In this chapter we deal with the distributed computing principles of wireless communication: We make the simplifying assumption that all n nodes are in the communication range of each other, i.e., the network graph is a clique. Nodes share a synchronous time, in each time slot a node can decide to either transmit or receive (or sleep). However, two or more nodes transmitting in the same time slot will cause interference. Transmitting nodes are never aware if there is interference because they cannot simultaneously transmit and receive.

13.1 Basics

The basic communication protocol in wireless networks is the medium access control (MAC) protocol. Unfortunately it is difficult to claim that one MAC protocol is better than another, because it all depends on the parameters, such as the network topology, the channel characteristics, or the traffic pattern. When it comes to the principles of wireless protocols, we usually want to achieve much simpler goals. One basic and important question is the following: How long does it take until one node can transmit successfully, without interference? This question is often called the wireless leader election problem, with the node transmitting alone being the leader.

Clearly, we can use node IDs to solve leader election, e.g., a node with ID i transmits in time slot i. However, this may be incredibly slow. There are better deterministic solutions, but by and large the best and simplest algorithms are randomized.

Throughout this chapter, we use a random variable X to denote the number of nodes transmitting in a given slot.

Algorithm 13.1 Slotted Aloha

1: **Every node** v executes the following code:
2: **repeat**
3:    transmit with probability $1/n$
4: **until** one node has transmitted alone

Theorem 13.2. *Using Algorithm 13.1 allows one node to transmit alone (become a leader) after expected time e.*

Proof. The probability for success, i.e., only one node transmitting is

$$Pr[X = 1] = n \cdot \frac{1}{n} \cdot \left(1 - \frac{1}{n}\right)^{n-1} \approx \frac{1}{e},$$

where the last approximation is a result from Theorem 13.29 for sufficiently large n. Hence, if we repeat this process e times, we can expect one success.

$\square$

Remarks:

- The origin of the name is the ALOHAnet which was developed at the University of Hawaii.

- How does the leader know that it is the leader? One simple solution is a "distributed acknowledgment". The nodes just continue Algorithm 13.1, including the ID of the the leader in their transmission. So the leader learns that it is the leader.

- One more problem?! Indeed, node v which managed to transmit the acknowledgment (alone) is the only remaining node which does not know that the leader knows that it is the leader. We can fix this by having the leader acknowledge v's successful acknowledgment.

- One can also imagine an unslotted time model. In this model two messages which overlap partially will interfere and no message is received. As everything in this chapter, Algorithm 13.1 also works in an unslotted time model, with a factor 2 penalty, i.e., the probability for a successful transmission will drop from $\frac{1}{e}$ to $\frac{1}{2e}$. Essentially, each slot is divided into t small time slots with $t \to \infty$ and the nodes start a new t-slot long transmission with probability $\frac{1}{2nt}$.

13.2 Non-Uniform Initialization

Sometimes we want the n nodes to have the IDs $\{1, 2, \ldots, n\}$. This process is called initialization. Initialization can for instance be used to allow the nodes to transmit one by one without any interference.

Theorem 13.3. *If the nodes know n, we can initialize them in $O(n)$ time slots.*

Proof. We repeatedly elect a leader using e.g., Algorithm 13.1. The leader gets the next free number and afterwards leaves the process. We know that this works with probability $1/e$. The expected time to finish is hence $e \cdot n$.

$\square$

Remarks:

- But this algorithm requires that the nodes know n in order to give them IDs from $1, \ldots, n$! For a more realistic scenario we need a uniform algorithm, i.e, the nodes do not know n.

13.3   Uniform Initialization with CD

Definition 13.4 (Collision Detection, CD)**.** *Two or more nodes transmitting concurrently is called interference. In a system with collision detection, a* **receiver** *can distinguish interference from nobody transmitting. In a system without collision detection, a receiver cannot distinguish the two cases.*

The main idea of the algorithm is to partition nodes iteratively into sets. Each set is identified by a label (a bitstring), and by storing one such bitstring, each node knows in which set it currently is. Initially, all nodes are in a single set, identified by the empty bitstring. This set is then partitioned into two *non-empty* sets, identified by '0' and '1'. In the same way, all sets are iteratively partitioned into two non-empty sets, as long as a set contains more than one node. If a set contains only a single node, this node receives the next free ID. The algorithm terminates once every node is alone in its set. Note that this partitioning process iteratively creates a binary tree which has exactly one node in the set at each leaf, and thus has n leaves.

Algorithm 13.5 Initialization with Collision Detection

1: **Every node** v executes the following code:
2: $nextId := 0$
3: $myBitstring :=$ ''   ◁ initialize to empty string
4: $bitstringsToSplit := ['']$ ◁ a queue with sets to split

5: **while** $bitstringsToSplit$ is not empty **do**
6:    $b := bitstringsToSplit.\text{pop}()$

7:    **repeat**
8:       **if** $b = myBitstring$ **then**
9:          choose r uniformly at random from $\{0, 1\}$
10:          in the next two time slots:
11:          transmit in slot r, and listen in other slot
12:       **else**
13:          it is not my bitstring, just listen in both slots
14:       **end if**
15:    **until** there was at least 1 transmission in both slots
16:    **if** $b = myBitstring$ **then**
17:       $myBitstring := myBitstring + r$ ◁ append bit r
18:    **end if**

19:    **for** $r \in \{0, 1\}$ **do**
20:       **if** some node u transmitted alone in slot r **then**
21:          node u becomes ID $nextId$ and becomes passive
22:          $nextId := nextId + 1$
23:       **else**
24:          $bitstringsToSplit.\text{push}(b + r)$
25:       **end if**
26:    **end for**
27: **end while**

Remarks:

- In Line 20 a transmitting node needs to know whether it was the only one transmitting. This is achievable in several ways, for instance by adding an acknowledgement round. To notify a node v that it has transmitted alone in round r, every node that was silent in round r sends an acknowledgement in round $r + 1$, while v is silent. If v hears a message or interference in $r + 1$, it knows that it transmitted alone in round r.

Theorem 13.6. *Algorithm 13.5 correctly initializes n nodes in expected time $O(n)$.*

Proof. A successful split is defined as a split in which both subsets are non-empty. We know that there are exactly $n - 1$ successful splits because we have a binary tree with n leaves and $n - 1$ inner nodes. Let us now calculate the probability for creating two non-empty sets from a set of size $k \geq 2$ as

$$Pr[1 \leq X \leq k-1] = 1 - Pr[X = 0] - Pr[X = k] = 1 - \frac{1}{2^k} - \frac{1}{2^k} \geq \frac{1}{2}.$$

Thus, in expectation we need $O(n)$ splits. $\qquad\square$

Remarks:

- What if we do not have collision detection?

13.4 Uniform Initialization without CD

Let us assume that we have a special node ℓ (leader) and let S denote the set of nodes which want to transmit. We now split every time slot from Algorithm 13.5 into two time slots and use the leader to help us distinguish between silence and noise. In the first slot every node from the set S transmits, in the second slot the nodes in $S \cup \{\ell\}$ transmit. This gives the nodes sufficient information to distinguish the different cases (see Table 13.7).

	nodes in S transmit	nodes in $S \cup \{\ell\}$ transmit
$\|S\| = 0$	✗	✔
$\|S\| = 1, S = \{\ell\}$	✔	✔
$\|S\| = 1, S \neq \{\ell\}$	✔	✗
$\|S\| \geq 2$	✗	✗

Table 13.7: Using a leader to distinguish between noise and silence: ✗ represents noise/silence, ✔ represents a successful transmission.

Remarks:

- As such, Algorithm 13.5 works also without CD, with only a factor 2 overhead.

- More generally, a leader immediately brings CD to any protocol.

- This protocol has an important real life application, for instance when checking out a shopping cart with items which have RFID tags.

- But how do we determine such a leader? And how long does it take until we are "sure" that we have one? Let us repeat the notion of *with high probability*.

13.5 Leader Election

Definition 13.8 (With High Probability). *See also Definition 7.16. Some probabilistic event is said to occur **with high probability** (**w.h.p.**), if it happens with a probability $p \geq 1 - 1/n^c$, where c is a constant. The constant c may be chosen arbitrarily, but it is considered constant with respect to Big-O notation.*

Theorem 13.9. *Algorithm 13.1 elects a leader w.h.p. in $O(\log n)$ time slots.*

Proof. The probability for not electing a leader after $c \cdot \log n$ time slots, i.e., $c \log n$ slots without a successful transmission is

$$\left(1 - \frac{1}{e}\right)^{c \ln n} = \left(1 - \frac{1}{e}\right)^{e \cdot c' \ln n} \leq \frac{1}{e^{\ln n \cdot c'}} = \frac{1}{n^{c'}}.$$

$\square$

Remarks:

- What about uniform algorithms, i.e. the number of nodes n is not known?

Theorem 13.11. *By using Algorithm 13.10 it is possible to elect a leader w.h.p. in $O(\log^2 n)$ time slots if n is not known.*

Algorithm 13.10 Uniform leader election

1: **Every node** v executes the following code:
2: **for** $k = 1, 2, 3, \ldots$ **do**
3:　　**for** $i = 1$ **to** ck **do**
4:　　　　transmit with probability $p := 1/2^k$
5:　　　　**if** node v was the only node which transmitted **then**
6:　　　　　v becomes the leader
7:　　　　　**break**
8:　　　　**end if**
9:　　**end for**
10: **end for**

Proof. Let us briefly describe the algorithm. The nodes transmit with probability $p = 2^{-k}$ for ck time slots for $k = 1, 2, \ldots$. At first p will be too high and hence there will be a lot of interference. But after $\log n$ phases, we have $k \approx \log n$ and thus the nodes transmit with probability $\approx \frac{1}{n}$. For simplicity's sake, let us assume that n is a power of 2. Using the approach outlined above, we know that after $\log n$ iterations, we have $p = \frac{1}{n}$. Theorem 13.9 yields that we can elect a leader w.h.p. in $O(\log n)$ slots. Since we have to try $\log n$ estimates until $k \approx n$, the total runtime is $O(\log^2 n)$. □

Remarks:

- Note that our proposed algorithm has not used collision detection. Can we solve leader election faster in a uniform setting with collision detection?

13.6　Fast Leader Election with CD

Algorithm 13.12 Uniform leader election with CD

1: **Every node** v executes the following code:
2: **repeat**
3:　　transmit with probability $\frac{1}{2}$
4:　　**if** at least one node transmitted **then**
5:　　　all nodes that did not transmit quit the protocol
6:　　**end if**
7: **until** one node transmits alone

Theorem 13.13. *With collision detection we can elect a leader using Algorithm 13.12 w.h.p. in $O(\log n)$ time slots.*

Proof. The number of active nodes k is monotonically decreasing and always greater than 1 which yields the correctness. A slot is called successful if at most half the active nodes transmit. We can assume that $k \geq 2$ since otherwise we would have already elected a leader. We can calculate the probability that a time slot is successful as

$$Pr\left[1 \leq X \leq \left\lceil \frac{k}{2} \right\rceil\right] = P\left[X \leq \left\lceil \frac{k}{2} \right\rceil\right] - Pr[X = 0] \geq \frac{1}{2} - \frac{1}{2^k} \geq \frac{1}{4}.$$

Since the number of active nodes at least halves in every successful time slot, $\log n$ successful time slots are sufficient to elect a leader. Now let Y be a random variable which counts the number of successful time slots after $8 \cdot c \cdot \log n$ time slots. The expected value is $E[Y] \geq 8 \cdot c \cdot \log n \cdot \frac{1}{4} \geq 2 \cdot c \cdot \log n$. Since all those time slots are independent from each other, we can apply a Chernoff bound (see Theorem 13.28) with $\delta = \frac{1}{2}$ which states

$$Pr[Y < (1 - \delta)E[Y]] \leq e^{-\frac{\delta^2}{2}E[Y]} \leq e^{-\frac{1}{8} \cdot 2c \log n} \leq n^{-\alpha}$$

for any constant α.

$\square$

Remarks:

- Can we be even faster?

- Let us first briefly describe an algorithm for this.

- In the first phase the nodes transmit with probability $1/2^{2^0}, 1/2^{2^1}, 1/2^{2^2}, \ldots$ until no node transmits. This yields a first approximation on the number of nodes.

- Afterwards, a binary search is performed to determine an even better approximation of n.

- Finally, the third phase finds a constant approximation of n using a biased random walk. The algorithm stops in any case as soon as only one node is transmitting, which will become the leader.

Lemma 13.15. *If $j > \log n + \log \log n$, then $Pr[X > 1] \leq \frac{1}{\log n}$.*

Algorithm 13.14 Fast uniform leader election

1: $i := 1$
2: **repeat**
3:    $i := 2 \cdot i$
4:    transmit with probability $1/2^i$
5: **until** no node transmitted
  {End of Phase 1}
6: $l := i/2$
7: $u := i$
8: **while** $l + 1 < u$ **do**
9:    $j := \lceil \frac{l+u}{2} \rceil$
10:    transmit with probability $1/2^j$
11:    **if** no node transmitted **then**
12:      $u := j$
13:    **else**
14:      $l := j$
15:    **end if**
16: **end while**
  {End of Phase 2}
17: $k := u$
18: **repeat**
19:    transmit with probability $1/2^k$
20:    **if** no node transmitted **then**
21:      $k := k - 1$
22:    **else**
23:      $k := k + 1$
24:    **end if**
25: **until** exactly one node transmitted

Proof. The nodes transmit with probability $1/2^j < 1/2^{\log n + \log \log n} = \frac{1}{n \log n}$. The expected number of nodes transmitting is $E[X] = \frac{n}{n \log n}$. Using Markov's inequality (see Theorem 13.27) yields $Pr[X > 1] \leq Pr[X > E[X] \cdot \log n] \leq \frac{1}{\log n}$. $\qquad\square$

Lemma 13.16. *If $j < \log n - \log \log n$, then $P[X = 0] \leq \frac{1}{n}$.*

Proof. The nodes transmit with probability $1/2^j > 1/2^{\log n - \log \log n} = \frac{\log n}{n}$. Thus, the probability that a node is silent is at most $1 - \frac{\log n}{n}$. Hence, the probability for a silent time slot, i.e., $Pr[X = 0]$, is at most $(1 - \frac{\log n}{n})^n = e^{-\log n} = \frac{1}{n}$. $\qquad\square$

Corollary 13.17. *If $i > 2\log n$, then $Pr[X > 1] \leq \frac{1}{\log n}$.*

Proof. This follows from Lemma 13.15 since the deviation in this corollary is even larger. $\qquad\square$

Corollary 13.18. *If $i < \frac{1}{2}\log n$, then $P[X = 0] \leq \frac{1}{n}$.*

Proof. This follows from Lemma 13.16 since the deviation in this corollary is even larger. $\qquad\square$

Lemma 13.19. *Let v be such that $2^{v-1} < n \leq 2^v$, i.e., $v \approx \log n$. If $k > v + 2$, then $Pr[X > 1] \leq \frac{1}{4}$.*

Proof. Markov's inequality yields

$$Pr[X > 1] = Pr\left[X > \frac{2^k}{n}E[X]\right] < Pr\left[X > \frac{2^k}{2^v}E[X]\right]$$

$$< Pr[X > 4E[X]] < \frac{1}{4}.$$

$\qquad\square$

Lemma 13.20. *If $k < v - 2$, then $P[X = 0] \leq \frac{1}{4}$.*

Proof. A similar analysis is possible to upper bound the probability that a transmission fails if our estimate is too small. We know that $k \leq v - 2$ and thus

$$Pr[X = 0] = \left(1 - \frac{1}{2^k}\right)^n < e^{-\frac{n}{2^k}} < e^{-\frac{2^{v-1}}{2^k}} < e^{-2} < \frac{1}{4}.$$

$\qquad\square$

Lemma 13.21. *If $v - 2 \leq k \leq v + 2$, then the probability that exactly one node transmits is constant.*

Proof. The transmission probability is $p = \frac{1}{2^{v \pm \Theta(1)}} = \Theta(1/n)$, and the lemma follows with a slightly adapted version of Theorem 13.2. $\qquad\square$

Lemma 13.22. *With probability $1 - \frac{1}{\log n}$ we find a leader in Phase 3 in $O(\log\log n)$ time.*

Proof. For any k, because of Lemmas 13.19 and 13.20, the random walk of the third phase is biased towards the good area. One can show that in $O(\log \log n)$ steps one gets $\Omega(\log \log n)$ good transmissions. Let Y denote the number of times exactly one node transmitted. With Lemma 13.21 we obtain $E[Y] = \Omega(\log \log n)$. Now a direct application of a Chernoff bound (see Theorem 13.28) yields that these transmissions elect a leader with probability $1 - \frac{1}{\log n}$. $\square$

Theorem 13.23. *The Algorithm 13.14 elects a leader with probability of at least $1 - \frac{\log \log n}{\log n}$ in time $O(\log \log n)$.*

Proof. From Corollary 13.17 we know that after $O(\log \log n)$ time slots, the first phase terminates. Since we perform a binary search on an interval of size $O(\log n)$, the second phase also takes at most $O(\log \log n)$ time slots. For the third phase we know that $O(\log \log n)$ slots are sufficient to elect a leader with probability $1 - \frac{1}{\log n}$ by Lemma 13.22. Thus, the total runtime is $O(\log \log n)$.

Now we can combine the results. We know that the error probability for every time slot in the first two phases is at most $\frac{1}{\log n}$. Using a union bound (see Theorem 13.26), we can upper bound the probability that no error occurred by $\frac{\log \log n}{\log n}$. Thus, we know that after Phase 2 our estimate is at most $\log \log n$ away from $\log n$ with probability of at least $1 - \frac{\log \log n}{\log n}$. Hence, we can apply Lemma 13.22 and thus successfully elect a leader with probability of at least $1 - \frac{\log \log n}{\log n}$ (again using a union bound) in time $O(\log \log n)$.
$\square$

Remarks:

- Tightening this analysis a bit more, one can elect a leader with probability $1 - \frac{1}{\log n}$ in time $\log \log n + o(\log \log n)$.

- Can we be even faster?

13.7 Lower Bound

Theorem 13.24. *Any uniform protocol that elects a leader with probability of at least $1 - \frac{1}{2^t}$ must run for at least t time slots.*

Proof. Consider a system with only 2 nodes. The probability that exactly one transmits is at most

$$Pr[X = 1] = 2p \cdot (1 - p) \leq \frac{1}{2}.$$

Thus, after t time slots the probability that a leader was elected is at most $1 - \frac{1}{2^t}$. $\qquad\square$

Remarks:

- Setting $t = \log\log n$ shows that Algorithm 13.14 is almost tight.

13.8 Uniform Asynchronous Wakeup

Until now we have assumed that all nodes start the algorithm in the same time slot. But what happens if this is not the case? How long does it take to elect a leader if we want a uniform and anonymous (nodes do not have an identifier and thus cannot base their decision on it) algorithm?

Theorem 13.25. *If nodes wake up in an arbitrary (worst-case) way, any algorithm may take $\Omega(n/\log n)$ time slots until a single node can successfully transmit.*

Proof. Nodes must transmit at some point, or they will surely never successfully transmit. With a uniform protocol, every node executes the same code. We focus on the first slot where nodes may transmit. No matter what the protocol is, this happens with probability p. Since the protocol is uniform, p must be a constant, independent of n.

The adversary wakes up $w = \frac{c}{p}\ln n$ nodes in each time slot with some constant c. All nodes woken up in the first time slot will transmit with probability p. We study the event E_1 that exactly one of them transmits in that first time slot. Using the inequality $(1 + t/n)^n \le e^t$ from Lemma 13.29 we get

$$
\begin{aligned}
Pr[E_1] &= w \cdot p \cdot (1 - p)^{w-1} \\
&= c\ln n \,(1 - p)^{\frac{1}{p}(c\ln n - p)} \\
&\le c\ln n \cdot e^{-c\ln n + p} \\
&= c\ln n \cdot n^{-c} e^{p} \\
&= n^{-c} \cdot O(\log n) \\
&< \frac{1}{n^{c-1}} = \frac{1}{n^{c'}}.
\end{aligned}
$$

In other words, w.h.p. that time slot will not be successful. Since the nodes cannot distinguish noise from silence, the same argument applies to every set of nodes which wakes up. Let E_α be the event that all n/w time slots will not be successful. Using the inequality $1 - p \leq (1 - p/k)^k$ from Lemma 13.30 we get

$$Pr[E_\alpha] = (1 - Pr(E_1))^{n/w} > \left(1 - \frac{1}{n^{c'}}\right)^{\Theta(n/\log n)} > 1 - \frac{1}{n^{c''}}.$$

In other words, w.h.p. it takes more than n/w time slots until some node can transmit alone.

$\square$

13.9   Useful Formulas

In this chapter we have used several inequalities in our proofs. For simplicity's sake we list all of them in this section.

Theorem 13.26. *Boole's inequality or union bound: For a countable set of events $E_1, E_2, E_3, \ldots$, we have*

$$Pr[\bigcup_i E_i] \leq \sum_i Pr[E_i].$$

Theorem 13.27. *Markov's inequality: If X is any random variable and $a > 0$, then*

$$Pr[|X| \geq a] \leq \frac{E[X]}{a}.$$

Theorem 13.28. *Chernoff bound: Let $Y_1, \ldots, Y_n$ be a independent Bernoulli random variables let $Y := \sum_i Y_i$. For any $0 \leq \delta \leq 1$ it holds*

$$Pr[Y < (1 - \delta)E[Y]] \leq e^{-\frac{\delta^2}{2}E[Y]}$$

and for $\delta > 0$

$$Pr[Y \geq (1 + \delta) \cdot E[Y]] \leq e^{-\frac{\min\{\delta, \delta^2\}}{3} \cdot E[Y]}$$

Theorem 13.29. *We have*

$$e^t \left(1 - \frac{t^2}{n}\right) \leq \left(1 + \frac{t}{n}\right)^n \leq e^t$$

for all $n \in \mathbb{N}, |t| \leq n$. Note that

$$\lim_{n \to \infty} \left(1 + \frac{t}{n}\right)^n = e^t.$$

Theorem 13.30. *For all p, k such that $0 < p < 1$ and $k \geq 1$ we have*

$$1 - p \leq (1 - p/k)^k.$$

Chapter Notes

The Aloha protocol is presented and analyzed in [Abr70, BAK$^+$75, Abr85]; the basic technique that unslotted protocols are twice as bad a slotted protocols is from [Rob75]. The idea to broadcast in a packet radio network by building a tree was first presented in [TM78, Cap79]. This idea is also used in [HNO99] to initialize the nodes. Willard [Wil86] was the first that managed to elect a leader in $O(\log \log n)$ time in expectation. Looking more carefully at the success rate, it was shown that one can elect a leader with probability $1 - \frac{1}{\log n}$ in time $\log \log n + o(\log \log n)$ [NO98]. Finally, approximating the number of nodes in the network is analyzed in [JKZ02, CGK05, BKK$^+$16]. The lower bound for probabilistic wake-up is published in [JS02]. In addition to single-hop networks, multi-hop networks have been analyzed, e.g. broadcast [BYGI92, KM98, CR06], or deployment [MvRW06].

Bibliography

[Abr70] Norman Abramson. THE ALOHA SYSTEM: another alternative for computer communications. In *Proceedings of the November 17-19, 1970, fall joint computer conference*, pages 281–285, 1970.

[Abr85] Norman M. Abramson. Development of the ALO-HANET. *IEEE Transactions on Information Theory*, 31(2):119–123, 1985.

[BAK$^+$75] R. Binder, Norman M. Abramson, Franklin Kuo, A. Okinaka, and D. Wax. ALOHA packet broadcasting: a retrospect. In *American Federation of Information Processing Societies National Computer Conference (AFIPS NCC)*, 1975.

[BKK$^+$16] Philipp Brandes, Marcin Kardas, Marek Klonowski, Dominik Pająk, and Roger Wattenhofer. Approximating the Size of a Radio Network in Beeping Model.

In *23rd International Colloquium on Structural Information and Communication Complexity, Helsinki, Finland*, July 2016.

[BYGI92] Reuven Bar-Yehuda, Oded Goldreich, and Alon Itai. On the Time-Complexity of Broadcast in Multi-hop Radio Networks: An Exponential Gap Between Determinism and Randomization. *J. Comput. Syst. Sci.*, 45(1):104–126, 1992.

[Cap79] J. Capetanakis. Tree algorithms for packet broadcast channels. *IEEE Trans. Inform. Theory*, 25(5):505–515, 1979.

[CGK05] Ioannis Caragiannis, Clemente Galdi, and Christos Kaklamanis. Basic Computations in Wireless Networks. In *International Symposium on Algorithms and Computation (ISAAC)*, 2005.

[CR06] Artur Czumaj and Wojciech Rytter. Broadcasting algorithms in radio networks with unknown topology. *J. Algorithms*, 60(2):115–143, 2006.

[HNO99] Tatsuya Hayashi, Koji Nakano, and Stephan Olariu. Randomized Initialization Protocols for Packet Radio Networks. In *13th International Parallel Processing Symposium & 10th Symposium on Parallel and Distributed Processing (IPPS/SPDP)*, 1999.

[JKZ02] Tomasz Jurdzinski, Miroslaw Kutylowski, and Jan Zatopianski. Energy-Efficient Size Approximation of Radio Networks with No Collision Detection. In *Computing and Combinatorics (COCOON)*, 2002.

[JS02] Tomasz Jurdzinski and Grzegorz Stachowiak. Probabilistic Algorithms for the Wakeup Problem in Single-Hop Radio Networks. In *International Symposium on Algorithms and Computation (ISAAC)*, 2002.

[KM98] Eyal Kushilevitz and Yishay Mansour. An Omega(D log (N/D)) Lower Bound for Broadcast in Radio Networks. *SIAM J. Comput.*, 27(3):702–712, 1998.

[MvRW06] Thomas Moscibroda, Pascal von Rickenbach, and Roger Wattenhofer. Analyzing the Energy-Latency

Trade-off during the Deployment of Sensor Networks. In *25th Annual Joint Conference of the IEEE Computer and Communications Societies (INFOCOM)*, *Barcelona, Spain*, April 2006.

[NO98] Koji Nakano and Stephan Olariu. Randomized O (log log n)-Round Leader Election Protocols in Packet Radio Networks. In *International Symposium on Algorithms and Computation (ISAAC)*, 1998.

[Rob75] Lawrence G. Roberts. ALOHA packet system with and without slots and capture. *SIGCOMM Comput. Commun. Rev.*, 5(2):28–42, April 1975.

[TM78] B. S. Tsybakov and V. A. Mikhailov. Slotted multiaccess packet broadcasting feedback channel. *Problemy Peredachi Informatsii*, 14:32–59, October - December 1978.

[Wil86] Dan E. Willard. Log-Logarithmic Selection Resolution Protocols in a Multiple Access Channel. *SIAM J. Comput.*, 15(2):468–477, 1986.

Chapter 14

Labeling Schemes

Imagine you want to repeatedly query a huge graph, e.g., a social or a road network. For example, you might need to find out whether two nodes are connected, or what the distance between two nodes is. Since the graph is so large, you distribute it among multiple servers in your data center.

14.1 Adjacency

Theorem 14.1. *It is possible to assign labels of size $2\log n$ bits to nodes in a tree so that for every pair u, v of nodes, it is easy to tell whether u is adjacent to v by just looking at u and v's labels.*

Proof. Choose a root in the tree arbitrarily so that every non-root node has a parent. The label of each node u consists of two parts: The ID of u (from 1 to n), and the ID of u's parent (or nothing if u is the root). $\square$

Remarks:

- What we have constructed above is called a *labeling scheme*, more precisely a labeling scheme for adjacency in trees. Formally, a labeling scheme is defined as follows.

Definition 14.2. *A **labeling scheme** consists of an **encoder** e and a **decoder** d. The encoder e assigns to each node v a label*

$e(v)$. *The decoder d receives the labels of the nodes in question and returns an answer to some query. The largest size (in bits) of a label assigned to a node is called the **label size** of the labeling scheme.*

Remarks:

- In Theorem 14.1, the decoder receives two node labels $e(u)$ and $e(v)$, and its answer is YES or NO, depending on whether u and v are adjacent or not. The label size is $2 \log n$.

- The label size is the complexity measure we are going to focus on in this chapter. The run-time of the encoder and the decoder are two other complexity measures that are studied in the literature.

- There is an interesting connection between labeling schemes for adjacency and so-called *induced-universal graphs*: Let $\mathcal{F}$ be a family of graphs. The graph $U(n)$ is called *n-induced-universal for $\mathcal{F}$* if all $G \in \mathcal{F}$ with at most n nodes appear as a node-induced subgraph in $U(n)$. (A node-induced subgraph of $U(n) = (V, E)$ is any graph that can be obtained by taking a subset V' of V and all edges from E which have both endpoints in V'.)

- In the movie Good Will Hunting, the big open question was to find all graphs of the family of homeomorphically irreducible (non-isomorphic, no node with degree 2) trees with 10 nodes, $\mathcal{T}_{10}$. What is the smallest induced-universal graph for $\mathcal{T}_{10}$?

- For a graph family $\mathcal{F}$, if there is a labeling scheme for adjacency with distinct node labels and label size $f(n)$, then there is an n-induced-universal graph for $\mathcal{F}$ of size at most $2^{f(n)}$. Since the size of $U(n)$ is exponential in f it is interesting to study the label size carefully: If f is $\log n$, the size of $U(n)$ is n, whereas if f is $2 \log n$ the size of $U(n)$ becomes n^2!

- What about adjacency in general graphs?

Theorem 14.3. *There is a labeling scheme for adjacency in general graphs with the label size of $\lfloor \frac{n}{2} \rfloor + \lceil \log n \rceil \approx \frac{n}{2}$.*

Proof. Let the label of each node be comprised of:

- a distinct ID i between 0 and $n-1$ ($\lceil \log n \rceil$ bits);

- for $j = i+1 \mod n, \ldots, i + \lfloor \frac{n}{2} \rfloor \mod n$, one bit indicating adjacency to the node with the ID j.

Then, for any pair of nodes, one of the node labels will contain the bit indicating adjacency. The bit can be found based on the ID's. $\qquad \square$

Theorem 14.4. *Any labeling scheme for adjacency in general graphs has a label size of at least $\approx \frac{n}{2} \in \Omega(n)$ bits.*

Proof. Let $\mathcal{G}_n$ denote the family of graphs with n nodes. A graph in $\mathcal{G}_n$ can have at most $\binom{n}{2}$ edges. When taking into account that the order of the nodes is irrelevant, it can be shown that $|\mathcal{G}_n| \geq 2^{\binom{n}{2}}/n!$. Indeed, $|\mathcal{G}_n|$ converges towards $2^{\binom{n}{2}}/n!$ for large n.

Assume there is a labeling scheme for adjacency in graphs from $\mathcal{G}_n$ with label size s. First, we argue that the encoder e must be injective on $\mathcal{G}_n$: Since the labeling scheme is for adjacency, e cannot assign the same labels to two different graphs.

There are 2^s possible labels for any node, and for every $G \in \mathcal{G}_n$ we can choose n of them. Thus, we obtain that

$$|\mathcal{G}_n| \leq \left(\!\!\binom{2^s}{n}\!\!\right) = \binom{2^s + n - 1}{n}$$

Canceling out the $n!$ term and taking the logarithm on both sides of the inequality we conclude that $s > \frac{n-1}{2} \in \Omega(n)$. $\qquad \square$

Remarks:

- The lower bound for general graphs is a bit discouraging; we wanted to use labeling schemes for queries on large graphs!

- The situation is less dire if the graph is not arbitrary. For instance, in degree-bounded graphs, in planar graphs, and in trees, the bounds change to $\Theta(\log n)$ bits.

- What about other queries, e.g., distance?

- Next, we will focus on rooted trees.

14.2   Rooted Trees

Theorem 14.5. *There is a $2 \log n$ labeling scheme for ancestry, i.e., for two nodes u and v, find out if u is an ancestor of v in the rooted tree T.*

Proof. Traverse the tree with a depth first search, and consider the obtained pre-ordering of the nodes, i.e., enumerate the nodes in the order in which they are first visited. For a node u denote by $l(u)$ the index in the pre-order. Our encoder assigns labels $e(u) = (l(u), r(u))$ to each node u, where $r(u)$ is the largest value $l(v)$ that appears at any node v in the sub-tree rooted at u. With the labels assigned in this manner, we can find out whether u is an ancestor of v by checking if $l(v)$ is contained in the interval $(l(u), r(u)]$. $\qquad\square$

Algorithm 14.6 Naïve-Distance-Labeling(T)

1: Let l be the label of the root r of T
2: Let $T_1, \ldots, T_\delta$ be the sub-trees rooted at each of the δ children of r
3: **for** $i = 1, \ldots, \delta$ **do**
4:    The root of T_i gets the label obtained by appending i to l
5:    Naïve-Distance-Labeling(T_i)
6: **end for**

Theorem 14.7. *There is an $O(n \log n)$ labeling scheme for distance in trees.*

Proof. Apply the encoder algorithm Naïve-Distance-Labeling(T) to label the tree T. The encoder assigns to every node v a sequence $(l_1, l_2 \ldots)$. The length of a sequence $e(v)$ is at most n, and each entry in the sequence requires at most $\log n$ bits. A label $(l_1, \ldots, l_k)$ of a node v corresponds to a path from r to v in T, and the nodes on the path are labeled $(l_1), (l_1, l_2), (l_1, l_2, l_3)$ and so on. The distance between u and v in T is obtained by reconstructing the paths from $e(u)$ and $e(v)$. $\qquad\square$

Remarks:

- We can assign the labels more carefully to obtain a smaller label size. For that, we use the following *heavy-light decomposition*.

Algorithm 14.8 Heavy-Light-Decomposition(T)

1: Node r is the root of T
2: Let $T_1, \ldots, T_\delta$ be the sub-trees rooted at each of the δ children of r
3: Let $T_{\max}$ be a largest tree in $\{T_1, \ldots, T_\delta\}$ in terms of number of nodes
4: Mark the edge $(r, T_{\max})$ as *heavy*
5: Mark all edges to other children of r as *light*
6: Assign the names $1, \ldots, \delta - 1$ to the light edges of r
7: **for** $i = 1, \ldots, \delta$ **do**
8:    Heavy-Light-Decomposition(T_i)
9: **end for**

Theorem 14.9. *There is an $O(\log^2 n)$ labeling scheme for distance in trees.*

Proof. For our proof, use Heavy-Light-Decomposition(T) to partition T's edges into heavy and light edges. All heavy edges form a collection of paths, called the *heavy paths*. Moreover, every node is reachable from the root through a sequence of heavy paths connected with light edges. Instead of storing the whole path to reach a node, we only store the information about heavy paths and light edges that were taken to reach a node from the root.

For instance, if node u can be reached by first using 2 heavy edges, then the 7th light edge, then 3 heavy edges, and then the light edges 1 and 4, then we assign to v the label $(\mathbf{2}, 7, \mathbf{3}, 1, 4)$. For any node u, the path $p(u)$ from the root to u is now specified by the label. The distance between any two nodes can be computed using the paths.

Since every parent has at most $\Delta < n$ children, the name of a light edge has at most $\log n$ bits. The size (number of nodes in the sub-tree) of a light child is less than half the size of its parent, so a path can have less than $\log n$ light edges. Between any two light edges, there could be a heavy path, so we can have up to $\log n$ heavy paths in a label. The length of such a heavy path can be described with $\log n$ bits as well, since no heavy path has more than n nodes. Altogether we therefore need at most $O(\log^2 n)$ bits. $\square$

Remarks:

- One can show that any labeling scheme for distance in trees needs to use labels of size at least $\Omega(\log^2 n)$.

- The distance encoder from Theorem 14.9 also supports decoders for other queries. To check for ancestry, it therefore suffices to check if $p(u)$ is a prefix of $p(v)$ or vice versa.

- The lowest common ancestor is the node w that is on $p(u)$ and $p(v)$ and on the shortest path between u and v; the separation level of u and v is the distance of w to the root.

- Two nodes are siblings if their distance is 2 but they are not ancestors.

- The heavy-light decomposition can be used to shave off a few bits in other labeling schemes, e.g., ancestry or adjacency.

14.3   Road Networks

Labeling schemes are used to quickly find shortest paths in road networks.

Remarks:

- A naïve approach is to store at every node u the shortest paths to all other nodes v. This requires an impractical amount of memory. For example, the road network for Western Europe has 18 million nodes and 44 million directed edges, and the USA road network has 24 million nodes and 58 million directed edges.

- What if we only store the next node on the shortest path to all targets? In a worst case this stills requires $\Omega(n)$ bits per node. Moreover, answering a single query takes many invocations of the decoder.

- For simplicity, let us focus on answering distance queries only. Even if we only want to know the distance, storing the full table of n^2 distances costs more than 1000TB, too much for storing it in RAM.

- The idea for the encoder is to compute a set S of *hub* nodes that lie on many shortest paths. We then store at each node u only the distance to the hub nodes that appear on shortest paths originating or ending in u.

- Given two labels $e(u)$ and $e(v)$, let $H(u,v)$ denote the set of hub nodes that appear in both labels. The decoder now simply returns $d(u,v) = \min\{\text{dist}(u,h) + \text{dist}(h,v) : h \in H(u,v)\}$, all of which can be computed from the two labels.

- The key in finding a good labeling scheme now lies in finding good hub nodes.

Algorithm 14.10 Naïve-Hub-Labeling(G)

1: Let P be the set of all n^2 shortest paths
2: **while** $P \neq \emptyset$ **do**
3:     Let h be a node which is on a maximum number of paths in P
4:     **for** all paths $p = (u, \ldots, v) \in P$ **do**
5:         **if** h is on p **then**
6:             Add h with the distance $\text{dist}(u,h)$ to the label of u
7:             Add h with the distance $\text{dist}(h,v)$ to the label of v
8:             Remove p from P
9:         **end if**
10:     **end for**
11: **end while**

Remarks:

- Unfortunately, algorithm 14.10 takes a prohibitively long time to compute.

- Another approach computes the set S as follows. The encoder (Algorithm 14.11) first constructs so-called *shortest path covers*. The node set S_i is a shortest path cover if

S_i contains a node on every shortest path of length between 2^{i-1} and 2^i. At node v only the hub nodes in S_i that are within the ball of radius 2^i around v (denoted by $B(v, 2^i)$) are stored.

Algorithm 14.11 Hub-Labeling(G)

1: **for** $i = 1, \ldots, \log D$ **do**
2:     Compute the shortest path cover S_i
3: **end for**
4: **for** all $v \in V$ **do**
5:     Let $F_i(v)$ be the set $S_i \cap B(v, 2^i)$
6:     Let $F(v)$ be the set $F_1(v) \cup F_2(v) \cup \ldots$
7:     The label of v consists of the nodes in $F(v)$, with their distance to v
8: **end for**

Remarks:

- The size of the shortest path covers will determine how space efficient the solution will be. It turns out that real-world networks allow for small shortest path covers: The parameter h is the so-called *highway dimension* of G, is defined as $h = \max_{i,v} F_i(v)$, and h is conjectured to be small for road networks.

- Computing S_i with a minimal number of hubs is NP-hard, but one can compute a $O(\log n)$ approximation of S_i in polynomial time. Consequently, the label size is at most $O(h \log n \log D)$. By ordering the nodes in each label by their ID, the decoder can scan through both node lists in parallel in time $O(h \log n \log D)$.

- While this approach yields good theoretical bounds, the encoder is *still* too slow in practice. Therefore, before computing the shortest path covers, the graph is contracted by introducing *shortcuts* first.

- Based on this approach a distance query on a continent-sized road network can be answered in less that $1\mu s$ on current hardware, orders of magnitude faster than a single random disk access. Storing all the labels requires roughly 20 GB of RAM.

- The method can be extended to support shortest path queries, e.g., by storing the path to/from the hub nodes, or by recursively querying for nodes that lie on the shortest path to the hub.

Chapter Notes

Adjacency labelings were first studied by Breuer and Folkman [BF67]. The $\log n + O(\log^* n)$ upper bound for trees is due to [AR02] using a clustering technique. In contrast, it was shown that for general graphs the size of universal graphs is at least $2^{(n-1)/2}$! Since graphs of arboricity d can be decomposed into d forests [NW61], the labeling scheme from [AR02] can be used to label graphs of arboricity d with $d \log n + O(\log n)$ bit labels. For a thorough survey on labeling schemes for rooted trees please check [AHR].

Universal graphs were studied already by Ackermann [Ack37], and later by Erdős, Rényi, and Rado [ER63, Rad64]. The connection between labeling schemes and universal graphs [KNR88] was investigated thoroughly. Our adjacency lower bound follows the presentation in [AKTZ14], which also summarizes recent results in this field of research.

Distance labeling schemes were first studied by Peleg [Pel00]. The notion of highway dimension was introduced by [AFGW10] in an attempt to explain the good performance of many heuristics to speed up shortest path computations, e.g., Transit Node Routing [BFSS07]. Their suggestions to modify the SHARC heuristic [BD08] lead to the hub labeling scheme and were implemented and evaluated [ADGW11], and later refined [DGSW14]. The $\Omega(n)$ label size lower bound for routing (shortest paths) with stretch smaller than 3 is due to [GG01].

Bibliography

[Ack37] Wilhelm Ackermann. Die Widerspruchsfreiheit der allgemeinen Mengenlehre. *Mathematische Annalen*, 114(1):305–315, 1937.

[ADGW11] Ittai Abraham, Daniel Delling, Andrew V. Goldberg, and Renato Fonseca F. Werneck. A hub-based labeling algorithm for shortest paths in road networks. In *SEA*, 2011.

[AFGW10] Ittai Abraham, Amos Fiat, Andrew V. Goldberg, and Renato Fonseca F. Werneck. Highway dimension, shortest paths, and provably efficient algorithms. In *SODA*, 2010.

[AHR] Stephen Alstrup, Esben Bistrup Halvorsen, and Noy Rotbart. A survey on labeling schemes for trees. To appear.

[AKTZ14] Stephen Alstrup, Haim Kaplan, Mikkel Thorup, and Uri Zwick. Adjacency labeling schemes and induced-universal graphs. *CoRR*, abs/1404.3391, 2014.

[AR02] Stephen Alstrup and Theis Rauhe. Small induced-universal graphs and compact implicit graph representations. In *FOCS*, 2002.

[BD08] Reinhard Bauer and Daniel Delling. SHARC: fast and robust unidirectional routing. In *ALENEX*, 2008.

[BF67] Melvin A Breuer and Jon Folkman. An unexpected result in coding the vertices of a graph. *Journal of Mathematical Analysis and Applications*, 20(3):583 – 600, 1967.

[BFSS07] Holger Bast, Stefan Funke, Peter Sanders, and Dominik Schultes. Fast routing in road networks with transit nodes. *Science*, 316(5824):566, 2007.

[DGSW14] Daniel Delling, Andrew V. Goldberg, Ruslan Savchenko, and Renato F. Werneck. Hub labels: Theory and practice. In *SEA*, 2014.

[ER63] P. Erdős and A. Rényi. Asymmetric graphs. *Acta Mathematica Academiae Scientiarum Hungarica*, 14(3-4):295–315, 1963.

[GG01] Cyril Gavoille and Marc Gengler. Space-efficiency for routing schemes of stretch factor three. *J. Parallel Distrib. Comput.*, 61(5):679–687, 2001.

[KNR88] Sampath Kannan, Moni Naor, and Steven Rudich. Implicit representation of graphs. In *STOC*, 1988.

[NW61] C. St. J. A. Nash-Williams. Edge-disjoint spanning trees of finite graphs. *J. London Math. Soc.*, 36:445–450, 1961.

[Pel00] David Peleg. Proximity-preserving labeling schemes. *Journal of Graph Theory*, 33(3):167–176, 2000.

[Rad64] Richard Rado. Universal graphs and universal functions. *Acta Arith.*, 9:331–340, 1964.

Chapter 15

Exercises

Chapter 1

Exercise 1 ("Reduce" Algorithm)

In Chapter 1, a distributed algorithm ("Reduce") for coloring an arbitrary graph with $\Delta + 1$ colors in n synchronous rounds was presented (Δ denotes the largest degree, n the number of nodes of the graph).

a) What is the message complexity, i.e., the total number of messages the algorithm sends in the worst case?

> **Hint:** Note that the "undecided" messages sent in Line 6 are actually not needed. A node could just as well send no message at all. Therefore neglect these messages in your analysis!

b) Let m be the number of edges. Can you come up with an exact number of messages being sent?

Exercise 2 (TDMA)

You have learned about coloring and TDMA (time division multiple access) in Chapter 1. We will now present two applications to show you the relevance of coloring. Consider some nodes, which are placed as shown in Figure 15.1. These nodes exchange messages using some kind of wireless communication.

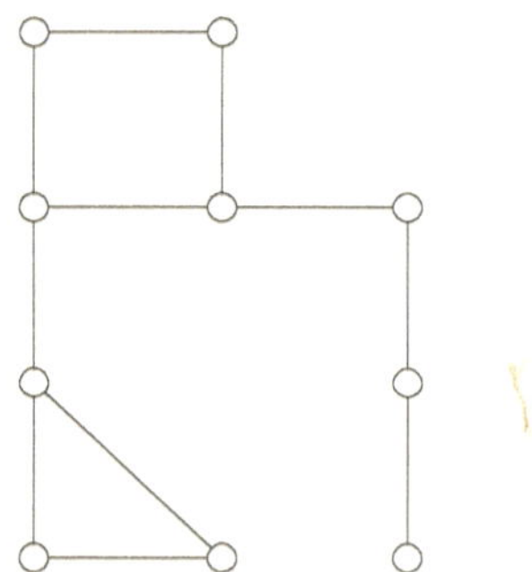

Figure 15.1: The wireless network

a) If two neighboring nodes send a message at the same time, then none will receive a message (because the messages interfere). We now want to allocate these nodes slots such that they can communicate without any interference. Hence, your task is to color the nodes of this specific instance with as few colors as possible to maximize the amount of messages that can be exchanged.

b) You have upgraded to a faster wireless communication method. But it is a bit more susceptible to errors. In addition to two neighboring nodes not being allowed to send a message simultaneously, there is another constraint. If two (or more) of my neighbors send a message, then I can no longer decode either message correctly. How can you model this? How many colors do you need now?

c) We now present a different area in which coloring is useful. Students can choose the lectures they want to attend. These lectures should not take place at the same time to allow the students to attend the lectures they have chosen. You are now given a list of students and the lectures they want to attend and are supposed to schedule these lectures to as few slots as possible.

  - Arnold wants to attend Principles of Distributed Computing, Statistical Learning Theory, and Ubiquitous Computing.
  - Berta wants to attend Principles of Distributed Computing and Graph Theory.
  - Christina wants to attend Cryptography.
  - Don wants to attend Statistical Learning Theory and Ubiquitous Computing.
  - Emil wants to attend Graph Theory and Cryptography.
  - Flo wants to attend Principles of Distributed Computing and Cryptography.

Exercise 3 (Coloring Rings and Trees)

The combination of Algorithms 1.17 and 1.21 colors any (directed) tree consisting of n nodes with 3 colors in $O(\log^* n)$ rounds. It consists of two phases: In the first phase (Algorithm 1.17), the initial coloring consisting of all node IDs is reduced to 6 colors, in the second phase (Algorithm 1.21), the 6 colors are further reduced to 3. Note that, in order to decide when to switch from Phase 1 to Phase 2, the nodes running the algorithms actually count $\log^* n$ rounds. However, this is only possible if the nodes are aware of the total number of nodes n. If n is unknown the nodes do not know when the first phase is over: A node v running Algorithm 1.17 cannot simply decide to be done once its color is in $\mathcal{R} = \{0, \dots, 5\}$ since its parent w might still change its color in the future. Even if the color of w is also in $\mathcal{R}$, w might receive a message from its parent that forces w to change its color once more (potentially to node v's color!).

In the following, we want to overcome this problem and make Algorithms 1.17 and 1.21 work even if the nodes are unaware of n. To make our lives easier we try to find a solution for the ring topology before we tackle the problem on trees. Formally, a ring is a graph $G = (V, E)$, where $V = \{v_1, \dots, v_n\}$ and $E = \{\{v_i, v_j\} \mid j = i+1 \,(\mathrm{mod}\, n)\}$. You can assume that G is a *directed* ring, i.e., nodes can distinguish between "left" and "right".[1]

a) Show how the log-star coloring algorithm for trees can be adapted for rings given that the nodes know n.

b) Now adapt your algorithm from a) so that it also works if the ring nodes do not know n. Preserve the running time of $O(\log^* n)$!

   Once the color of node v in the ring is in $\mathcal{R}$, it wants to reduce the number of colors used to 3. Show how this reduction phase works even if the first phase may not have terminated in some other parts of the ring![2]

   Hint: You can use additional colors to segment the ring and switch phases locally.

c) Based on the previous exercise, propose a uniform algorithm that colors any directed tree in $O(\log^* n)$ rounds with at most 3 colors! A distributed algorithm is called *uniform* if it works without the knowledge of the number of nodes n.

---

[1] Note that this assumption is stronger than *sense of direction*, which merely requires that nodes can distinguish their neighbors.

[2] Note that a node cannot wait until it knows that all other nodes are ready to start the second phase as this would require time in the order of n.

Chapter 2

Exercise 4 (License to Match)

In preparation for a highly dangerous mission, the participating agents of the gargantuan Liechtensteinian secret service (LSS) need to work in pairs of two for safety reasons. All members in the LSS are organized in a tree hierarchy. Communication is only possible via the official channel: an agent has a secure phone line to his direct superior and a secure phone line to each of his direct subordinates. Initially, each agent knows whether or not he is taking part in this mission. The goal is for each agent to find a partner.

a) Devise an algorithm that will match up a participating agent with another participating agent given the constrained communication scenario. A "match" consists of an agent knowing the identity of his partner and the path in the hierarchy connecting them. Assume that there is an even number of participating agents so that each one is guaranteed a partner. Furthermore, observe that[3] the phone links connecting two paired-up agents need to remain open at all times. Therefore, you cannot use the same link (i.e., an edge) twice when connecting agents with their partners.

b) What are the time and message (i.e., "phone call") complexities of your algorithm?

Exercise 5 (License to Distribute)

We consider another day at the office of the LSS as in Exercise 4. After the above mission was successful, the involved agents collected a large number of sensitive documents. Some agents might have a lot of them and others have none. Now they need to distribute the documents throughout the agency such that each person in the LSS has the same amount of data to process.

a) Assume that there are n agents in the LSS and that there is also a total of n documents. Devise a way for the agents to distribute their sensitive data: in the end, each agent should have exactly one document. The communication scheme is the same as above.

---

[3] in the case of an emergency where they lose contact

b) How good is your algorithm with respect to time and number of messages? You may assume that arbitrarily many documents can be sent in a single message.

Exercise 6 (Restructuring the LSS)

Recall the organizational structure of the LSS: each member of the LSS can communicate only with his direct superior and his direct subordinates over a secure phone line. On top of this tree hierarchy sits L, the "big boss". Members who do not have any subordinates are the field agents. All others (including L) are office workers. Let the total number of LSS members be $n > 1$.

a) In an effort to improve the efficiency of the LSS, L suspects that there are too many office workers and not enough field agents to save the world. To that end, she needs to know exactly how many people in the company are office workers and how many are field agents. Devise an efficient asynchronous, distributed algorithm, started by L, to determine those numbers.

b) What are the time and message complexities of your algorithm? Because of political turbulences, Liechtenstein is now being split into two countries, Lichtstein and Lampenstein, who each want to have their own secret services, LiSS and LaSS, respectively. The politicians agree to create two groups of people out of the original LSS. The goal is that each new group collectively has the capacity to perform the same jobs as the LSS before. The jobs were such that, in the original LSS, every member knew how to execute his own task and all the tasks of his direct contacts (i.e. the direct superior's and subordinates' tasks). And since a person is only allowed single citizenship, he can only be part of either the LiSS or the LaSS. Note that we do not care about the internal structure of the future LiSS and LaSS at this point, only about membership.

c) Devise an asynchronous algorithm that assigns each member of the LSS to either LiSS or LaSS. The algorithm is initiated by L and should terminate in time $O(depth(T))$, where T refers to the LSS structure.

d) Same task as above. Now the algorithm may be synchronous, is started by all members simultaneously and should terminate in time $O(\log^* n)$, where n is the number of members in the original LSS. You may use the algorithms from Chapter 2 as a black box. Show that your algorithm correctly solves the problem in the specified amount of time.

e) If Liechtenstein had been split into several countries, how many such entities could have been created maximally and why?

Chapter 3

Exercise 7 (Leader Election in an "Almost Anonymous" Ring)

a) Is deterministic leader election possible in a synchronous ring in which all but one processors have the same identifier? Either give an algorithm or prove an impossibility result.

b) Consider a synchronous ring in which exactly two nodes have identifier A and all the other nodes have identifier B. Is deterministic leader election possible in this setting? Either give an algorithm or prove an impossibility result.

Exercise 8 (Anonymous Leader Election in Special Graphs)

The goal of this task is to gain some more insights into the feasibility of solving leader election. We assume nodes communicate in synchronous rounds. The graph is *anonymous*, i.e., the nodes do not have unique IDs.

A node that terminates may no longer send any messages or change its internal state. The whole algorithm terminates when all nodes have terminated. Once the algorithm terminates, there must be exactly one node that is in the "leader" state. All other nodes must know that there is a unique leader.

Let us first consider an anonymous tree with n nodes. All nodes are initially unaware of their function (root, leave, inner node) in the tree and are in the same state (undecided). Your task is to come up with an algorithm such that:

1. Exactly one node becomes the root.

2. All nodes with only one neighbor become leaves.

3. All the remaining nodes become inner nodes.

a) Prove that there is no deterministic algorithm that can solve the given task.

b) Can you find such an algorithm if we require the underlying graph to have an odd number of nodes? Either prove that no such algorithm exists, or state an algorithm that solves the problem. In the latter case, also provide the time complexity and prove the correctness of the algorithm.

Now let us consider the torus graph. The torus graph consists of a grid of m by n nodes. Each node has four neighbors (north, east, south, west). The nodes on the border of the grid are connected to their counterpart of the opposing border (see Figure 15.2).

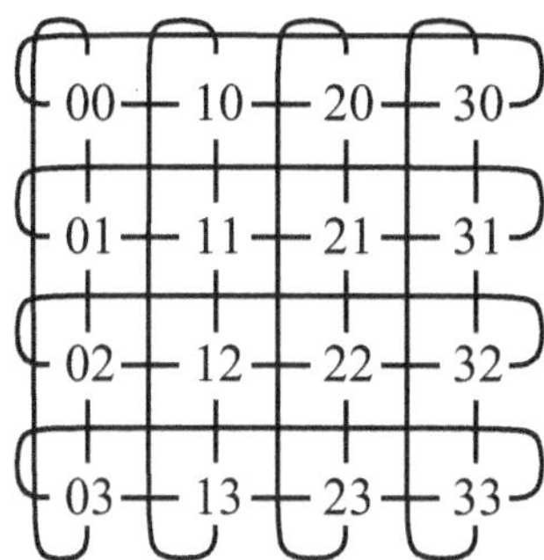

Figure 15.2: Sample of a torus graph with $m = n = 4$ nodes

c) Is there a deterministic, non-uniform[4], and anonymous algorithm to elect a leader in such a graph? Prove impossibility or give an algorithm.

d) If the size of the grid (m, n) is unknown, is it possible to compute the size of the grid? Prove impossibility or give an (uniform) algorithm.

e) Now assume that an arbitrary node is removed from the graph and its neighbors are interconnected (north-south and east-west). Is anonymous leader election possible in this graph? Prove impossibility or give an algorithm.

    Hint: Can a node determine if it is lying in the same row or column as the node that has been removed?

---

[4] An algorithm is called uniform if the number of nodes is **not** known to the algorithm.

Exercise 9 (Distributed Computation of the AND)

Consider an anonymous ring where each processor has a single bit as input. You can assume that nodes can distinguish between their neighbors, i.e., when a node v receives a message, v knows which neighbor has sent the message (note that nodes may not know a consistent clockwise or counterclockwise orientation of the ring!).

a) Prove that there is no uniform synchronous algorithm for computing the AND of all input bits.

b) Present an asynchronous (non-uniform) algorithm for computing the AND; the algorithm should send $O(n^2)$ messages in the worst case.

c) Present a synchronous (non-uniform) algorithm for computing the AND; the algorithm should send $O(n)$ messages in the worst case. What is the time complexity of your algorithm?

Chapter 4

Exercise 10 (Sorting Networks)

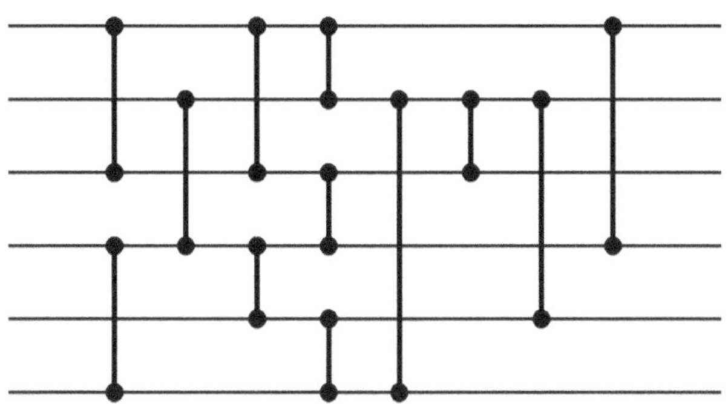

Figure 15.3: A Sorting Network?

For each of the following questions, prove or disprove the given claim.

a) The network of width 6 and 12 comparators in Figure 15.3 above is a sorting network, that is, it sorts each input sequence of numbers correctly.

b) Given any correct sorting network, adding another comparator at the end does **not** destroy the sorting property.

c) Given any correct sorting network, adding another comparator at the front does **not** destroy the sorting property.

d) Every correct sorting network needs to have at least one comparator between each two consecutive wires.

e) A network which contains all $\binom{n}{2}$ comparators between any two of the n wires, in whatever order they are placed, is a correct sorting network.

f) Given any correct sorting network, adding another comparator anywhere does not destroy the sorting property.

g) Given any correct sorting network, inverting it (i.e., feeding the input into the output wires and traversing the network "from right to left") results in another correct sorting network.

Exercise 11 (Sorting with Hypercubes)

a) You are given the labeled hypercube H_3 of dimension 3 in Figure 15.4 and you are asked to construct a correct sorting network with eight wires using comparators only between wires whose corresponding vertices in H_3 are connected by an edge. (For example, you may compare wire 0 and 1 but not wire 1 and 2). Explain why this is not possible.

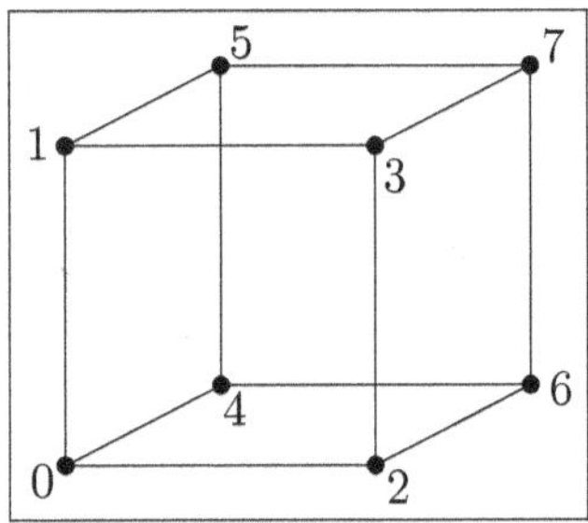

Figure 15.4: Hypercube H_3 of dimension 3

b) Now you may change the labeling of the vertices in H_3. Prove that this allows you to construct a correct sorting network using comparators only between wires whose corresponding vertices in H_3 are connected.

c) Argue how to assign labels to a hypercube H_d of dimension d to allow the construction of a correct sorting network.

d) Now, instead of normal comparators, you may use *directed* comparators that move the larger element to the upper ($\uparrow$) or to the lower wire ($\downarrow$) of the two connected wires. Show how you can construct a correct sorting network with three wires (named 0, 1, and 2), if it is forbidden to have a comparator between wire 1 and 2.

e) Explain how you can transform a sorting network using directed comparators into a sorting network using only normal comparators.

f) Give a correct sorting network with four wires using directed comparators only between wires whose corresponding vertices in H_2 are connected by an edge.

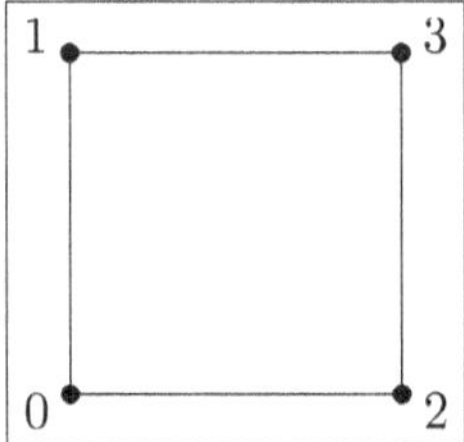

Figure 15.5: Hypercube H_2 of dimension 2

Exercise 12 (Low Cost Sorting)

Consider a network of four nodes: v_1, v_2, v_3 and v_4. Each node is given an input number. An algorithm on this network executes in synchronous rounds. In each round, each node can participate in a compare-and-exchange operation with at most one neighbor. See Figure 15.6 for an example. The cost of running an algorithm for

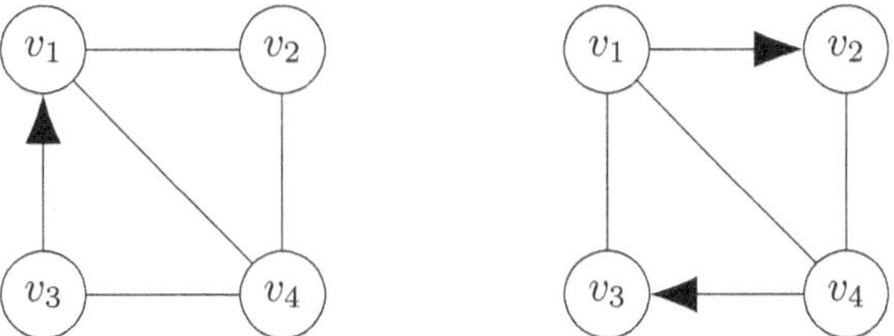

Figure 15.6: An example network where all pairs of nodes have edges between them except v_2 and v_3. After compare-and-exchange between a pair of nodes (represented by an arrow), the smaller value moves to the node at the head of the arrow, the larger to the node at the tail. In the first round, compare-and-exchange occurs between v_1 and v_3, the smaller value moving to node v_1. In the second round, compare-and-exchange occurs between v_2 and v_1, and between v_3 and v_4.

t rounds on a network of m edges is $m \cdot t^2$. For questions **a)** and **b)**, give exact instead of asymptotic bounds.

a) Consider the problem of finding the minimum of the input numbers in a network with four nodes v_1, v_2, v_3 and v_4.

  (a) Give a lower bound on the number of *edges* any network needs to put the minimum number at v_1.

  (b) Give a lower bound on the number of *rounds* any algorithm needs to put the minimum number at v_1.

  (c) Give a network and an algorithm for placing the minimum number at v_1 so that the cost $m \cdot t^2$ is minimum.

b) Now consider the problem of sorting the input numbers in a network with four nodes v_1, v_2, v_3 and v_4 so that node v_i gets the ith smallest number.

  (a) Give a lower bound on the number of *rounds* any algorithm needs to sort the numbers.

  (b) Give a network and an algorithm to sort the numbers minimizing the cost $m \cdot t^2$ (better cost gives more points).

c) Now you are given n nodes. Describe how to design a network and a sorting algorithm minimizing the cost $m \cdot t^2$. Please use the big-O notation for this part (better asymptotic cost gives more points).

Chapter 5

Exercise 13 (Shared Sum)

In Chapter 5, we discussed how shared registers can be employed efficiently to allow each process to announce a value to all other processes. Now we look at a different scenario: Each process p_i computes a local variable x_i and we want to make the sum $x := \sum_{i=1}^{n} x_i$ available to all processes.

We want to guarantee the following: If a process updates x_i, it should first ensure that x is updated accordingly before proceeding. However, we do not want to use a large number of registers or a huge register. In the following, you are given a single register that can store $O(\log n)$ bits (the choice of the constant is up to you). Moreover, we assume that "x cannot become too large", i.e., the x_i (and thus x) are of size polynomial in n and hence can be encoded using $O(\log n)$ bits.

a) Give a solution using a shared register supporting the fetch-and-add operation with a constant update and access complexity. If possible, prevent both lockouts and deadlocks.

b) Give a solution using a compare-and-swap register, also with constant access complexity. If successful, an update should need a constant number of steps (otherwise the process may retry). Are lockouts excluded?

c) Give a solution using a load-link/store-conditional register. Compare it to the preceding solutions.

d) Assume now that the return value of compare-and-swap is not whether the operation succeeded, but the value stored in the register after the operation. Can the problem still be solved? Prove your claim!

Exercise 14 (Space Efficient Binary Tree Algorithm)

The adaptive collect algorithm using binary trees from Chapter 5 requires to store a complete binary tree of depth $n - 1$, resulting in exponential memory requirements.

Suppose the algorithm is modified the following way: Whenever a process leaves a splitter with result **left** or **right** it flips a coin to replace this result by **left** or **right** with probability 1/2 each. Prove that for this randomized variant of the algorithm it is *with high probability*[5] sufficient to allocate memory polynomial in n.

Exercise 15 (Shared Clustering Coefficient)

Definition (Clustering Coefficient). *The **local clustering coefficient** $C(v_i)$ of a vertex v_i is defined as the probability that a randomly chosen pair of neighbors of v_i are neighbors of each other, i.e.,*

$$C(v_i) = \frac{\#\ edges\ between\ neighbors\ of\ v_i}{\binom{|\mathcal{N}_{v_i}|}{2}},$$

*where $\mathcal{N}_{v_i}$ is the set of neighbors of v_i. The **clustering coefficient** $C(G)$ of a graph $G = (V, E)$ is the average of the local clustering coefficients of all the vertices $v_i \in V$.*

For this task we look at the parallel computation of clustering coefficients of a graph $G = (V, E)$ using a set of n processor cores. The graph G has $|V| = n$ nodes and a node degree of at most 10. All processor cores can access a read-only shared memory M. This memory contains the graph G in the following form: For each vertex $v_i \in V$, the memory holds a list M_i containing the indices of v_i's neighbors, i.e. $M_i[j]$ is the index of the j-th neighbor of v_i. Note that the size of a list M_i equals the degree of v_i.

a) Give a shared memory algorithm to compute all local clustering coefficients $C(v_i)$, $i = 1, \ldots, n$, in G (assuming that all processor cores can run in parallel). What is your algorithm's time complexity?

b) Once the local clustering coefficients have been computed, the graph clustering coefficient can be computed by averaging them. Assume that we have one shared read-write memory register R of capacity $O(\log n)$ bits. Given that any processor core $i \in \{1, \ldots, n\}$ knows its local clustering coefficient $C(v_i)$, outline an algorithm that uses R to compute $C(G)$ as fast as possible, and give its time complexity.

c) Assume now that we have an unlimited number of shared read-write memory registers R_k, $k = 1, 2, \ldots$, each with capacity $O(\log n)$ bits. Again, given that any processor core

---

[5]I.e., with probability at least $1 - 1/n^c$ for a choosable constant $c > 0$.

$i \in \{1, \ldots, n\}$ knows $C(v_i)$, outline a fast algorithm that computes $C(G)$ using these registers, and give its time complexity.

d) Is your solution in **c)** asymptotically optimal? Give an informal explanation of why it is optimal, or why it is not.

Chapter 6

Exercise 16 (Concurrent Ivy)

Consider the tree for the Ivy shared variable protocol in Figure 15.7. There are three concurrent requests placed by the nodes v_1, v_2 and v_3. The token is initially held by the circled node labeled r. We assume synchronous execution.

a) Give the order of serviced requests.

b) Draw the tree after the last request has been served.

c) Show that in an asynchronous setting, Ivy incurs at most an $O(\log n)$ overhead in amortized message complexity.

Figure 15.7: Tree for Question 16.

Exercise 17 (Tight Ivy)

In Theorem 6.12 it was shown that, on average, acquiring a lock requires at most $\log n$ steps, where n is the number of processors.

Show that this bound on the number of steps is tight by constructing a tree consisting of n nodes in which each request requires $\log n$ steps if all requests are performed sequentially by suitable nodes in the tree.[6]

---

[6]Hints: Assume that n is a power of 2. Construct a tree whose topology remains the same with respect to the token holder after each request.

Exercise 18 (Ivy on Trees)

In Chapter 6, you saw the Ivy protocol for unweighted complete graphs. In this task we apply the Ivy protocol to weighted trees: you start with a weighted tree, and the weight of any pointer is the distance between the corresponding nodes in the tree. In other words, we will consider the performance of the Ivy algorithm from Chapter 6 on a complete weighted graph where the distance between any two nodes is defined by the distance on an underlying tree.

a) Show that Ivy on the tree given in Figure 15.8a, with the corresponding complete graph in Figure 15.8b, has a *competitive ratio* of at least $2 - \varepsilon$. Give therefore a recurring sequence of requests so that the ratio of *ivy cost* and the *optimal cost* is at least $2 - \varepsilon$. For a sequence of requests, the *ivy cost* is defined as the sum of distances traversed by the Ivy algorithm between the consecutive requests, whereas the *optimal cost* is the sum of the shortest distances between the consecutive requests. Note that your ε should be arbitrarily small.

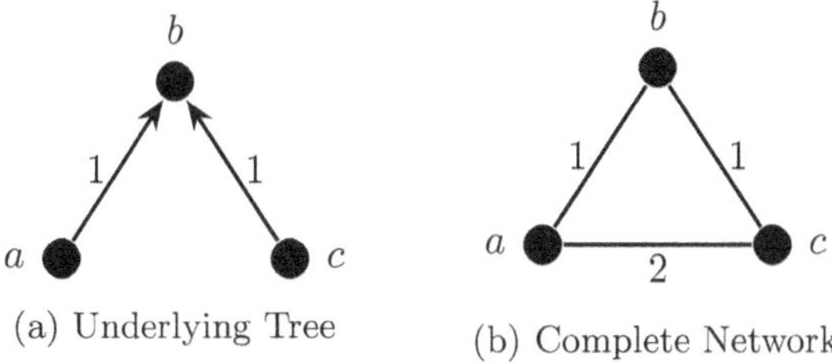

(a) Underlying Tree   (b) Complete Network

Figure 15.8: A small example

b) Show that Ivy is always 2-competitive for the tree in Figure 15.8a, i.e., the ratio of *ivy cost* and *optimal cost* is at most 2 for any finite sequence of requests.

c) Show that Ivy is $\Omega(n)$ competitive on general weighted trees where n is the number of nodes in the tree.

   Hint: You only need edge weights of 1 and ε in the tree.

Chapter 7

Exercise 19 (Deterministic Maximal Independent Set)

In Chapter 7, we discussed a slow but simple deterministic maximal independent set (MIS) algorithm (Algorithm 7.3) in which the decisions of the nodes are based on their identifiers. The time complexity of this algorithm is $O(n)$.

We might hope that if the nodes with the largest degrees, i.e., the largest number of neighbors, decide to enter the MIS, the set of undecided nodes reduces the most. In the following algorithm we try to exploit the knowledge of the node degrees:

Assume that each node knows its degree and also the degrees of all its neighbors. If a node has a larger degree than all its undecided neighbors, it joins the MIS and informs its neighbors. Once a node v learns that (at least) one of its neighbors joined the MIS, v decides not to join the MIS.

Naturally, the algorithm does not make any progress if two or more neighboring nodes share the largest degree. As this is a difficult problem, we will assume in the following that this situation does not occur, i.e., if a node v has the largest degree, then no neighboring node has the same degree as v.[7]

a) Draw a graph that illustrates that this algorithm has a large time complexity for trees! Give a (non-trivial) lower bound on the (worst-case) time complexity for trees consisting of n nodes!

   Hint: A lower bound of $\omega(\log n)$ is sufficient to show that this algorithm is worse than the Fast MIS algorithm for trees, you do not need to find a lower bound of $\Omega(n)$.

   Hint: A runtime of $\omega(f(n))$ means that the runtime is *"asymptotically **strictly** larger than f(n)"*.

b) Construct a graph that shows that the time complexity of this algorithm is even worse for arbitrary graphs than for trees! What is the time complexity?

---

[7]The motivation for this constraint is that if we prove that the time complexity is large even if there is no conflict in each step, then being able to break ties clearly does not help.

c) We will now modify the algorithm: The degree of a node v in any given round is only the number of *undecided* neighbors. Prove (tight) lower and upper bounds for this modified algorithm on arbitrary graphs!

Exercise 20 ((Local) Reductions)

Many problems can be seen as—more or less obvious—variants of others and therefore can be solved by clever use of the same algorithms. In this exercise, you may use the algorithms derived in Chapter 7 as subroutines.

a) The *edge coloring* problem is defined as follows: Given a graph $G = (V, E)$, assign each edge $e \in E$ a color $c(e)$ such that no two adjacent edges (i.e., edges sharing a node) have the same color! As usual, the problem should be solved not only fast, but also using a small number of different colors. Give a $2\Delta - 1$ edge coloring algorithm running in time $O(\log n)$ w.h.p.!

> **Hint:** Δ denotes the largest degree of all nodes in G, i.e., $\Delta = \max_{v \in V} d(v)$.

b) Given a graph $G = (V, E)$, a *dominating set* is a subset $D \subseteq V$ such that each node either is in D or has a neighbor in D. The *minimum dominating set* problem is to find a dominating set of minimum cardinality. Give a $3/2$-approximation algorithm for this problem on rings which takes $O(\log^* n)$ time!

c) A family of graphs of *bounded independence* is a set of graphs where, for each node, the largest independent set in the one-hop neighborhood (i.e., the direct neighbors) has a size that is bounded by a constant C. Give a C-approximation algorithm to the minimum dominating set problem on graphs of bounded independence running in time $O(\log n)$ w.h.p.!

Chapter 8

Exercise 21 (Coloring Rings)

In Chapter 1, we proved that a ring can be colored with 3 colors in $\log^* n + O(1)$ rounds. Clearly, a ring can only be (legally) colored with 2 colors if the number of nodes is even.

    a) Prove that even if the nodes in a ring know that the number of nodes is even, coloring the ring with 2 colors requires $\Omega(n)$ rounds![8]

Since coloring a ring with 2 colors apparently takes a long time, we again resort to the problem of coloring rings using 3 colors.

    b) Assume that a *maximal independent set* (MIS) has already been constructed on the ring, i.e., each node knows whether it is in the independent set or not. Give an algorithm to color the ring with 3 colors in this scenario! What is the time complexity of your algorithm? Deduce from this a lower bound for computing an MIS!

Exercise 22 (Ramsey theory)

In the classic example for Ramsey theory ($R(3,3)$), it is asked how many people you can invite to a party so that are no three people that mutually know each other, and no three people which are mutual strangers. This can work with five persons, but it will never work with 6, i.e. $R(3,3) = 6$. This could be important for planning a party, since three people that mutually do (not) know each other will form their own subgroup during the party and rarely interact with the other guests. In more mathematical terms this is a coloring problem: Consider the complete Graph K_n with n nodes. Can you assign each edge to one of two colors (for example red and blue), so that there is no K_3 as a subgraph where all edges have the same color? As stated above, you can do this with K_5, but not with K_6: $R(3,3) = R(K_3, K_3) = 6$.

    a) However, parties with only 5 people are pretty boring. You change your concept to allow bigger parties: From now on,

---

[8]As in Chapter 8, the message size and local computations are unbounded and all nodes have unique identifiers from 1 to n.

you want that if three people come together, there is always at least one mutual stranger to the other two. On the other hand, you now raise the number of people that are mutual strangers: There should be no group of p people that mutually do not know each other. How many people (depending on p) can attend your party at most?[9]

---

[9]If you have trouble finding a solution, start with $p = 2$ and $p = 3$.

Chapter 9

Exercise 23 (Communication Complexity of Set Disjointness)

In Chapter 9 we studied the communication complexity of the equality function. Now we consider the disjointness function: Alice and Bob are given subsets $X, Y \subseteq \{1, \ldots, k\}$ and need to determine whether they are disjoint. Each subset can be represented by a string. E.g., we define the ith bit of $x \in \{0,1\}^k$ as $x_i := 1$ if $i \in X$ and $x_i := 0$ if $i \notin X$. Now define disjointness of X and Y as:

$$DISJ(x,y) := \begin{cases} 0 & : \text{there is an index } i \text{ such that } x_i = y_i = 1 \\ 1 & : \text{else} \end{cases}$$

a) Write down M^{DISJ} for the $DISJ$-function when $k = 3$.

b) Use the matrix obtained in $a)$ to provide a fooling set of size 4 for $DISJ$ in case $k = 3$.

c) In general, prove that $CC(DISJ) = \Omega(k)$.

Exercise 24 (Distinguishing Diameter 2 from 4)

In Chapter 9 we stated that when the bandwidth of an edge is limited to $O(\log n)$, the diameter of a graph can be computed in $O(n)$. In this problem, we show that we can do faster in case we know that all networks/graphs on which we execute an algorithm have either diameter 2 or diameter 4. We start by partitioning the nodes into sets: Let $s := s(n)$ be a threshold and define the set of high degree nodes $H := \{v \in V \mid d(v) \geq s\}$ and the set of low degree nodes $L := \{v \in V \mid d(v) < s\}$. Next, we define: An H-dominating set $\mathcal{DOM}$ is a subset $\mathcal{DOM} \subseteq V$ of the nodes such that each node in H is either in the set $\mathcal{DOM}$ or adjacent to a node in the set $\mathcal{DOM}$.

Note: We define $N_1(v)$ as the closed neighborhood of vertex v (v and its adjacent nodes).

Assume in the following, that we can compute an H-dominating set $\mathcal{DOM}$ of size $\frac{n \log n}{s}$ in time $O(D)$.

a) What is the distributed runtime of Algorithm 2-vs-4? In case you believe that the distributed implementation of a step is

---

Algorithm 15.9 "2-vs-4".   Input: G with diameter 2 or 4
Output: diameter of G

1: **if** $L \neq \emptyset$ **then**
2:     choose $v \in L$ { We know: This takes $O(D)$.}
3:     **compute** a BFS tree from each vertex in $N_1(v)$
4: **else**
5:     **compute** an H-dominating set $\mathcal{DOM}$ {Use: Assumption}
6:     **compute** a BFS tree from each vertex in $\mathcal{DOM}$
7: **end if**
8: **if** all BFS trees have depth 2 or 1 **then**
9:     **return** 2
10: **else**
11:     **return** 4
12: **end if**

---

not known from the lecture, find a distributed implementation for this step!

Hint: The runtime depends on s and n.

b) Find a function $s := s(n)$ such that the runtime is minimized (in terms of n).

c) Prove that if the diameter is 2, then Algorithm 2-vs-4 always returns 2.

Now assume that the diameter of the network is 4 and that we know vertices u and v with distance 4 to each other.

d) Prove that if the algorithm performs a BFS from at least one node $w \in N_1(u)$ it decides "the diameter is 4".

e) In case $L \neq \emptyset$: Prove that the algorithm performs a BFS of depth at least 3 from some node w.

Hint: use **d)**.

f) In case $L = \emptyset$: Prove that the algorithm performs a BFS of depth at least 3 from some node w.

g) Give a high-level idea, why you think that this does not violate the lower bound of $\Omega(n/\log n)$ presented in Chapter 9!

h) Assume $s = \frac{n}{2}$. Prove or disprove: If the diameter is 2, then Algorithm 2-vs-4 will always compute some BFS tree of depth exactly 2.

Chapter 10

Exercise 25 (Distributed Network Partitioning)

In this exercise, we will derive an asynchronous distributed version of the cluster construction algorithm presented in Chapter 10.

Assume that (in $O(n)$ time and using $O(m + n \log n)$ messages) a rooted spanning tree has already been computed. We further assume that the constant ρ in the algorithm is 2. Moreover, you can ignore the intercluster edges in this exercise, i.e. the number of intercluster edges does not have to be reduced once the clusters are built.

Just like the centralized algorithm, the distributed algorithm repeatedly applies the following two steps to construct a partitioning:

1. Find a (cluster) leader.

2. Construct a cluster C, considering all edges E (not just spanning tree), remove all the nodes $v \in C$ and remove all the edges $\{u, v\}$ for which $u \in C$ or $v \in C$ or both.

We shall now develop how this algorithm can be executed in an asynchronous setting. Given a leader, we need to build the cluster by adding more and more nodes to the cluster. The root of the spanning tree can be used as the first leader.

a) Describe how a leader constructs a cluster! Let C denote the constructed cluster. Show that the time complexity to construct the cluster is bounded by $O(|C|)$!

   Hint: If the radius of C is r, show that the time complexity is $O(r^2) \subseteq O(\log^2 |C|) \subset O(|C|)$!

b) Let $E' \subseteq E$ be the set of edges that can be removed in Step 2. Show that the construction of cluster C can be accomplished using $O(|E'|)$ messages!

   Hint: Use the observation that edges closer to the leader have to be traversed more often, but there are more edges with a greater distance to the leader!

c) Once a cluster has been constructed, we need to find the next leader in the remaining graph. Show how this task can be done in $O(n)$ time using $O(n)$ messages for all rounds in total.

> **Hint:** Think about how all nodes in the graph can be visited in $O(n)$ time using $O(n)$ messages in total using the spanning tree! How can this tree-traversal scheme be used to find the cluster leaders every time a new cluster has been built?

d) Putting everything together, show that the entire partitioning requires $O(n)$ time and uses $O(m)$ messages![10]

---

[10]The construction phase of the spanning tree is (clearly) not considered in these bounds.

Chapter 11

Exercise 26 (Self-stabilizing Spanning Tree)

In this exercise, we are searching for efficient, self-stabilizing spanning tree algorithms. Thus, the spanning tree will be adapted if the topology changes or nodes and/or links fail.

a) Prove an (asymptotically) optimal lower bound on the time complexity of any self-stabilizing spanning tree algorithm!

b) If the transformation from the Chapter 11 is applied to the Bellman-Ford BFS algorithm (see Algorithm 2.13), is the time complexity of the resulting self-stabilizing algorithm optimal? On average, how much more information per round must be transmitted compared to the original algorithm?

c) Assume that the diameter D is known to the leader (i.e., the root of the constructed tree) Can you give an algorithm stabilizing—up to constant factors—in the same time, but sending not more information in each round than the unmodified Bellman-Ford algorithm? If yes, can your approach be generalized to other algorithms? If no, prove a corresponding lower bound!

Chapter 12

Exercise 27 (Scale Free Networks)

Different studies of the structures of social networks have reported that the degree distribution of the underlying connectivity graphs asymptotically follow a power law, i.e., the probability of a node in a social network to have degree k is given by:

$$Pr[k] = ck^{-\alpha} \quad \text{where } c \text{ is a normalization constant}$$

a) Is the diameter of two graphs with the same node-degree distribution equal (not necessarily power law graphs)?

b) Remember the rumor game from Chapter 12: Two players choose a node on the graph, where they start their rumor. The player that is closer to a node in the graph can spread its rumor to the node. Winner is the player who can spread his rumor to more nodes. In a power law network, is it the optimal strategy to always choose the node with the highest degree?

For the following problems you may use the *Chernoff bound:* [11]

Theorem 15.10 (Chernoff Bound).
Let $X := \sum_{i=1}^{n} X_i$ be the sum of n independent $0-1$ random variables X_i. Then the following holds:

$$Pr[X \le (1-\delta)\mathbb{E}[X]] \le e^{-\mathbb{E}[X]\delta^2/2} \qquad \text{for all } 0 < \delta \le 1$$

Exercise 28 (Greedy Routing in the Augmented Grid)

Recall the network from Chapter 12 where nodes were arranged in a grid and each node had an additional directed link to a randomly chosen node. Consider the case where $\alpha = 2$, i.e., the random link of node u connects it to node w with probability

---

[11]Chernoff-type and similar probability bounds are very powerful tools that allowed to design a plethora of randomized algorithms that *almost* guarantee success. Frequently this "almost" makes a huge difference in e.g., running time and/or approximation quality.

$d(u, w)^{-2} / \sum_{v \in V \setminus \{u\}} d(u, v)^{-2}$. In Chapter 12, we saw that for this α, with probability $\Omega(1/\log n)$, in each step we get to the next phase when we employ greedy routing. Hence, the expected number of steps is in $O(\log^2 n)$. Prove that the same bound on the number of steps holds w.h.p.!

Exercise 29 (Diameter of the Augmented Grid)

Now consider $\alpha = 0$, i.e., the targets of the random links are chosen completely uniformly at random. In Chapter 12, a proof of the fact that such a network has diameter $O(\log n)$ w.h.p. was sketched. We will now fill in the details.

a) Show that $\Theta(n/\log n)$ many nodes are enough to guarantee with high probability that at least one of their random links connects to a given set of $\Omega(\log^2 n)$ nodes. Prove this (i) by direct calculation and (ii) using the Chernoff bound.

    Hint 1: For (i), use that $1 - p \le e^{-p}$ for any p.

    Hint 2: Use that you can choose the constant in the O-notation for the $O(n/\log n)$ many nodes!

b) Suppose for some node set S we have that $|S| \in \Omega(\log^2 n) \cap o(n)$ and denote by H the set of nodes hit by their random links. Prove that H together with its grid neighbors contains w.h.p. $(5 - o(1))|S|$ nodes!

    Hint: Observe that *independently* of all previous random choices, each new link has at least a certain probability p of connecting to a node whose complete neighborhood has not been reached yet. Then use the Chernoff bound on the sum of $|S|$ many variables.

c) Infer from **b)** that starting from $\Omega(\log^2 n)$ nodes, with each hop the number of reached nodes w.h.p. more than doubles, as long as we have still $O(n/\log n)$ nodes (regardless of the constants in the O-notation).

    Hint: Play with the constant c in the definition of w.h.p. and use the union bound $(\Pr[a \wedge b] \le \Pr[a] + \Pr[b])$.

d) Conclude that the diameter of the network is w.h.p. in $O(\log n)$.

Chapter 13

Exercise 30 (Determining the Median)

Consider a radio packet network with n nodes and without collision detection. Furthermore, assume that each node has a token of size $O(\log n)$ (a number) and is equipped with memory of size $O(\log n)$. Present a uniform algorithm which allows the nodes to determine the median in $O(n)$ time slots w.h.p.

Hint 1: You can assume that n is odd and each token is unique.

Hint 2: Initializing first and then trying to determine the median simplifies the task.

Hint 3: With a memory of size $O(\log n)$ the nodes can count up to n.

Exercise 31 (Maximum)

Assume a uniform wireless network with collision detection in which every node is given a number. Give a $O(\log^2(n))$ algorithm that finds the highest number w.h.p.

Hint 1: Use the fast Leader Election with CD algorithm from the script.

Hint 2: Use the ideas in the proof of the fast Leader Election with CD algorithm and the union bound to prove that your algorithm succeeds w.h.p.

Chapter 14

Exercise 32 (Flow labeling schemes)

In this exercise, we focus on flow labeling schemes. Let $G = \langle V, E, w \rangle$ be a weighted undirected graph where, for every edge $e \in E$, the weight $w(e)$ is integral and represents the capacity of the edge. For two vertices $u, v \in V$, the flow between them (in either direction), denoted $\mathrm{flow}(u, v)$, can be defined as follows. Denote by G' the multigraph obtained by replacing each edge e in G with $w(e)$ parallel edges of capacity 1. A set of paths P in G' is edge-disjoint if each edge (with capacity 1) appears in no more than one path $p \in P$. Let $\mathcal{P}_{u,v}$ be the collection of all sets P of edge-disjoint paths in G' between u and v. Then $\mathrm{flow}(u, v) = \max_{P \in \mathcal{P}_{u,v}}\{|P|\}$.

Consider the family $\mathcal{G}(n, \hat{\omega})$ of undirected weighted connected n-vertex graphs with maximum integral capacity $\hat{\omega}$. We will find flow labeling schemes for this family. Given a graph $G = \langle V, E, w \rangle$ in this family and an integer $1 \leq k$, define the relation:

$$R_k = \{(x, y) | x, y \in V, \ \mathrm{flow}(x, y) \geq k\}.$$

a) Show that[12] for every $k \geq 1$, the relation R_k induces a collection of equivalence classes on V, $C_k = \{C_k^1, \ldots, C_k^{m_k}\}$, such that $C_k^i \cap C_k^j = \emptyset$ (if $i \neq j$) and $\bigcup_i C_k^i = V$. What is the relationship between C_k and C_{k+1}?

According to the solution of **a)**, given G, one can construct a tree T_G corresponding to its equivalence relations. The k'th level of T corresponds to the relation R_k. The tree is truncated at a node once the equivalence class associated with it is a singleton. For every vertex $v \in V$, denote by $t(v)$ the leaf in T_G associated with the singleton set $\{v\}$.

For two nodes x, y in a tree T rooted at r, we define the separation level of x and y, denoted $\mathrm{SepLevel}_T(x, y)$, as the depth of $z = lca(x, y)$, the least common ancestor of x and y. I.e., $\mathrm{SepLevel}_T(x, y) = \mathrm{dist}_T(z, r)$, the distance from z to the root.

b) Show that if there exists a labeling scheme for distance in trees with labeling size $\mathcal{L}(\mathrm{dist}, T)$, then there is a labeling scheme for separation level with labeling size $\mathcal{L}(\mathrm{SepLevel}, T) \leq$

---

[12] As a convention, $\mathrm{flow}(x, x) = \infty$.

$\mathcal{L}(\text{dist}, T) + \lceil \log m \rceil$ where m is the number of nodes in the tree.

c) Recall there is an $O(\log^2 m)$ labeling scheme for distance in unweighted trees of size m. Show that $\mathcal{L}(\text{flow}, \mathcal{G}(n, \hat{\omega})) = O(\log^2(n\hat{\omega}))$.

Assume there is an $O(\log^2 m + \log \omega \log m)$ labeling scheme for weighted distance in integer-weighted trees of size m with max. weight size ω.

d) Find a more careful design of the tree T_G which can improve the bound on the label size to $\mathcal{L}(\text{flow}, \mathcal{G}(n, \hat{\omega})) = O(\log n \log \hat{\omega} + \log^2 n)$.

Hint: Consider the nodes of degree 2 in T_G.

Exercise 33 (1-Bit Adjacency Labels)

We want to label nodes for determining adjacency (whether two nodes are neighbors) based only on their node labels. Each label is exactly 1 bit, i.e. every node is labeled with either 0 or 1. Clearly, many nodes will have the same label. Assume there are no queries asking whether a node is adjacent to itself. If we can obtain one graph from another by shuffling node ID's, the graphs are considered identical.

a) Determine the largest k, such that there is a 1-bit adjacency labeling scheme for *all* graphs with k nodes.

b) Consider graphs with exactly 10 nodes. Give a 1-bit adjacency labeling scheme such that you can label as many graphs as possible. How many different graphs with 10 nodes can you label?

c) How many graphs with exactly 20 nodes can you label (using the same labeling scheme as in B)?

Index

9 798628 688267